HEART BROKE OPEN

HEART BROKE OPEN

SAHARA SUN

HEART BROKE OPEN

*A courageous healing journey
through the heart of Lyme disease*

SAHARA SUN

Copyright © 2016 by Sahara Sun
All rights reserved.
Published by Shen Press

All rights reserved. No part of this book may be reproduced in any form or by any means, electronic or mechanical, including photocopying or recording, or by any information and storage retrieval system, without written permission of the publisher.

ISBN: 0997295600 (paperback)
ISBN-13: 978-0997295603 (Shen Press)
ISBN-13: 978-0-9972956-1-0 (e book: Kindle / mobi)
ISBN-13: 978-0-997-2956-2-7 (ebook: ePub)

Library of Congress Control Number: 2016906584
Shen Press
Printed in the United States
Editing by Jill D. Twist
Cover Design by Ardel Chisholm, LincTech Media and Sahara Sun
Interior Design by Jane Perini, Thunder Mountain Design
Author photo: © Kecia Joy on top of Haleakalā

Permissions:
'This is the Day' (Jaya Lakshmi c2005)
"I will Survive" Hal Leonard Permissions
I Will Survive
Words and Music by Dino Fekaris and Frederick J. Perren
Copyright © 1978 UNIVERSAL - POLYGRAM INTERNATIONAL PUBLISHING, INC. and PERREN-VIBES MUSIC, INC.
All Rights Controlled and Administered by UNIVERSAL - POLYGRAM INTERNATIONAL PUBLISHING, INC.
All Rights Reserved Used by Permission
Reprinted by Permission of Hal Leonard Corporation
"You Are My Sunshine" by Jimmie Davis
Copyright © 1940 by Peer International Corporation
Copyright Renewed.
Used by Permission.
All Rights Reserved.

To respect the rights and privacy of others, I have changed the names and places of all individuals and altered some identifying details.

Find out more at: www.Sahara-Sun.com

Dedicated to all the Lyme Warriors who are too weak and sick to be heard. May my story be your story, and may my voice be your voice. We are a tribe of warriors fighting to stay alive! It was your love, strength, and courage that gave me the inspiration to share my own story for you.

Also

Mom and Dad, I love you and am so grateful for your own unwavering dedication to our family.

Table of Contents

Introduction..13
Divine Medicine Passages...25

PART 1: THE PORTAL..29

Journey Medicine...30
CHAPTER 1 Leap of Faith...31

Crow Medicine...36
CHAPTER 2 Transplant Shock...37

Medicine of Being..42
CHAPTER 3 Mongoose on My Stomach..................................43

Turtle Medicine..52
CHAPTER 4 Home..53

Mourning Dove Medicine...62
CHAPTER 5 The Axe..63

Ocean Medicine...68
CHAPTER 6 Heart Broke Open...69

Pono Medicine...76
CHAPTER 7 Pono Journey...77

Solar Medicine...84
CHAPTER 8 Psychic Download...85

Aloha Medicine..92
CHAPTER 9 Burnt Pizza...93

Storm Medicine..100
   CHAPTER 10 The Hermitage...101

Owl Medicine..108
   CHAPTER 11 Aftermath..109

Mountain Medicine..114
   CHAPTER 12 The House of the Rising Sun.................................115

Mana Medicine..122
   CHAPTER 13 Star Beings...123

Whale Medicine..132
   CHAPTER 14 Flesh, Bone, and Being...133

Dream Medicine..138
   CHAPTER 15 The Flare..139

Pachamama Medicine..146
   CHAPTER 16 Closure Through Prayer...147

PART 2: THE HEALING GAUNTLET..151

Ghost Medicine..152
   CHAPTER 17 Facing Ghosts..153

Dog Medicine..162
   CHAPTER 18 Banished Queen..163

Angel Medicine...172
   CHAPTER 19 Divine Assistance..173

Death Medicine...182
   CHAPTER 20 Unmarked Grave...183

Eagle Medicine..190
   CHAPTER 21 Miracles and Blessings..191

Butterfly Medicine......198
CHAPTER 22 Metamorphosis......199

Tree Medicine......204
CHAPTER 23 Standing Tall Being......205

PART 3: DIVINE GUIDANCE......211

Hawk Medicine......212
CHAPTER 24 On My Knees......213

Phoenix Medicine......220
CHAPTER 25 Paradise......221

Gratitude Medicine......226
CHAPTER 26 The Bridge Man......227

Trust Medicine......236
CHAPTER 27 The Invitation......237

Orca Medicine......242
CHAPTER 28 Planes, Trains, and Orcas......243

Deer Medicine......246
CHAPTER 29 The Driver's Seat......247

Test Medicine......256
CHAPTER 30 The Final Exam......257

Grace Medicine......264
CHAPTER 31 State of Grace......265

Belief Medicine......274
CHAPTER 32 A Worthy Vessel......275

Acknowledgement......281
Biography......285

*May your heart break open unto itself.
Again. And again. And again...*

Introduction

I AM ABOUT TO SHARE with you a most arduous journey that takes place over the course of six months from winter 2014 through early summer. It is a blip of time on a greater, twenty-four-year journey to heal a mysterious illness that has plagued me since I was a teenager. Even though I now have a diagnosis and name to what was a phantom plague, my journey to heal still continues to this day.

My journey to heal has become most epic in the sense that, even though I have been trying to heal my body, another part of me understood that I needed to also heal my spirit. I have been able to see into the spiritual realm since I was born, and my curiosity to explore this mysterious, unseen spirit world has also been part of my quest. Though this ability was a source of fear I carried throughout my childhood, I knew I had to overcome this fear to fully explore the hidden mysteries of this world. It is this lifelong quest that has led me to spiritual experiences in Ecuador, Peru, and eight trips to Hawaii that lasted at least a month each. I visited sweat lodges, teepee ceremonies, and twenty years of retreats. I participated in, experienced and learned Shamanic Rites of Initiation, Peyote and San Pedro ceremonies, Native American traditions, hours of meditating all over the world, sacred geometry healing, and spiritual healing trainings from teachers all over the world.

This quest has led me down the path of the wounded healer. The archetype of the healer that has to heal themselves first before healing another. My own healing experience with a chronic illness became the guinea pig to understanding and exploring the realm of spiritual healing. My training in holistic healing, medicinal plant research, and the Taoist philosophy of five element acupuncture has also shaped my expedition to heal my soul so that I could heal another.

The spiritual healing lessons I have learned on this life's journey have become deep wisdom for my soul. It is wisdom that has seeped into the marrow of my being. It is the wisdom to understand how to listen to Spirit and trust in the messages. I used these teachings, my own intuition, and the love in my heart to experience Spirit speaking through everything. This wisdom didn't necessarily come to me through neon signs or shocking revelations. Although that did happen at times, messages from the Universe were often subtle, coming in the form of a comment from a grocery store clerk, a stone that fell inside my shoe, or a random phone call from a friend. I understood the power for any encounter to be a possible message from God, Universe, and Spirit guiding me along my way.

The wisdom I learned is the art of listening beyond what my ears could hear, to see beyond what my eyes could see, and to feel with all of my heart. This was both the challenge and the reward of my healing journey: How can I follow my heart without fear? How can I learn to love with all of my heart? How can I learn to follow the breadcrumbs of my soul's path—those synchronicities, chance encounters, and little nudges that the Universe uses to teach me?

Although this story is about healing my body, its messages are universal to healing one's soul. You may be on a journey to heal your heart rather than your body, or to find your passion in life, to step into your future, or to heal your past. Whatever our journey, we all need courage to walk our own path, to thrive authentically in the world with all of our hearts. This story is my own personal journey to heal myself in body, mind, and spirit, and I share it with you in hopes that through my own peril, my own revelations, and my reclaimed hope that you, too, find the wisdom you seek within your soul.

Over half of my adult life was spent in one doctor's office or another, recovering from one odd medical issue to another strange malady, with no concrete answer to my mystery illness. It started one day (we suspect) when I was 16 years old. When I woke, for some reason, I couldn't walk right. My legs simply wouldn't work. It wasn't like they were paralyzed, but I just couldn't make the connection with my brain to get them to do what I wanted them to do. As a doctor, this mysterious illness drove my father crazy. Every test under the sun was conducted on me over the next five years, all with inconclusive results. Meanwhile, I continued to live a normal life, but a life interspersed with bouts of a strange illness that made me crash with fatigue, severe fatigue. Countless doctors, their misdiagnoses, and their endless head scratching that reverted to the old, "it must be in her head" diagnosis, rendered me feeling helpless with modern medicine. To date, it has been a twenty-four-year journey that has culminated, finally, but only in the last three years, with a proper diagnosis. Lyme disease.

Acquiescing to the old standby of treatment for this chronic disease, I endured antibiotics, anti-parasitics, antimalarial, and antifungal medications for nine months preceding the day where this book begins. The experience was harrowing at best. Caught in a nightmare from the side effects of the pharmaceuticals as well as the neurotoxins excreted by the Lyme bacteria, I was overwhelmed by the daunting number of symptoms I was enduring. I was overwhelmed into a state of shock, awe, and excruciating suffering. In addition, I faced the challenge that all Lyme patients must face: most of my symptoms were invisible to everyone else but me.

I would experience a myriad of neurological misfires, muscles twitching, random pain in odd places, ears ringing, rooms spinning. But to an observer, I looked totally healthy. How could someone feel so horrible when they looked totally normal? It was difficult for most people to comprehend, and it left me isolated from many fair-weather friends and family, because it was too difficult for them to understand.

My pharmaceutical treatment came to a screeching halt upon my realization that I would not survive taking those drugs for another two to five years, as was prescribed. The drugs were killing me, literally; they would have destroyed my kidneys if I kept taking them. In desperation for survival, for my life, I knew this plain fact: something had to change, or else, death was going to change me.

When you have Lyme disease, there are so many health issues that you experience at once, yet they seem unrelated. A problem with my wrists, a leaky gut, anxiety, rare tumors, hand trembling, neck pain, strange visual disturbances, extremely low blood pressure, and astonishing fatigue were only some of the maladies I experienced along my twenty-four year journey to healing. In spite of their quantity, none of these symptoms were ever pieced together as symptoms of Lyme disease.

Then, the year before I turned 40, I underwent a seemingly unrelated surgery to remove several rare tumors. The surgery brought the dormant Lyme bacteria out from hibernation, after which they began ravaging my body yet again. My biggest nightmare had returned.

Ten years prior, I experienced the ravages of this illness when the stresses of naturopathic medical school brought my body crashing down. Bedridden for two years, dropping out of medical school, I was reeling from the loss of a marriage, home, my dreams, and the life I once knew. The fact that this mystery illness was blooming yet again became a spiritual awakening, all the way to the depths of my soul; and yet, I wanted to believe that the likelihood of undergoing such pain again was impossible.

Freeing myself from the grips of this illness ten years ago, especially in such a painful time, was hard enough. I thought I finally celebrated the end of my long journey toward healing when I completed acupuncture school and board exams, and my divorce was finalized. I thought I had transcended these dark hours to embrace life anew. I didn't want to look back, nor even think that my nightmare could return.

But it had returned.

When the Lyme bacteria reared its ugly head after almost a decade of hibernation, the extreme level of grief, shock, horror, and fear shrouded all my hopes and dreams. I had no choice but to face this illness yet again. The pages that follow are the courageous journey I took into the heart of Lyme disease to be rid of it once and for all.

Though the hardships I encountered on this journey were many, the gifts I received were also abundant. By using the Divine wisdom and lessons I learned to transcend my own personal healing journey, I have been able to "pay it forward" as a medical intuitive, acupuncturist, and spiritual healer. It is my deep understanding that one cannot help heal that which they have not healed within themselves. God had more healing for me to do within my own body and my own soul, so that I could understand the deepest, clearest path to heal, not just human ailments, but humanity. Out of this twenty-four-year journey, my healing practice was born, and it has been an honor to help others on their journey to fully heal.

So there I was, reliving my biggest nightmare. My partner Alex was not prepared for the onslaught of emotions and physical devastation that was about to occur to my body. He was witnessing the woman he loved shriveling away, eaten from the inside out by little bacteria, and there was nothing he could do about it. He tried to understand the torture and frustration of this illness, but justifiably, imagining what went on inside my body was difficult for him to comprehend—especially when my illness was invisible to his eyes. Instead, he experienced my inner illness only as it manifested outwardly. Any damage occurring inside my brain, he experienced as my emotional upsets, scattered thinking, and lack of presence. Honestly, considering the extent of internal damage this disease inflicted on my body, I am surprised I am here to tell this story.

There have been countless times during this journey when wishing for death was easier than the thought of enduring the constant level of severe pain and neurological misfires happening everywhere in my body. To put this into perspective, imagine how every nerve cell in one's body is connected to some muscle, neurotransmitter, pain receptor, or sensory receptor. Now consider that every single one of these nerve cells is susceptible to being damaged or affected by the bacteria and co-infections that cause Lyme disease, as well as the neurotoxin these bacteria excrete. Nothing is exempt. It is overwhelming even to try to explain how every part of my body was experiencing some symptom from this war, let alone fight the war.

How do you explain to a person who sees you as fine, who thinks you are fine that you can't see or hear them clearly? How do you explain that there is pain everywhere—and I mean *every*where? How do you explain that the simplest body movement sends shrieks of pain rattling through the nervous system, and any emotional upset rumbles through your body like an earthquake?

How do you explain your level of fatigue, that to even lift your mug of tea to your lips must first be deliberated and weighed against the consequential pain to come from such a simple gesture? On top of all that, how do you explain the sudden and unexpected changes in my body? At any given moment, I might've felt my heartbeat suddenly become irregular, or felt dizzy from moving too fast, or felt my lungs expand but not fill with enough air. At any given moment, fatigue would take my energy, sequestering it into unreachable places.

Randomly, one of my legs forgot how to work, changing my gate into an unsteadiness that made me appear drunk. Another time, with no explanation, one of my hands forgot how to hold knitting needles, and the only solution was to just put them down. At any given moment, I might've realized—experienced—that a wall was closer than I thought, or that the wall was not there at all when I grabbed for it. Thoughts didn't arise, although I knew they were in there trying to come out. The name of a person who I had known for years would simply slip into some vault in my mind that I had no access to, leaving me unable to find the name inside my brain. Sentences would disappear from my brain even as I spoke them. Emptiness clung to unexpressed brain synapses, leaving behind only the constant awareness of twitching and nervous ticks that no one could see or feel but me. The neurological ramifications alone are enough to drive a person mad, and trying to explain it, to convey the extent of this disease is just as difficult as experiencing it first-hand.

As my pharmaceutical treatment progressed, I became trapped inside my own body—isolated from everyone else—watching myself fall apart physically, mentally, and spiritually from a disease that no one could see but me. But this time, at least there was a diagnosis; at least this time there was treatment. Though this knowledge brought me some level of reassurance, this was nothing compared to the detriment of the treatment, which turned out to be almost worse than the symptoms. Meanwhile, my agony in enduring the side effects of the pharmaceuticals, was getting in the way of Alex's busy life. We had been together four years and living in the little cottage on Lost Lake, Washington for the last two years. From my perspective, his actions told me that he valued his life more than helping me get better.

The disease, and my suffering from it, had driven a huge wedge into our relationship. In my mind, any smaller incidents that occurred in our relationship during that time were only aggravated by my constant and relentless suffering from Lyme disease. Something had to change.

"I can't swallow another pill. I can't do it!" I cried, pleading with Alex, the Universe, anyone who would hear me. I swallowed fourteen different pharmaceuticals at varying doses on a daily basis, in addition to herbs, vitamins, juices, tinctures, detox teas, and more. My stomach couldn't handle one more pill, not one more.

"Let's pray over them together," Alex said. "Then you can get them down. You need to take these, don't you?" He was trying to help me.

We first met under a starry spring night on the Makah Indian Reservation, sharing in a sacred Inipi ceremony also known as a Sweat Lodge.

Our relationship began in a spirit-centered way, and through our own inner wounds, limitations, and oppositions we still formed a beautiful bond that grew slowly over time. Before meeting him, I had a premonition I would meet a man that evening at the Sweat Lodge. Over the course of the next four years, we created beautiful memories together, that is, until my illness reared its ugly head again. Then, like a flower at the end of the summer, our relationship budded, blossomed—we tasted the nectar—and now it was withering and dying. Death was surrounding me at our home on Lost Lake, and the pressure to change was paramount to my survival.

Holding the mound of pills in both hands, holding them up to God, praying that they would be easy on my body, I acquiesced and swallowed them. But in spite of the pills, in spite of the prayers that Alex and I spoke together, I became steadily sicker. The realization that I was dying, not only from Lyme disease, but also from these drugs, was a realization that consumed every part of me. I felt like I was being eaten alive, and I was conscious of every bite being taken from my body, mind, and soul.

"What will you do instead?" Alex asked me one morning when I finally refused to take my pills.

"I don't know," I said, "but this isn't working. I can't do this for another five years, or even two years. I just can't. This isn't the way." Sobbing in hopeless despair, I sat across the room from him, and we began discussing my options. Even then, even in our discussions, I disliked how we sat so far apart.

The pharmaceuticals weren't working, I knew that much. Now, having lost all hope in Western medicine after countless misdiagnoses, treatments, herbs, supplements, and anything that someone suggested might help, I decided to embark on an epic journey to find a new place to live, with a new lifestyle and new climate that seemed more conducive to someone with Lyme disease. This was my newest hope in getting well: live in paradise and eventually my body would heal.

Had I known what that road ahead of me held—the road I was so eager to walk down—perhaps I would have chosen to stick with the pharmaceuticals and accept a graceful death.

But on that morning, a mound of pills staring me down, I realized that although I had been walking this same old road since I was sixteen years old, Alex had only been on this journey with me for a short, nine months. I had already lost a husband to these Lyme bacteria; I didn't want to lose Alex as well. My level of desperation was at an all-time high. I had to do something drastic to save my life and to save my relationship with Alex.

When one dreams of an idea, a place to be, something to become, the illusion of this dream is always the source of joyous feelings surrounding it. For me, this dream had been Hawaii. Climbing out of my bed eight years prior, I travelled to Hawaii for a rejuvenating vacation and fell in love. I fell in love with the Aloha spirit, the sunshine and carefree way of playing while I lived there. And while I lived there, I fell in love with *me*.

It was my first time to the Islands, and I had traveled to the Big Island by myself, where my intended two-week stay stretched into two glorious months. I refused to return to my life in Seattle, pushing my flight back regardless of penalty costs.

"I like me better here!" Sobbing and lamenting, I declared this to a new friend during my final hours in Hawaii before my flight took me back to the mainland.

That precious two-month period of time was cemented in my mind for the next eight years, and all the while, I hoped to return, to catch a glimpse of that girl who appeared in Hawaii. I did return, many times over, sometimes for weeks and other times for months. Every chance I had, I returned, crying tears of joy when the plane landed on those islands, and crying tears of sorrow every time the plane lifted away to bring me back to the mainland.

The mainland had a way of sucking me into its fast pace, of filling me with a sense of urgency, as if something was wrong if I wasn't in a hurry. I have never resonated with this sense of urgency, which is why I have always sought out chances to live in the country. Finding a little, 750-square foot lake cottage on Lost Lake in Washington offered this alternative way of life, one with boundless quiet and natural surroundings.

When I came to live at Lost Lake, I didn't intend to land in the midst of fellow healers or other people who also wished to experience life from a spiritual and conscious perspective. So many beautiful things emerged during my experiences of that land and community, and yet, I was still stuck on that girl I left on the Hawaiian Islands. I couldn't shake her. I dreamed of her, especially on the cold, wet, dark days of the Pacific Northwest. When the sun hadn't shined for weeks, I yearned to be back in Hawaii. It is the only place I have ever known to call me.

And so, when the urgency to save my life became more important than any sense of security, the portal opened again for me to return to Hawaii. The message had been clear: it was time to go. So much of me wanted to keep my healing practice, my home, and my relationship just the way it was, to visit Hawaii for a few months to see if my health would actually improve. Yet, once the energy started to move my thoughts in that direction, it was like a snowball propelling itself down a hillside, getting larger and larger and picking up more momentum along the way. Friends encouraged me to jump fully, to give myself a chance to commit to being there, rather than simply dipping my toe in the water.

The haze of pharmaceuticals, neurotoxins, exhaustion, and fearing an impending death clouded my own intuition and discernment of these upcoming choices. Yet, my jump to Maui became a path that I could not turn back on, not for one second, and it happened so fast that the life that I had merely slipped through my fingers, quicker and more wildly than I could consciously comprehend.

My friends and my partner alike were encouraging me, and since they were the closest people to me, I believed and trusted in guidance greater than myself. This was the path; this was *my* path. And so, I shut down my beautiful healing sanctuary nestled in the woods, got rid of most of what I worked so hard to acquire, packed up the belongings that

I thought I might need in Hawaii, left the rest for Alex to watch over, said goodbye to my seven animals, said goodbye to a struggling relationship, and leaped fully into the unknown.

This giant leap of faith began a pilgrimage to heal all of me, not just my body, in which the pain and heartache I had endured up to that point would lead me into a sense of grace and peace I had spoken about with my patients, but had yet to fully integrate into my body, mind, and soul.

In the following pages, I share with you a six-month piece of my own healing journey in hopes that it gives you inspiration, direction, courage and hope to embark on your own. Whatever dark depths you must face, this story shows that there is light at the end of the tunnel. This light's source is from no other place than your own soul. My own journey to heal from Lyme disease and incredible obstacles of heartbreak have led me to find my own light and home within myself. It is with this knowledge that I hope your own heart breaks open, releasing your natural light into the world, to stay open forever. It is with your light and my light that we will bring health, peace, and change for humanity.

Divine Medicine Passages

EVERY SOUL, WHETHER LIVING in this lifetime or the next, will walk unforged paths into the recesses of their hearts. This is where true transformational healing happens. From the beginning, I knew that my own healing journey would require much more courage, strength, and support than what I alone could provide. So, as I embarked onto this healing journey into the unknown, my eyes, ears, and heart were opened to the many sacred teachers and guides of this earth. Every cloud, mountain, animal, plant, storm, and culture I experienced had something to teach me. I became aware of them, and their presence became medicine for my soul.

Signposts that lighted my path were presented through an old cedar tree on Lost Lake in Washington, which I knew only as Grandmother Cedar, the whales off the coast of Maui, the divine helpers that came during my treatment in the Nevada desert, and the energy of the place I landed, on Orcas Island. God was everywhere on my journey, and once I opened up to the omnipotent power that held and supported me, I felt guided through each stage and challenge by sage wisdom that subtly spoke to me.

Since in my mind, God, the Universe, Divine and Spirit are seemingly the same entity, I use these terms interchangeably throughout my story. To me, these words refer to the same source of supreme power coursing through every molecule of every being. My heart is opened to this unseen presence guiding, protecting, and loving me through every synchronistic encounter on my journey.

Each chapter in this book is prefaced with a short excerpt on a particular sign or symbol that revealed its greater meaning to me on the many miles of road I traveled. My own inner antennae were constantly picking up hidden messages and meanings through every encounter on my path. Each encounter, though often subtle, prompted deep inner contemplation in my mind to uncover its hidden message and lesson. Sometimes these lessons were obvious for me to interpret, like an owl flying overhead meant I need to look for my life, even in the dark. But always, when my awareness was drawn to a mountain, a bee, a deer, or a concept, I understood its presence as a messenger of the Universe, here to teach me a lesson for growth, change, and healing. Nothing was random. I would meditate with the divine medicine being offered and use it to navigate my way into the depths of my healing.

Each Divine Medicine passage offered in this book was inspired by an experience that actually happened on my journey, and offered a wisdom that I share with you now. I have woven these encounters into my story, so you, the reader, can see how they might apply to your own healing journey.

I could have tried to control the outside world, but it was my inside world where I had the ability to chose.

PART ONE

THE PORTAL

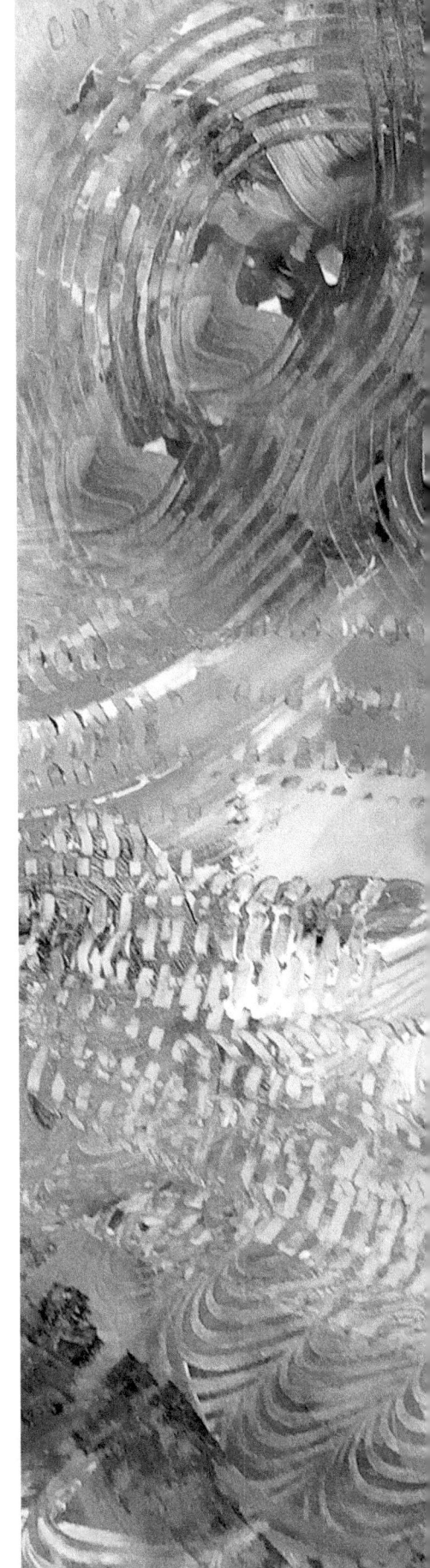

Journey Medicine

Stepping onto a journey with hopes to create authentic change summons both courage and fear in the traveler. By setting out, the traveler submits to the unknown. But there is guidance: if the traveler opens his or her heart, guiding messages of the Universe can enter. Through this opening, whatever lingers in the soul, whatever is tethered to one's old ways of thinking or being, are freed. Journey Medicine inspires curiosity to seek rather than to control. It tests your strength of spirit, courage, and faith. *Is there a journey that is beckoning you on your life's path? Are you too afraid to take the first step? Are you feeling stagnant, stuck in the same problems but hoping that change will happen of its own accord? Do you need to take action?* When Journey Medicine comes into your life, it is time to take the first step. It is time to be accountable for the life you have created. If you are not happy with the way your life is right now, let Journey Medicine be your guide into an unexplored realm of physical and spiritual healing. Journey Medicine summons an opening of the heart to trust in something greater than we, as humans, can comprehend. It summons a power within ourselves to seek change, to live the best life that we can, and to dream of a better way to live our authentic truth. If a journey is beckoning you, let your curiosity be the catalyst for change. *Are you curious enough to take the first step?*

CHAPTER 1

Leap of Faith

ASKING THE UNIVERSE for snow was my last request before heading to tropical weather. I received it. Though early for snow that time of year, only days after Thanksgiving, evergreen branches bore the weight of beautiful white crystals, refracting light in a sparkling dance of sun and snow against bright blue sky. My favorite kind of winter day was gifted, nature's sendoff to me, and it was a picturesque gift I still remember. Living on the beautiful, non-motor Lost Lake, which is nestled in the foothills of the Cascade Mountains, I already had the pleasure of waking to its beauty each day; but when swelling clouds threatened to dump the feeling of death into my body, I had no choice but to say goodbye.

The cool crisp air was a welcomed surprise this time of year. The warmer temperature of the Pacific Northwest winters generally lent itself to misty, wet, bone chilling cold that left me walking with my head down to avoid huge rain drops falling from the trees. It was this feeling, being weighted down, that began my pilgrimage to find my new home: a home where I would heal from what ailed me in that damp, cold, rainy climate. In short, I was about to set out on a journey to find a home of sunshine and warmth that I hoped would lift and rejuvenate my spirits.

"Let me say goodbye to Grandmother Cedar one more time," I said to my partner, Alex.

Bundled in my red, down jacket and token white hat I had adorned for the last 10 years, I stepped into her presence, offering my deepest gratitude and thanks. The icy deck was slippery, but Grandmother Cedar held strong to her beauty and strength, even under the added weight of snow. She was likely 15 feet in diameter, a rare gem even in the tree-filled Pacific Northwest, especially in an old logging town. She had been my council and teacher for the previous several years, and it was she who told me I needed to go. I had helped others to also sit under her branches to soak in her sage wisdom. They also learned how to surrender within one's own center because of this tree.

It was she who taught me what it meant to be okay right where I was, and it was this ancient being who nudged me to find my own roots and health. And it was she who I held one last time, Grandmother Cedar, breathing with her, sinking my heart into hers, exhaling gratitude and inhaling solidity and strength for this new path opening ahead of me.

"You've already said goodbye to her a thousand times," Alex replied. "We have to go or we'll hit traffic."

Alex was loading my luggage in the car for the airport, a solid one-hour drive without traffic. His arms, muscled from working in the lumber yard, always made lifting heavy burdens look easy. Still, there was an uneasiness about him that morning, a nervousness and sadness.

All the energy of the morning, the snow, the lake, and Alex's sad heart echoed in me. Everything around us held nostalgia. The mist, which would be the last time I saw that mist on the lake. The chicken coop, that was my coop, and I had to leave it behind. My cats and dogs, I was their mother, how could I walk away from all of that? My healing practice, not only was I leaving all of my financial security, I was letting my patients down. My friends and community, all healers, all people who understood my connection to energy, spirits, and nature, I wouldn't see them anymore either. At my home at Lost Lake I was free to be me—well, almost me—and I was leaving all that behind.

Together, Alex and I made plans for him to join me in Maui, a few weeks after I arrived. He talked of staying for several months, helping me get settled and taking time to nurture our relationship, and ourselves individually.

"What are you feeling right now?" Alex asked me one late evening after returning home from yet another of his long days. Just before he'd returned home, I had managed to put myself to bed after a bath. After doing deep healing work all day long in my practice, I could barely walk or even lift a finger in the evening hours.

This was during the thick of my treatment. The pharmaceuticals were killing the bacteria that caused my Lyme disease, but in doing so, the bacteria released their contents, which were full of neurotoxins.

In moments like those, I could hear Death beckoning from another dimension, like Charon, the ominous boatman on the River Styx in Hades, slowly rowing towards me. I felt that boat in the mist; I even felt the two gold coins in my hand as payment for my ride through the Underworld. All there was left to do was hand over my payment, and I was sure Charon would gladly have taken me to my death.

So that night, when Alex had asked me how I felt, I tried to put all of these feelings into words.

"I am feeling so much right now I can't even describe it to you." I can only imagine that I appeared to Alex like a corpse, with him standing there as if at my wake.

The partner he loved so dearly was dying right before his eyes. Alex's dear friend and father figure, David, was also dying, though the ravages of metastasized cancer were more visible, eating away at him to an emaciated, eminent death. All of Alex's emotional energy was going towards this one man. Though I wanted Alex to hold space for his friend's passing, and to have that precious time with David, I needed him desperately as I went through my own treatment, a battle that has been likened to chemotherapy.

I tried so very hard to stay afloat and take care of myself, so I didn't become another burden to him. Still, through all that effort, I felt like a burden. The treatment was killing me and I was dying alone, it seemed.

"So, you don't need me to do anything then?" Alex asked again, when his question fell along the bedside where I lay in a seemingly catatonic state. In my foggy neurotoxic haze, I couldn't find my words; I couldn't emote anything.

I could feel him eager to eat the dinner I had managed to prepare for him, sit down in his comfy chair, and watch one of his favorite television shows to settle himself down for the night. Days bled together with Alex's work, exercise, volunteering, helping out his friends and holding vigil for David. At the end of the long day there wasn't much left for Alex to give, either to me or to himself.

"I am so weak," I said. "I can't even talk right now. I wish I could. I miss you."

I remember trying to hold his hand. He'd been standing over our bed at the time, but I knew his mind was still with David. His distant presence at that moment was symbolic of so many things for me. To me, he always seemed to have one foot in and one foot out the door.

Alex and I were astrologically direct opposites, he an Aquarius and I a Leo. Aquarians rule from the head, deal with matters of analytics, logic and the mind, whereas Leos rule from the heart, with passion, joy, and adoration. This astrological difference was reflected in our rhythms and ways of doing things day to day, our thoughts, perspectives and how we loved one another. We butted heads often during our daily lives and yet, we were magnetized to one another. Opposites attract, and for four years, that magnetism held us together.

It seemed that we were two souls with a fated destiny played out through many lifetimes—that of unrequited love. Sensing this fate intuitively even then, on that night, I was determined to change its course. Instead of looking at our relationship from a discerning perspective, I perceived it through the eyes of hope and determination. It was my forged illusion that he would follow me wherever I need to go, and that our bond and our love was going to get us through my illness. Hindsight is always twenty-twenty, right?

Alex had loaded the luggage and our three wiener dogs, Frankie, Sampson, and Delilah all eagerly jumped in for the adventure in the car. My heart flip flopped like a yo-yo inside my chest as I stared into their big brown eyes. These three dogs were my babies and I was about to leave them for several months.

"Are you ready?" Alex asked as he shut the back of the SUV.

"I'm ready." I said, gulping my fear down with the hardboiled eggs I had made us for the ride to the airport.

Fed up with the constant chronic illness, not understanding the war that was going on inside of my body, the only thing Alex could do was release me to the Aloha spirit. He would realize that life with me was better than life without me. Still, nothing could have prepared me for the journey that awaited the moment the plane lifted off the ground.

Crow Medicine

Crows are incredibly intelligent birds. They can remember a person simply by the sight or smell of one's hair, hat, or home. They can signal to their crow friends when that person is near by using certain vocal messages that signal whether he or she is a friend or foe. Crows are a symbol and reminder that there is magic in the world. They have the ability to find shining things on the earth and hoard them in their nests. Many lost heirlooms have been found in crow's nests. Their ability to always find something shining is their medicine, and it is here to teach us and invite us to find the light and magic within our own lives. Crows teach us to look for the signs that lead us to shining places in life. *Do you need to find things that are bright and good in your world? Or do you only think about darkness and despair, instead of finding value in all things?* Their vocal ability when signaling to other crows also teaches us that sometimes we have to ask and sometimes we need to shout for what we need. There is always someone listening to our calls, even if it is just the trees. Crows live in huge communities and roost together at night. Their days revolve around the sun, which serves as a reminder of how to live within community according to our own rhythms within each day. *Are you isolating yourself because you are afraid you don't fit in with your community and the rest of the world? Do you need to engage with others to find your flock? Have you forgotten that there is still magic in the world?* Crow Medicine is our reminder of the seen and unseen, and it will help us find what we are looking for—as long as we use our voices to ask for help.

CHAPTER 2

Transplant Shock

"I LOVE YOU SO MUCH!" Alex's tears glistened across his wet chiseled face, trickling through his five-o'clock shadow. His slicked back hair, gathered in a ponytail only amplified his handsome bone structure and piercing blue eyes. Through our nearly five-year relationship, I relished every moment I laid my head on his chest. Our height difference allowed me to hear his heartbeat every time I hugged him, and to feel the embrace of his huge arms taking me in. I loved our hugs—I cherished them—and felt I could linger in them forever. He was always the first to break away from our embraces. This was something I noticed, but never mentioned to him.

"I love you, too," I said. "So, so much. Don't worry, I'll see you in a few weeks." Rubbing his big, strong chest, the home of his heart chakra, I said, "It's going to be okay." I was fighting back my own tears the whole time, but I told myself not to fall apart now. So, after leaving Lost Lake together as a family with our dogs, I had no idea that our embrace at the airport was going to be the last time those arms would enfold me, ever again.

On the way to the airport, crows had followed along with our car, as if escorting us down the I-5 corridor through Seattle. Their dark silhouettes beckoned my eyes upward toward the heavy, grey sky, and they drew my awareness up through the clouds where I knew the sun shined brightly.

The crows' presence offered me this sendoff message: keep magic in your heart. *It is going to be okay. Stay focused.* In response, I told myself,

'You have been divinely guided this far', even though I was gripping Alex's hand in fear of my journey ahead. In spite of the crow's medicine, I was terrified; my push for survival had driven me to make choices that felt so surreal and insane now that I lived them. Every detail of the hours before I got on that plane was played out in slow motion.

I was about to take the ride of my life. Like a player in a big game, I had to stay focused. I was so hopeful seeing Alex's tears, his passion and feeling his embrace that I was oblivious to the other passengers hustling from their arrival or to their departure at SeaTac International Airport.

Walking through the security lines, we were quickly reaching that fated impasse where we'd part ways. I wanted to say, "Let's just forget this whole idea, I want to stay here with you. I don't want to leave you."

It was all so surreal, but what was happening all around me, in the airport and in my body, was completely real. It was the kind of pain that made my stomach turn at the mere thought of what was about to happen. We would part ways, Alex and I, and I had allowed it, even encouraged it to happen.

When I reached the fated security checkpoint, I couldn't bear to look back at the empty place where Alex once stood and held me in his embrace. But I did, and like Lot's wife, I turned to look back and only saw emptiness where there once stood love. My heart sunk. I didn't turn into a pillar of salt like Lot's wife, but the shock of what I was about to do cemented itself in me. Panic began to stir. *What have I done?*

Everything I did, I did for my own survival. I had to get my body better or else the feasting bacteria were going to kill me. This constant awareness of looming death screamed agony through the pain, neurological twitches, hallucinations, visual disturbances, ringing ears, confusion, and the distorted perception of everything. Every second of every day, this awareness of impending death clamored throughout my cells and into the depths of my soul. Yet, the devastation that was happening on the inside was invisible to everyone, even Alex. My mission was to be rid of this illness once and for all, so I could finally and completely stop the nightmare I had been living and begin to create the life of my dreams.

As the plane shunted me through a portal in the starry sky over the Pacific Ocean, the roots that held me in the Pacific Northwest for the previous decade were ripped out of me in an emotion-packed sensation unlike anything I had ever experienced. My thoughts wreaked havoc on my heart and stirred up my stomach.

Oh my god, what have I done? This was a total mistake, I love Alex so much, and I don't want to go down this path without him, without our family intact. Maybe I should have gone to Reno, to that medical center for people with Lyme disease instead. But I can't turn back now, I'm already on the plane, my car will be waiting for me when I arrive on Maui. What have I done? What in the hell was I thinking? I am too sick to be doing this. This was a mistake. But I have to commit to this, I've jumped and I can't go back.

I was not prepared for the emotional onslaught that took place on that plane and ravaged my energy body, nervous system, and heart. I had imagined joyous tears flowing with elation as had happened all the other times I flew to Hawaii. Yet, the exact opposite emotions flowed out through my tears. They were tears of fear, of the realization that I was completely untethered, flying wilding through the cosmos.

My ego and mind felt so very alone. My spirit was trying its very best to hold steady, lovingly guiding me to a place where I could not see for myself. The pangs of higher altitude and low oxygen sent my cells into agony, kidneys screaming at me in pain, and a blanket of exhaustion tucked me in for a bumpy, emotional ride into the night. The plane landed close to midnight.

A small firecracker of a woman stood watching me struggle with my five pieces of luggage at the airport curb, and finally said, "Hello, you must be Sahara!" Her frenetic energy was stuffed into such a small, tightly packed body that she seemed ready to explode at any minute. The warm, salty breeze immediately heightened my awareness, and I knew even in the dark that the ocean was nearby.

"Aloha!" I said, embracing her with the familiar heartwarming hug of mine, which I give to anyone I feel gratitude towards. Renee, as I already knew from our previous conversations, was the property manager for the house in which I had rented a room for the month.

Days prior when she called me on the mainland to let me know that she would help me get settled, she offered to pick me up from the airport. Touched by this kind gesture from the first islander to extend an Aloha welcome to me, I already felt such appreciation for this woman and her car—a chariot so unlike that boat of Death I had felt calling me recently—awaiting to take me to my lodging.

We loaded my things into her Nissan Pathfinder and headed towards Kihei, the beach town on Maui known for its heat and tourists. Hesitant to land in the hot, dry, touristy part of the island, this was where I felt the Universe and the spirits of this land call me. I had agreed to the journey into the unknown, but part of me was kicking and screaming along the way. The same resistance and fear that caused me to panic on the plane was still coursing through my veins even with the warm ocean breeze and the realization that I had landed in paradise.

I was desperate to talk to Alex. I already ached for him in every cell of my being. Checking the time, I calculated it was 4 a.m. back at our lake house in Washington. Calling Alex was going to have to wait until morning, his morning, which, for the first time in four years, was different from mine. The chasm had already started to grow between us, and I found myself echoing into the abyss with no sound to be returned. Desolation and despair were growing in me and I was doing my very best to keep it all under control.

After a short drive, Renee unloaded my luggage at the front of the small ranch house I would call home for the next month, which was within walking distance to a beautiful Maui beach. Stepping out of the car, a welcoming committee of three large dogs and two, seemingly exhausted, sun-drenched women greeted me. The women were not as interested as the dogs in getting to know me, not just yet.

Inside my new home, a small wooden plaque with a simple engraving sat on the counter: "Ahunui." *I wonder what that means,* I thought. I knew that the carpets had been cleaned because all of the furniture was still piled upside down on top of the bed, my bed. But my arrival prompted quick movement by Renee and the other two women to put the furniture back in place.

Hiding my pangs of panic, dread, and incredible grief that had sprouted in me during the flight, it took everything inside of me to simply "act normal." I was too weak to help them, but none of these women knew about my health condition. I feared that explaining my shortfalls within moments of meeting them would start things out on the wrong foot, so, full of emotional and physical pain, I joined in and set up the furniture.

And all the while I did so, I felt I didn't want to be there, not yet, and that realization was a shock for me. Finally I was there, in Hawaii, and now all I wanted was Alex, my home by Lost Lake, my animals (my babies), and the familiarity of the life I once had—even if that familiarity was filled with physical pain and suffering.

Yet, standing there in that house, in walking distance to the beach, I realized I had gone through the portal and emerged on the other side—in Hawaii. I couldn't go back. And even if I did go back, I knew even then that my life would never be the same as it was. Not ever again.

Finally, after fixing the furniture, I bid goodbye to the welcoming committee. "Good night ladies," I said. "It was nice to meet you." After paying Renee the full month's rent in cash, I hurried off to my new bedroom, where, behind the closed door, I tried to reassure myself of the days to come. *You will wake in the morning with the sunshine, beach and Aloha spirit. You will be okay. This pain is only temporary.* Still, that first night in Maui, I cried myself into an exhausted sleep.

Medicine of Being

No matter where we are in life, physically or emotionally, there is always an invitation for us to embrace stillness and deep presence in our current situation. When our hearts are full of so many misgivings and our minds are swirling into the future and the past, the sacred medicine that is available to our soul gets missed in the process of wanting, desiring, pining, grieving, longing, aspiring, and all the other things that drive a person on most days. The natural rhythms of the earth and the stillness of the present moment is where the lessons linger for transformation and true authentic change. It is where we find the love of who we are meant to be, all by simply *being. Where in life are you forgetting to just be? What pulls you away from peace in your heart or keeps you in a loop of continual anxiety and fret? How are your current circumstances teaching you even before you take the next step on your life's journey? Where are you not listening, what aspects of your life are you ignoring?* When the Medicine of Being comes into your life, understand that this awareness is an unveiling of a path unique to you and your life. When your cell phone isn't working or the cable goes out, take this as a sign to be still with your thoughts. When there is traffic and you can't get to your destination, there might just be something at play to help you become present. Any event that stops the forward momentum of the fast-paced world is divinely placed to teach you something. Being Medicine allows magic to be revealed in places we didn't expect, and allows healing to transcend from the physical realm into the lessons of the soul.

CHAPTER 3

Mongoose on My Stomach

I AWOKE TO THE SAME AWFUL FEELINGS that were tearing at my gut the previous night. My first thought upon waking was, *what have I done?* I was in panic, resistance, and regret because I remembered my intuition, which had shown me glimpses of this journey ahead, after saying goodbye to Alex. Somehow, I sensed even then that this was going to be a very long journey. Still, I managed to make a morning cup of coffee, using supplies that were not my own, intending forgiveness before permission as my new roommates slept late that morning.

The covered front porch housed an old, worn leather couch. I hunkered down into the cracked leather and watched the gentle, ethereal light of the sunrise make its ascent into the Maui blue sky. I had made it to the land of Aloha. But pieces of me felt shattered all over the planet, mainly at my home on Lost Lake. So many times before I had come to Hawaii and learned deep lessons in my soul. What was in store for me this time? I contemplated, *is this really my new home?* I was going to give myself three months to make that decision. In the meantime, my focus was recovering from my illness. The shaking in my body from the panic attack on the plane was still rumbling without amnesty.

The mourning doves chortled their morning conversation, a familiar sound that awoke memories of my previous trip to Hawaii eight years prior. It was my first time to Hawaii, to the Big Island, and I went alone.

Recalling my first initiation onto the islands, my jet lag and early morning hours on Maui carried over to the Big Island in my memories. There were lessons I learned back then that I knew I needed to apply to my journey now. Taking those first steps onto the tarmac in Kona, I knew that the lessons I had learned and would soon learn in Hawaii would enter into the depths of my soul.

※

Eight years prior, dry, volcanic dust blew billows of brown red plumes through the rising heat, creating mirages everywhere I looked. The bright sky of the Big Island was a stark contrast to the Seattle grey, where I had already spent two years bedridden from a still undiagnosed illness, staring out of my bedroom window and wondering what life was like out in the "real" world. Once I felt strong enough, my first trip into the "real world" was to the Big Island of Hawaii. The red earth below my feet felt like mars, and the sun's rays actually penetrated my skin instead of just warming it. It felt miraculous!

I had never really traveled alone before that trip. My classmate from acupuncture school, Shana, invited me to come stay at an old, retired retreat center down on the south side of the island, to an area known as Ho`okena. With my luggage in tow, Shana picked me up in her old Honda Civic hatchback, the classic Hawaii car. Hot, sticky, tired, and in a car that felt the same way, we headed south through the volcanic smog, which I learned was called Vog.

The beautiful drive meandered through thick tropical jungles, lianas hanging everywhere, mango trees bursting with fruit, bougainvillea vines, and lush landscapes at every glance. The hour drive from the airport took us into dryer and dryer weather, during which I stopped only for a few provisions, thinking I'd see the place first to get a better idea of what I would need.

The turnoff to Ho`okena was an amazing two-mile decent to the ocean and Old King's Trail. The expansive ocean view with farms, horses and cattle took my breath away, that time and every time thereafter.

As we descended to sea level black lava rock and banyan trees with their supportive root systems greeted the entrance onto the Old King's Trail. I would learn that this trail once went around the entire island and was the main thoroughfare for daily life. This part of the road led to two places: The Place of Refuge and the Women's village. The Place of Refuge was used as a "pardon" for any criminals to escape. If they were accused of a crime (any small grievance was punishable by death) they had the opportunity to outrun their prosecutors to this place of refuge. If they made it, they could live out their days there safely. If they didn't, death would find them on the Old King's Trail.

The road was built of lava rock. Huge boulders that radiated heat day and night. Driving this path, we came to what seemed like a dead end nestled in a small oasis of trees along the beach. Shana gunned her little Honda into the sand, navigating it along the beach and back onto another lava rock road toward a very remote part of the island, all the while warning me about many things about life in Hawaii.

"You have to watch out for scorpions, they'll come up through the sink and sting you while you do dishes. You have to watch out for the mongoose, they'll poo in your shoes and try to get into the house and tear stuff up. Don't try to talk to the locals down here, they won't like you, especially since you're blonde. Just wave and be mindful that this is their place. Watch out for the wasps, they come looking for water, so if you turn on the hose you'll be swarmed. There are wild dogs down here, too, and they'll attack you, so stay away from them. There are also wild boars, so don't walk the road at night...." This went on for a while, and with each of her warnings, my fear and panic swelled like the incoming tide on the other side of the road.

Later, I learned from a local (who was supposed to hate me according to Shana) that the patch of sandy beach, palm trees, and stone we drove through was actually an oasis, a women's village. No one would have known it just by looking at it. It seemed only as a small patch of woods, random rocks scattered about, leaf litter, with lianas threatening to encroach the cooling shade of the upper canopy. I had no idea sitting in that little Honda that I had landed in a sacred and healing place.

The women's village was used for any matters of the feminine. It was a place for birth, a place to rest during your moon time, a place for the old crone's to retire and live their days taking care of the new mothers and the young women taking care of them. There were birthing pools with grooves notched into stone with the grips of labor pains imprinting the lava over eons of time. There were storage areas, sleeping quarters, and more, all made with lava rock.

The quiet solitude of this place was not in my awareness driving with Shana. All I saw was fear and danger at every glance.

Finally, Shana and I arrived at the old retreat center, the last stop on Old King's Trail before it became impassable by car, where we were confronted with a two-story, turquoise building, dilapidated and echoing what once was. Signs of a life burgeoning with people and activity were remnants now to old screens in the windows, vines seeking their perfect crack in the foundation to take root, and old gardens withered away from lack of water, care, and love. There was an old water catchment, an outhouse, and an outdoor shower (which ended up being my favorite thing about the property).

Inside, the dark wood beams created a feeling of nighttime even in broad daylight. The kitchen was ample, a mish mash of cooking equipment accumulated over the years. Everything was on solar and it seemed adequate for meeting the bare minimum of living. Shana showed me the rest of the house with four bedrooms and a level roof to sit on at night and watch the stars. A deck for practicing yoga overlooked the ocean, where, when I eventually practiced there, I noticed salt residue at my feet.

After the tour, I turned to Shana for the "what's next" part of the journey.

"Well," she said, "I'll see you later. Have a good time."

What? What did she mean, "See you later"? My look must have said it all.

"Oh, I didn't tell you? I'm housesitting on the other side of the island for a month, so you'll be here by yourself. I have to go or I'll be late.

Have fun!" she called out as she headed to her little beat up car and skedaddled to her next thing.

What?! I was stunned.

Had I known she wasn't going to be there *with me*, I would have, 1) rented a car, 2) bought more food, 3) reconsidered the entire trip altogether.

But, I was there. Spirit was wielding something for me, and I felt it as such. This was time for me to be alone with only Spirit and nature to guide me. It was a two-mile walk to the beach, people, cell phone reception, or any type of communication with anyone. I was literally out in the middle of no man's land, a little place of refuge all to myself.

I had no idea how much my body had been running on the energy of the mainstream, how tired I was, how fried my nervous system had been until I was totally unplugged. I was unplugged from everything that I thought was security and necessary. I was unplugged from the life I was struggling with at the time. I was unplugged from any distraction that kept me from listening and looking deep within. There was no pets, no television, no phone, no car, and no agenda. It was just me, the mongoose, and the Hawaiian spirits I had learned were called 'Aumakuas.

That night, alone and in the dark, my initiation truly began. Madam Pele, the goddess of fire, lightning and wind, holding the powerful life force of the Big Island, made her presence known to me when a huge tropical storm blew through. The ferocity of the ocean surged its power onto the house and I knew I was no longer in charge.

I was on the second floor, praying I didn't get swept away in the night. The alarms on the solar panels and refrigerator were going off and I had no idea what to do. I had no flashlight and it was so pitch black I couldn't even see my hand in front of my face.

So I did the only thing I could do: lay on my bed and say over and over, "You are alright. You are going to be okay. You are safe." After that night, I now take a flashlight whenever I travel.

Slowly, each day, my energy body began to align with the rhythms of the Hawaiian tide, the moon, the sunrise and the sunset and I came to a deep inner peace and stillness that felt both healing and freeing.

I didn't want to leave. I wanted to stay there forever. Scheduled to stay for two weeks, I ended up staying at that retreat center for two months. During that time I befriended creatures great and small. I befriended native Hawaiians; their children called me "Auntie." The big, innocent, brown eyes of three little boys marveled at my blue eyes, touched my cheeks, lips, hair and chin. They had never seen blue eyes before.

Playing in the tide pools with three little boys and their father watching approvingly was medicine for the soul. There were no barriers of color, culture, or creed between us; there was only love and a fascination of the uniqueness that we each possessed. It was the Aloha spirit at its finest, and a magical memory.

At some point during the many walks down the hot, lava rock toward the beach, I noticed something about my gait. Though my body was starting to align with the energy of the land, being in deep peace, quiet, and surrender, my gait was still operating on the mainland—with a must-be-on-the-move mentality. Leaping over lava rocks, picking up sea urchin spines for art projects, looking into small pools of water where little fish waited for the tide to take them to better places, and listening to the ocean make music against the lava, I realized my walk was not in alignment with the energy of the land.

Instantly, upon this recognition, my gait changed from the mainstream, from the "I have somewhere I am supposed to be" mentality, to the "I *am* being" mentality. I slowed. I savored the present moment. I let go even more deeply to embrace a frequency that has long been forgotten in our modern world. The importance of "getting there" washed away in the tide, and it was replaced with "being here" and the perception of my world opening yet again.

Even though Shana warned me about the mongoose, a mix between a squirrel, a ferret, and a rat, as one of the many nuisances I might experience in Hawaii, the lessons of my Catholic upbringing taught me to love all creatures great and small. It felt wrong in my heart to loathe a creature that didn't choose to be on this island, but rather, were captured from India and transported here to reduce the rat population. It wasn't their fault they were on the island. They were just trying to survive like everything else on this planet.

"Okay, Mongoose," I shouted outside the house one day, "I love you. I respect you and am your friend. This is your land and I understand that I am a visitor. I thank you for letting me be here with you. I ask that you welcome me as your guest and know that I will take good care of you and this land while I am here. Thank you for protecting me. I will protect you as well. Mahalo."

I held my love for them in my heart, and felt it was returned: to everyone else who ventured onto that property, a mongoose would poo in their shoes. Every time. But they never once pooed in mine.

One day, I was napping in the afternoon shade of the lanai on a Tahitian couch, where the resident cat usually curled up with me. With my eyes closed, I felt little paws climb onto my belly and settle down. Thinking nothing of it, I didn't move. I only observed that she had come to rest as well. It wasn't until I heard a hiss from above my head that I emerged from my sleepy revelry. I looked up to see the cat, above me. Then, looking down to my stomach, I saw the red, beady eyes of a mongoose staring back at me, inches from my face.

A mongoose had been hanging out on my stomach the entire time!

Startled, the mongoose "eeked" and leapt off of me to hide in the rocks below. I couldn't believe it! Why would a mongoose come take a nap on me in the middle of the day?

Though mongoose were often loathed by the locals and seen only as pest-eating creatures, to me they seemed gentle. Something had shifted in me so much since coming to the Big Island that I felt the beauty emanating even from the vermin.

Moments like those are so magical. My energetic resonance had changed in those days with nothing to do, nowhere to go, just me, the mongoose and the ocean. The shift in the frequency brought profound beauty and moments of awe and splendor that I never looked for nor anticipated.

It was merely in the act of *being*, in my heart and in the moment, and being okay with where I was right there right now that allowed the shift to happen. I didn't have to try, strive for an outcome, or be something I was not. It was just in *being* that my awareness of life's beauty came, that miracles happened and that life became one magical awakening after another.

If I had been walking around in the fear I felt that first day in Shana's car, none of those magical moments would have happened. I would not have experienced that time with so much love and wonder. Realizing I had stepped into another dimension where time didn't exist, I savored *being* and simply loving.

The walk along that Old King's Trail connected me back to past lives, days of old where life was simple and sweet. I didn't care about my cell phone, my growing healing practice back on the Mainland, my crumbling marriage, or what was going to happen tomorrow. The level of deep presence that old retreat center and all the beings on it taught me was a gift. It was precious, and it was not something I could take with me.

Like the fountain of youth, the precious energy of that space only worked in that space and time. It would never be repeated again, although I would try years later. What I did take away from that time at Ho`okena was an understanding that how we walk in the world shapes our experiences, shapes the people we meet, how we love, and what we dream. It is all perspective, and it is a daily practice.

The sounds of a garbage truck groaning and clanking cans in the early morning hours broke the ethereal nuances of my morning daydream on the front porch on Maui. Ho`okena, the mongoose, and the time on the Old King's Trail reminded me of what I needed to summon in myself now.

Traveling a road full of unknowns and fighting an illness, I asked myself, "Why? How?" Why does this new chapter of my life have to start with healing my body? How am I going to do this in Hawaii? I knew I had the tools under my belt to love this journey, to develop the deep presence I learned down on the water at Ho`okena.

I need to surrender all fear and embrace where I am right now, I thought. The fear of facing this illness head on with the neurotoxins waiting to wage war on my body was terrorizing. Yet, the memory of *being* was still in me.

My cells remember the vibration of being, I thought. *It is a part of who I am now. When I fret and worry, that imprint is there too. It is a matter of choosing which one to resonate with. I may not be at that old Oceanside retreat, but I am in Hawaii, and its loving energy has something to show me.*

Giving myself a pep talk, recalling the lessons of my time with the mongoose, I asked quietly but out loud, "Do you want to walk through this day in fear and worry or do you want to walk through this day in splendor? You are in Hawaii for God sake!"

I could have tried to control the outside world, but it was my inside world where I knew I had the ability to choose.

You can stay in this fear or you can find love on this journey like you did eight years ago with the mongoose. You get to choose how you want to walk through this world. You get to choose to be here, right now, for your body. Embrace what gifts come, and surrender to whatever hardship await. You get to choose.

Turtle Medicine

Glimpses of turtles, alive or seen in images, connect us back to a place within ourselves of calm, rest, and peace. Known in Hawaiian as *Honu,* turtles are ancient, respected beings depicted as wise creatures in stories—slow and steady, and full of rich, simple advice to those who seek it. Born on the land, turtles return to their home in the water and navigate the seas, living sometimes hundreds of years. Turtles have several symbolic meanings beyond this depiction. First, their shells are their homes. This fact teaches us, even as humans without a hard turtle shell that we are already home within ourselves. Everything we need is already within us. Second, turtles stretch their necks out to forage for food, an act that translates to the human species' need to stick out our own necks in order to grab what life offers us and live up to our fullest potential. Third, their slow and steady pace teaches us patience, reminding us that all things come in good time. Pushing ourselves toward an outcome too forcefully or quickly goes against the natural rhythm of the earth. Turtle Medicine teaches us these lessons, and reminds us to go slow and pay attention to the little things in life. Turtles teach us that we are already home, each person within his or her own body. *Are you moving too fast? Too slow? Do you need time to retreat? Do you need to be bold and reach for something?* These are the questions that turtles ask of us.

CHAPTER 4

Home

THE INITIAL ILLUSORY MUSINGS of landing in paradise may easily conjure up images of me lounging on the beach, body surfing the ocean waves, getting tan, getting healthy. In reality, those first few days were a far cry from the quintessential Aloha welcome of a rum-filled tropical Mai Tai drink and a fragrant Plumeria flowered Lei. Though those two things represent Hawaii to so many people, I have never been greeted with either, not once.

Instead, I received the hot pavement and searing sunlight beating down upon my skin, which, only several days prior, was wrapped in sweaters, fleece, and goose-down. All my memories of crisp, white snow that I thought were imprinted deeply in my mind soon melted into images of heat waves along the road, the scorching sun, buying groceries, and acquiring my car at the sizable shipping port. I was shocked by the stark contrast between climates and all things that I considered "home" to where I was living now. It was a shock that tore my body down.

So often in those first few days I wished Alex, or anyone, was there to help me. Each day I turned my attention away from the screaming cells inside my body and hoped that the land of Aloha would heal me. I continued to hope that I would eventually just sit back, slather myself in coconut oil, and soak up the sun. The sun would heal me, I was sure of it, by charging my body with its solar power.

The change of pace would soothe me, and I would finally be free from the hell inside of my body. I had cried over those golden Hawaiian rays time and time again in the thick clouds of Seattle, and now those rays were shining above me and I was sure they would be the golden healing elixir I craved.

Five days passed in Maui, and my anxiety, pensiveness, and heartache had reared up a massive flare up of my illness. Rarely have I felt true panic, and when I have, it is an emotion that doesn't come easily. But the shock of what I had just done stirred panic for five days straight, and it was taking its toll on my mind and my body.

The nervous system, I'd learned, becomes fried and over-taxed with all of the Lyme bacteria ravaging any part of the body it wishes. The bacteria spew its neurotoxic waste all over the place, like a squashed grape releases its juices. When this happens, as it happened to me in Maui, glitches in the nervous system occur anywhere, anytime. These glitches presented themselves in the form of pain, speech impairment, proprioception issues, muscle twitches, gnawing internal shaking, cognitive problems, emotional upsets, and exhaustion.

As I experienced each of these symptoms, the level of panic welling up inside of me was horrific. My pain, still present and still unbearable even in Maui, helped me realize what I had actually done by moving there. I had stepped onto a path that was going to be arduous, a road less traveled; and I was doing it on my own, with a body that didn't work. Instead of a mantra full of surrender and unconditional, universal service, my mantra became: *What the hell was I thinking?*

"Did you hear from Alex yet?" Kerry, my housemate for the first few weeks of December, asked me one day.

"No," I replied. "He keeps telling me he is too busy, and maybe he'll call later." Speaking it out loud, I was still perplexed with his actions. "I don't get why he isn't making time to check in." Alex knew I was having a hard time from the brief conversations we'd had. I needed him, and he knew it. So where was he?

There were so many things I wanted to say to Alex in those first few days, so many realizations about our relationship that became clear to me: I contributed to our current state, taking him for granted, and pushing him where he didn't want to be pushed. I felt so much love for him when I realized what I had left behind, thousands of miles away in Washington.

Within the first few hours of my departure, I'd already begun grasping the severity of what I had done, and the potential ripple effect it would create. But now that I was actually in Hawaii, who knew how long it would take for me to get this message across to Alex. I couldn't reach him by phone, and the conversation I knew we needed to have would have to be face to face. He would need to come sooner than planned.

I wanted time with him on the beach, time to talk, to make love, to deepen our bond and clarify our vision for our relationship and our life together. I needed him. And every day that he wasn't there, I held tighter to a deep inner sadness that he wasn't where he should be, that we weren't where we should be in our relationship or in the world.

This was my continual complaint with Alex, that I needed him in a way he couldn't give to me. I knew this complaint made him feel inadequate, and many times it resulted in him pushing me further away.

Panic, lamentation, and the urge to fix this bad decision to leave him and our family in Washington—it was all right there in my solar plexus, the third chakra located in the abdomen. One of the seven energy centers held within the body, the third chakra is the transformer along the energetic highway that runs through our nervous system. It is the home within a home, the power center of our bodies, and it is the central place of stability and security within us. All of that panic and lamentation I felt toward Alex was there, in my abdomen, and it was a sick, punched-in-the-gut feeling.

But that nausea, lack of appetite, and the incredible hole I felt in my solar plexus was only the beginning of my suffering. My entire individuality, my ego's sense of security, all of it was under major siege.

No one knew me in my new home, no one saw me as anything other than another woman who came to Maui with big hopes of healing, finding or rejuvenating the love in my life, and living the Aloha lifestyle. There were no patients for me to help or take care of, no patients to thank me for the beautiful healing work I was capable of offering. There were no friends to hug and love on. My menagerie of animals that were my constant companions was almost three-thousand miles away from me. There was no partner to engage in love and affection, conversations, and walks. There was no pillow that I could call mine.

My identity, everything that made me unique, everything I had worked so hard to establish as a holistic healer, and all the security that I'd established in Washington was ripped out of my body on that plane ride. It had been ripped out from its place deep within my solar plexus, leaving behind an emptiness that I tried to fill at night by hugging myself in the fetal position.

Rather than rejuvenate my old self, I realized my old self could not be saved in the sacred dimension where these islands lingered. Rather than healing my body, mind and soul, I was experiencing another form of death—and I didn't want to die!

My entire being was in shock with my transplant to Hawaii, and my roots, like toes in frigid water, couldn't bear to dig deep into the paradise where I had landed. It was a conundrum. Feeling withered, exhausted, scared, alone, and overwhelmingly anxious to go home back to Alex's arms, I cried and sobbed myself to sleep almost every night during those first few weeks. And when I woke each morning, instead of rejuvenation, I felt incredible and overwhelming grief.

"I'm heading to the beach for a while," I told Kerry one day. I was already wearing my bathing suit and was carrying a beach bag full of bottled water, snacks, my journal, sun hat, and towels.

"Okay! See you later," she called back. "I'm taking the scooter to my

Ukulele lesson." Kerry was an independent, strong woman, free and eager to live life for herself. In short, she was a glaring reminder to me every day that I had forgotten how to trust in my own inner strength.

The white, soft, sandy beach opened up to a large crescent-shaped wall of lava rock that arced its way out into the crashing surf. The wall was just high enough to stop the siege of building waves from crashing onto the shore, and as a result, created calm, warm waters on the beach and within me.

The heads of turtles, known in Hawaiian as *Honu*, popped up periodically for breaths of air. The longer I stayed on the beach, the more I realized that Honu were everywhere. By watching their dance with the current, which was always in sync with the flow of the ocean waters, I was reminded that I still needed to settle into the rhythm of Hawaii.

There is medicine for me here, I thought. *Don't focus on what you left behind. Try to embrace this magical land. Learn the lessons that Maui has to teach. Look at those turtles, they are already home inside of their shell. You are already home inside of you, too.* I tried to convince myself of the very things I would have taught another. *Don't worry about what you are going to do, just let yourself be here for a little while.*

Settling into the sand that day, watching the Honu and soaking in the sun's golden elixir, I looked up into the sky. Watching the setting sun fill that Hawaiian sky with hues of pink and orange, I wondered, *Is this my new home? Is turtle telling me that I am home?*

I've come to learn that there are three types of home: first, there is the physical place where one lives; second, there is the place where your memories are ("home is where the heart is"); and third, home is a spiritual place within each person.

My heart had three homes for a very long time—Hawaii (my joyous spirit home), Kentucky (that place of where I had my family roots), and Washington (my heart community, my sense of familiarity with the land). For the decade since I've had these three homes, I've been torn between them. How many times had I asked myself, *How do I find a combination of all three? How can I choose any one of them, when any choice requires letting go of something else?*

Then, beyond these three homes, there was yet another home, within me. The solar plexus, that place that represented home to me like the turtle's shell represented home to the turtle. The shell of my solar plexus was crumbling. In route to Maui, I lost my inner compass, and now I was panicking far beyond any illusion of control. Still, I knew that Spirit, the Universe, God was trying to teach me something through the lesson of the turtle. I needed to open myself up to what was possible.

That day on the beach, I realized that moving to Maui meant learning about and rediscovering my home on all three levels; where I chose to put my roots down would always be my decision. But before I made that choice, I knew that attributes from all three of my homes needed to merge into one being within my body and within my life.

With my body in such a state of shock, it was challenging for me to see clearly on a spiritual and energetic level. Everything screamed of foreign land, and my resistance to embracing the Hawaiian paradise divulged itself everywhere I turned.

Something as simple as drinking water turned into a spiritual dilemma. When I compared the horrible-tasting drinking water of Kihei to the pristine, filtered well water at Lost Lake, I could barely drink it. Instead, I chose to purchase bottled water, in toxic plastic, nonetheless. Everything—not just the bottled water—was so expensive in Maui, a price shock that rendered me buying simply and cheaply over my previous choice of quality. Back in Washington, fresh organic produce was delivered to my door. But in Maui, where the beach was only several mere steps from my house, even the cost of fish was outlandish; small servings the size of my palm were all I could find in the grocery store. I missed the beautiful salmon that was so easily accessible in the Pacific Northwest, all fresh and reasonably priced. Now, in my new home, nothing looked good enough to buy.

I saw the connection between my dilemma over meeting my basic needs, such as food and water, to my present battle with my solar plexus. After all, I knew that this area of the body was also in charge of my appetite. All I wanted was my red soup pot to cook something comforting to ground me as it had so many times before. In order to acclimate to Maui, I knew that I needed to nourish myself physically and stop this self-obsessed misery once and for all. Chicken soup was the first authentic meal I cooked in Maui.

But as the days went on in Hawaii, I asked myself if I was prepared to completely rebuild my life. Could I do that by myself, considering the state of my health? Suddenly I realized how much of my life I had taken for granted in the Pacific Northwest. Up until the point I left for Hawaii, I had created a beautiful life, and it was that life from which I chose to walk away. I chose, although, it seemed to me in those first days in Maui, against my better judgment.

Lacking insight to understand the full value and the gifts that I had in Washington, so much of me in Maui now recoiled as I reviewed my past decisions. But through this review, I returned to one basic premise: I did not want to suffer silently with Lyme disease anymore, alone in agony, exhaustion, and pain every day. And so, once again, I understood my decision to leave Washington for Hawaii. Fleeing from the life I had built there was all I could do to save the life I had remaining inside of me. Physically, I had been falling apart for a long time. Now, in Maui, I was falling apart emotionally, physically, spiritually, and mentally. I was a total mess, wandering through the world of Maui like I was stranded on a deserted isle.

Through all of that wandering, I was still pleading with Alex to talk to me on the phone. As the days carried his silence I continued to think: *Where was Alex?*

All these things I was thinking, discovering, realizing about myself and my life, I wanted to share with my beloved. So much had become clear to me even in a few short days, and it was approaching eight days in Maui without a word from him except for the briefest good morning and good night texts. I'd take and send him pictures to show him things

I'd seen, to share with him, but often I got no response. Prior to my departure, Alex and I agreed to video call once a week, so at least I could see him and my babies, but he did not even respond to this agreed upon communication.

If I were a plant, I mused, *what I'd need is some soil to set new roots, some fresh water, sunlight, and air to breathe.* I told myself that if I could get past this panicked stage, perhaps these would be the exact things I found in Maui.

The warm foam built up in places where gentle waves broke, rolling themselves along the fine grains of soft sand. Getting pulled out of my reverie, I realized this place, known as the Fish Pond, was a sanctuary for Honu to offer me their turtle medicine. The sounds of the waves and the simplicity of that moment soothed what ailed me, at least momentarily. Still, the uncharted territory of emotion left me inept to process all that I was sensing and experiencing on my own. I was homesick like I've never felt before, with the realization that I didn't appreciate things until they were gone.

How I receive unconditional love is just as important as how I give it.

Mourning Dove Medicine

Doves carry the symbolic meaning for the Spirit of the Universe, our own spirit, and the love that guides us. They symbolize peace of the deepest, gentlest kind. Often depicted with the olive branch as a symbol for extending compassion, kindness and peace, doves are gentle creatures that summon gentleness within us. They are most talkative around 7:00 in the morning when, according to Chinese Medicine, is the time of the earth and the time to nurture and support our bodies. *Do you feel resistance to achieving inner peace? Are you aggravated, judging yourself or others?* The cooing of the dove often sounds sad, as if the dove is in mourning. They may be mourning, but they are still emanating peace. It is the reminder that even in the stirring of our own emotions peace is obtainable. *Are you sad? Are you allowing yourself to be sad? Can you be centered in your sadness and despair, allowing it to be there, to be kind to yourself about it and gentle with your words?* Dove Medicine acknowledges the tender hearts that yearn for love. Like a mother that sings to her child, the mourning dove will sing her sweet lullaby to your soul and lull you into your place of peace.

CHAPTER 5

The Axe

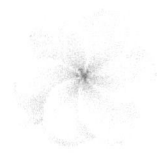*IT'S STILL ALL A SHOCK,* I remember thinking. *Trust that this journey is going to lead you to exactly what you have intended: setting down roots with a beautiful family, a lovely piece of land that will allow you to grow good food, have clean water, and live in a climate in which your body thrives. You are healthy,* I assured myself. *You feel settled in your currently unsettled spirit.*

I could feel my positive thoughts breaking through, but with every positive thought came the old, familiar, homesick one. Helplessly, I missed Alex so much. I still considered that house on Lost Lake where Alex lived to be my home. I wanted to go there, to be back in his arms, with my family of furry friends, chickens, Lake House, Grandmother Cedar and all the rest of the familiar things that created the life I'd had.

Then one phone call changed everything.

"I'd like to talk tomorrow around 10:00 a.m.," Alex texted me one day. "Would that work for you?" He was finally making time! Too preoccupied with my desire to hear from him, I didn't grasp the subtleties of his message.

"That would be great," I responded.

I was filled with relief. After eight long days of minimal contact, we were finally going to connect. I was so accustomed to having to be fit into his busy life that there was only one explanation I could surmise for his distance since my arrival in Maui. By nature, Alex was self-absorbed.

He would go days without showing a care for my needs. I was accustomed to this, but at the same time, I hoped my absence would have helped him come to the same realization I had: he had taken me for granted as I had done to him and of so many things in my life.

In my own delusion, Alex wanted to talk with me, finally and after all that time, because he was going to come to Hawaii early, to spend the holidays with me, when we'd figure out our next path in life. Then, I felt sure of it, I would return back to Washington with him. My knight in shining armor would bring me home. That is what I secretly wished. Still, I feared, would he really come for me?

The next morning couldn't have come slower. I woke early to the sounds of the mourning doves. They talked to me in the ways of Spirit and I meditated on what medicine they had to offer me before placing my feet on the ground for the day. *Be gentle with yourself and with Alex, I intended. Whatever he has to say, receive it with your heart and speak from your heart. Allow this to be peaceful.* I had so much that I wanted to express to him, my heart felt like it would burst.

With my morning coffee in hand, I hunkered down on the cracked leather couch outside. I waited. I was always waiting for Alex. Eager to talk to him, to tell him how much I loved him, how much I wanted to make our relationship work, it seemed even my cell phone felt my pensive grip. But I would never get the chance to say any of this to him.

Ring, ring......ring, ring

It was him! Finally!! It was only 7:00 a.m. in Hawaii, my housemates were still asleep, and the only thing I had to share him with that quiet morning was the cooing mourning doves.

"Aloha!" I whispered into the phone so as not wake my housemates.

"Hey," Alex replied. "How's it going?" This was his routine greeting when on the phone, not necessarily interested in hearing an answer, but only an automatic reply to my voice. I knew that he would sense a negative reaction in me, so I smiled, even though I knew he couldn't see it, and I tried to cover up my desperation of my ailing body, distraught mind, and shaken spirit.

"Good..." I said slowly.

We talked briefly about what I'd done in Maui those first few days. I told him about my beach time and my daily walks, the dogs at the house, my housemates, and how I got my car, Rupert, from the shipping yards.

"So," I said, full of hope, "do you think you can come in time for our anniversary?" With those words, I opened the door to our fated conversation.

This was the easiest and gentlest way I could bring up the subject, without seeming too attached or eager for his awaited answer. And even as I opened that door, I thought: *How odd that I still think this way around him after five years, this walking-on-egg-shells way.*

"Look," Alex began, and all he had to say came out at once. "I've decided that I don't want to be a part of any of this anymore. I'm out." Just like that, very much to the point, with no emotion except resolve. "I'm tired of this whole sickness crap. I'm tired of you always on the move. I don't want to have anything to do with you or Hawaii. I'm staying right here."

Most people in this situation might react with a sinking heart, a clogged throat, spreading panic. But me, my reaction went straight to survival. Instead of falling apart into a puddle, I matched his rigidity, hiding any authentic emotion that he might misconstrue as weakness. All of the feelings I'd wanted to share with him were suddenly washed away once he spoke those words and the floodgates opened. I had no chance to salvage any part of my point; it slipped from my fingers along with the life I had created for myself with him on Lost Lake. All of it went downstream in a torrent of emotion and hurt.

"That's it," I challenged, curtly meeting his thorny voice with my own.

"Yup," he said. "That is it. I'm done. I want out. The way I see it is this," and he began compartmentalizing all of our life together, "the animals are fine with me, I see no reason that I can't just keep them here where they're happy. You don't need them in Hawaii. Why don't you just start your own life there? Start from scratch." He said, "Fresh. I'll stay on here at the lake house with the animals."

Excuse me? Did he just swoop in and suggest I leave my three wiener dogs and four cats, a closet full of clothes, and a full house, all of which was mine before he moved in with me? Did he just tell me that our pets, my babies, would be happier with him than with me? Did he just try to claim the house, our *house, as his own?*

I was stunned, completely stunned. I was also hurt and angry that I was duped, tricked, manipulated and beguiled by his persuasive ways.

"There's no way to convince you otherwise?" Anger spoke through my words instead of the truth in my heart. I didn't want any of this to happen, at least I didn't think I did.

"I've made up my mind," Alex said. "I truly believe I am living my most authentic life now. I am on my spiritual path. You went through a portal when you went to Hawaii, and so did I on the way home from the airport. Things aren't the same anymore. I can't go create a life with you in Hawaii. I'm tired of all the chaos and sickness. I am just done."

There was nothing I could say. I knew intuitively once an Aquarian made up his or her mind, the deed was done. Done. It was like the wax seal of a king melted over the opening of a secret document.

So that was it. In one, fated phone call, all my ideas and all my hopes for returning home were gone. That wasn't my home anymore. I was no longer welcome there, with my animals and other creature comforts. There was no returning now. Going through that portal to Hawaii had severed our relationship. Destiny lit a match and burned everything—every definition of security and home I held in my head and heart—to the ground. Devastation replaced panic, despair replaced hope, grief replaced nostalgia, and keening replaced happiness. Not only had my solar plexus been ripped out of my body, but now my heart chakra had been ripped out too. My knight in shining armor wasn't coming to rescue me. I guess that knight didn't know how to sail such stormy seas.

"Can we please have a spirit-centered conversation so at least we can honor what we've had?" I had pleaded with him in the midst of a long-winded email, hoping to get him to at least talk to me. Days had passed and I still clung to the hope of some closure, some further understanding as to why Alex was so resolved.

Like an addict in major withdrawal, I needed a fix, just a taste of his love. Any kind of attention would do. I was desperate for closure and any shred of hope that may have still lingered for our relationship. What my heart really wanted was to honor each other's new path and to know that there was some shred of love that still lingered in Alex's heart. But I couldn't seem to find him or his love anywhere.

"I am truly stunned by you," he finally replied by email. "You refuse to get it. I am no longer responsible for your emotional needs and I no longer need to answer to you or talk to you. Whatever it is you are looking for, you're not going to find it with me. I have a better life now. Good luck with yours."

The warmth of his love was the pendulum that had swung from passionate, intense admiration and into the frigid world of cold, callus, and cruel. Alex took an axe and chopped down what we had built together. Still, I couldn't believe what I was reading. *How could he cut me out of his life like this, and so quickly?* Anger took hold of me, and in the preservation of my tender hurt heart, thorns of protection formed.

"This is the last shred of compassion and love I will extend to you," I wrote in an email to him. "I am going to get my babies back from you and never think of you again!" I was so deeply saddened that I wasn't going to get the goodbye from him that I thought our relationship deserved, and equally as saddened that I had reacted so poorly.

My whirling emotions led me down a bitter lane of shock that Alex premeditatedly took my babies, took our home, and sent me to an island in the middle of the Pacific Ocean to be a sick, orphaned castaway with no security or help. I could have seen the state of my life at that moment as divinely conspired for the greater good of my life, but my broken heart wasn't at the same place as my higher self. Not yet.

Ocean Medicine

Feminine in being, the Earth is capable of healing herself and all of humanity. She gives us opportunities to heal by delivering messages in nature and by aligning us with her own heart. The simple act of standing barefoot on the earth can reconnect a person to his or her own calm center. The deep expansive ocean is her lifeblood, a space that contains vast knowledge of this healing energy. Salty ocean water neutralizes negative energy, cleanses the soul, and brings us back to the peaceful, still serenity of the womb. Floating in healing oceanic waters, we can surrender all of the hurt and heartache we hold. Single water droplets have traveled around the world to meet us. A single water molecule could have been swallowed by Jesus or blessed by the Pope, and the memory of these encounters is carried within its liquid matrix. Each drop of water is capable of blessing us with the wisdom, love, and healing that a weary soul needs. Ocean Medicine shows us where we are rigid in life and where we must surrender and allow. Her medicine also helps us tap into the deep waters within each of us, where our own wisdom lingers. *Where in life are you not going with the flow? Where is there resistance, where do you hold on to an idea instead of letting life take you with the current? Which of your emotions need cleansing by these healing waters? Where do you ebb and flow? How can you honor your own tides that rise and fall in life?*

CHAPTER 6

Heart Broke Open

THE MORNING MAUI SUN, soft and golden, was still low in the sky. Slowly, it warmed the sand, and then a gentle breeze tickled the palm leaves above me. A gentle walk along the beach produced the standard breathless fatigue that I was so accustomed to in my unstable health. The walk was enough energetic output for the day, and afterwards, I surrendered myself into a daily meditation by the water's edge. Feeling the unresolved discomfort of diving into my inner suffering, I wanted to shirk the responsibility of what still lingered in my heart.

"If I'm going to heal all of me, I have to face this," I whispered to the wind, where no human ear could hear me.

The surf's reassuring rhythm lulled me into a meditative state. Eventually my own breath rode along with the rhythm of the vast ocean, keeping sync with the giant inhale and exhale of the cosmos. An omnipotent awareness coursed through me that morning and created in me a deep awareness of all sights, sounds, smells, and feelings.

The daily practice of channeling energy, activating the chakras, and getting them to spin in unison had been a part of my world for many years. Like practicing music scales on an instrument, I had learned to channel energy as a daily ritual for my life and for the healing work. Because of this practice, I knew the cells in my chakras were harboring emotions that I still needed to process. My cells seemed to be holding the weight of the galaxy. I repulsed the negativity coursing through these energy centers as I meditated and its weight threatened to crumble me at any minute. I knew I would need to use all the tools under my belt to help these chakras heal.

Sometimes I felt energy move around my body, through my cells, and back out into the cosmos. Other times I simply aimed to release my energy back to the earth, stars, wind, or fire. But that day, I was unable to get my heart chakra to cooperate with my meditative intention. The energy had stopped dead in its tracks, like it had come face to face with a large, impassible boulder. Nothing would move in my heart chakra, try as I might.

Exploring the recesses of my own heart, like checking under the hood of a car, I inspected the obstruction. Discovering the energetic paths running deep in my heart, I continued to meditate. In an instant it became clear. My heart was broken. It was broken like a cracked engine that is so irreparably damaged that it can no longer function. Realizing this, pain and tears poured out from me.

My association to the heart chakra has always been through the color green. Just as the trees express love in various shades of green, I saw the heart chakra with the same vibrant green, abundant with love. I knew my heart was like a shrine for self-love and carried the internal compass for my soul's path. But my heart chakra was covered in black. There was no color found in my heart that day on the beach. And not only was my heart chakra black and broken, but it revealed what had felt like lifetimes of pain. Exposed through the broken fissures of my heart, beyond the black pain, were cavernous recesses storing innumerable old wounds.

Another failed relationship, I thought. *Another man walking out because he was incapable of reaching the depths of himself that an intimate relationship requests. Another man who couldn't handle the Lyme disease. Alex didn't try to understand it or have compassion for it. Another man to abandon me. There is so much pain in my heart. How am I going to fix this?*

Rocking to and fro to the rhythm of the ocean waves, unremitting sobs broke my silence. I fell apart.

"My heart is just broken!" I cried out. The grips of pain coursed through my abdomen and took away my breath. Holding myself, rocking in shock and emotional agony I keened over the wounds with the ocean as my witness. Earlier that morning I was afraid that if I let these emotions out, the outpouring would never end. But it was too late to stop the flood. The wounds in my heart had been exposed and now that I saw them, there was no turning back.

The fissures in my heart were weeping and oozing with longing for the love that once was there. That longing seeped into the wounds of my failures, my disappointments, and my betrayals.

I have lost so many dreams over the years to this damn illness! I've given so much, and I've received so little in return. Why is this happening to me? Why do I feel so abandoned by everyone I love? Why do I feel so abandoned by the Universe?

"Why?!" I lamented to God.

The horrific realization that my heart had been run over, stepped on, and thrown out flooded through every part of me. I felt betrayed. Try as I might, I continued to feel the infinite universal energy within me hit the giant boulder that was my heart with a thud. The energy had reached an impasse in the caverns of my chest. Nothing was working right, and I grieved that too.

A man strolling by disrupted this revealing meditation. A surge of negative, seething emotions replaced my introspection, and in a flash, I realized that he had been serendipitously placed on my path so that I could see more deeply into the cracks of my heart.

I have hatred towards men! Oh, this isn't good. I don't want to hold this in my heart.

I'd been disappointed by men so many times in my life. It was a realization that I chose to explore inwardly. *What does this mean for my self-image?* And there it was, an answer: *Hatred toward myself.* That was the only explanation I could fathom. I allowed this to happen, I allowed men to treat me poorly, and I have blamed others for this allowance.

Syncing my breath to the rhythm of the waves, I discovered that I was willing to compromise myself in order to be loved. The wounded part of me didn't see that yet, but somewhere in me, my higher self was watching like a dove in the rafters of a church. I'd seen the signs in my relationship with Alex, I knew we had gone awry months ago but I didn't want to believe that what I saw was true.

The man on the beach had come and gone, but thoughts of the revelation he spurred still lingered. *That man was a teacher*, I realized.

The emotions and admissions contained in my heart were bubbling to the surface on that beach as the sweet ocean washed over my pain. Remembering all the suffering I had experienced recently, I realized my life had consumed my soul and seeped out of the cracks in my heart. The pain was like a geyser unleashing heartache, disappointment, and grief over what seemed to be lifetimes.

In spite of my revelation, I still felt duped. Alex banished me to another land as a way to break apart the union I held so sacred. This was the story my wounded heart formulated as truth in my mind.

The waves continued to swell gently in and out, in and out, and eventually, gentler thoughts floated into my mind. Was this the only way that my guiding spirits could separate me from Alex? As I reflected on our relationship, I realized that he always referred to his world as 'I', never using the word 'We' when referring to the two of us. The inauthenticity of our union was glaring to me then, and it seemed entirely possible that this situation was divinely conspired to separate us.

Recollecting, *he never really fully committed to this relationship and I didn't want to see it. The magnetic attraction I felt toward him, my fear of being alone, and my hope of making our relationship work had created my own delusional reality that we were okay.* The signs had been there that we were not. I saw that now.

With those realizations, it seemed as if black goo was oozing from the gaping fissures of my heart. I became overwhelmingly aware that I had been holding my heart closed. Afraid to feel the hurt I felt my heart contract instead. It had recoiled like a finger touching scalding water. I didn't want my heart to be open if it meant feeling such pain, but I knew it was inevitable if I was ever going to face what was going on inside of me. Only then would my heart be able to pour its love into the world like the petals of a rose unfolding and radiating beauty for all to see.

How do I get past this hurt, so my heart stays open? Is it possible to release so much pain? Can I love fully with my heart wide open and not fear that I need to protect it from hurt? Oh this is so hard!

With the incoming high tide, I came to the simple realization that my heart had been ignored for some time, not only by Alex, but by me. This insight prompted another, equally difficult discovery: the way I *thought* things needed to be was disguising and compromising my ability to see how things *actually* were, to see the truth. It was a ploy, all to validate my self-worth and insecurities about being loved. My eyes remained steadfast to these perceptions, all to keep my heart from getting hurt.

These continual insights on the beach sprung forth more grief, which surged through my broken heart like the high surf undulating unpredictable currents. Still, the ocean was calm that day, lapping its rhythmic breath onto the sand, which couldn't have been more different from the angry sea inside of me. I allowed the ocean's loving presence to wash over the wounds in my heart, cleaning out years of hurt and self-betrayal.

Somewhere in my heart I knew that Alex was not the one for me. My higher self and intuition knew this fact within the first few months of our budding relationship. But I refused to see it, and I set out on a crusade to win him even though I knew he was incapable of intimate love with me. I acted not from a deep, supportive, self-loving intention within me, but with a mission to prove that I could get someone to love me.

After all, the wounded eyes of my heart were convinced that loving *me* was impossible.

Seeing now what the gaping wound in my heart had exposed, I understood that my relationship with Alex may have seemed beautiful from the outside, but on the inside it was merely two people, who felt they were unlovable, trying to love and be loved. Around this fear, we had created a reality to confirm those hidden wounds within ourselves.

The way Alex had treated me was the outward manifestation of what I had been doing to myself on the inside. Each compromise, disappointment, and justification of our relationship was a betrayal to my heart and soul. I was the one that had betrayed my heart—me, not Alex—and I was the one who caused my heart to break open.

As my days in Maui progressed, my heart continued to ooze, weep, and fight itself to close rather than continue to stay open, as it had finally done that day on the beach. In spite of the emotional pain I felt, I was sure that the wounds in my heart would serve as stepping-stones to my new life, and a new way to heal a lifetime of hurt that had been pushed aside just like I had done so many times with my symptoms of Lyme disease.

And so, I began the arduous task of allowing this heart of mine to stay wide open. When it wanted to shut, I consciously kept it open. The pain of these wounds crept into my life through my words, and I shared these words with my housemates. Even still, I pined for the comforts of Alex's huge arms around me, just as I longed for my animals. The life I had created up until my time in Maui was burned to the ground—in hurt, heartache, and health issues. There was no home or partner to return to. Shock waves vibrated through me with the realization that my former life had slipped through my fingers.

Whether I was walking on the beach, having dinner with friends, or waking in the early morning and sobbing, hurtful memories and emotions would float into my awareness unannounced. Naturally, the visceral response from my heart was to seal shut. But I held it steady, open, and I embraced it like a mother comforting her child. As the wounds and painful emotions surfaced, I released the pain rather than suppressed it. I released my tears into the earth, the trees, the sky, the ocean, the sand, and the stars. I loved every bit of what was coming forth from my heart; I bravely allowed myself to feel it and then release it.

Mother Maui was teaching me the true essence of the heart chakra: keep my heart open no matter how much pain I felt. I was consciously embracing the spectrum of emotions flooding through me. The waves, the birds, the wind, the rainbows, serendipitous encounters, and deep connections with new friends all reflected the lesson to surrender, allow, embrace, and wonder. I felt that I had suddenly discovered the authentic heart inside of me. Although I ached with loss, I knew that being present with my emotions and loving what was there was the best thing that happened to me in a long time.

With my heart wide open, broken facets refracted light into places that were once dark, bringing the vital potential within me to the surface. This potential contained the seeds of my new life, which had been waiting to germinate for lifetimes, perhaps. The journey I had embarked upon suddenly took on a new meaning: I was on a quest to heal *every* part of me, starting with my heart.

My morning meditation on the beach continued daily. Channeling energy through my chakras like practicing the scales, I learned more and more about the nature of my heart and what I held inside my body. The concept that *healing is an inward journey* had transcended into a whole new revelation.

I imagined the energy surging through my body were flower petals opening and blossoming within. I wasn't being asked to open my heart to the world, but simply, to open unto itself. Once it could achieve that, then it could bubble over into the rest of the world. I had to love all of me, every part of me. And now that my heart had opened, I was determined to keep it open, no matter what.

Pono Medicine

There isn't a word in the English language that fully translates the Hawaiian word *Pono*. Instead, what we have as English speakers is more of a feeling and way of being that conveys the energy behind this word. Pono is the feeling when the soul is in proper alignment with the custodial relationship one has with the earth and all of its beings. Pono means living right by our hearts and the relationships that we have with ourselves, our loved ones, our coworkers, and our own moral code. If properly aligned with every thought, word, and deed, Pono allows us to live in integrity and harmony with the earth and the heart. Life is either lived in a Pono way or it's not. Any discord, disrespect, or adverse feelings are healed in the ancient Hawaiian ceremony of Ho'oponopono, in order to make things right. *Where in your life is Pono present? Where in your life is Pono absent?* This ancient healing art is extended beyond individual people, and into the greater vision for all of humanity. Health, healing and happiness require Pono in order to thrive. Most of the time we are not living in Pono with ourselves because we ache for a deep, unearthing forgiveness for our personal actions. *Where do you need to forgive yourself? Are you accountable for your choices? Can you love yourself like the earth loves you? Can you find an internal Pono relationship?* We can make our world Pono when healing happens. Pono is a way of life, a moral code to live right, to love wholly, and to live with integrity.

CHAPTER 7

Pono Journey

THE MAGIC OF MAUI was woven into its very air, water, food, and flowers. *Mana*, the Hawaiian word for 'power' and 'life force,' was present in all things of that land. I knew it was present in all things of every land, and was responsible for carrying the fated messages for my soul. Mana did not always guide me gently, but it always pointed me in the right direction when I sought to heal.

Hawaii had a way of entwining me with all the other living beings on its islands, and reminded me that all my experiences and chance encounters there were actually divinely conspired meetings. Whoever I came across, I saw as a teacher from whom I was meant to learn a valuable lesson. So, by opening up my heart to this healing opportunity in Hawaii, and anywhere else I would go, I knew magic would happen.

Unlike the many places on this earth where time felt like a modern construct of a modern lifestyle, in Hawaii, there was only "Island time." In Hawaii, the rhythm of life was different. I saw firsthand that time was measured with the rising and setting sun, the phases of the moon, high and low tides, and Aloha moments like sharing a good meal with friends. Entering the portal to Hawaii, I submitted to living the island lifestyle.

Days quickly turned into weeks, and slowly but surely, the continual so-called *chance* encounters with beautiful people started to soothe my broken heart and weary body. The surprising and endless twists and turns of my journey began to transform from a harrowing, terrifying free fall into a relatively fun ride. Within a few short weeks, already I felt so much transformation, growth, opening, and expansion.

Many of the gifts I experienced by living according to island time were the shared memories between housemates and friends that quickly turned to family. My housemates were comprised of an aquatic massage therapist, a graduate student, a business owner, and a lawyer. They were all women, divinely placed in my path. All a few years older than me, professional, and self-sufficient, these women worked continually on themselves to show the world all they had to offer. They were also all lesbian.

Their sexual preference didn't make any difference to me, but what I noticed was that they all carried an energy of power in their womanliness. Each day, one of the women would do something, say something or stand up for something that reminded me that I was a strong woman, too. I was a strong woman who would get through this devastating period in my life, and I was a strong woman on a journey to heal! These women were my personal source of Mana Spirit, my life preservers when I felt like I was drowning.

After our brief email correspondence, Alex abstained from nearly all communication with me. My texts, emails, and phone calls went either unanswered or replied to with simple, curt answers. Through these actions, or better put, lack of actions, he made himself clear that he had no desire to discuss our relationship any further. Our breakup felt like a death. I was devastated in spite of my meditations; unable to talk with him, I could only imagine how our breakup affected him.

How he could do this after five years, I wondered. *How could he not even talk to me, to even have a gracious goodbye? How could he do this when so much of our relationship was based upon honoring each other's Spirit? How could he be so cold and heartless when all he talked about was living from his heart?* I couldn't help but compare his actions with how most people viewed him: *Everyone thinks he is so great,* I thought, *and look what he is doing. He is living behind a huge façade, convincing everyone he is this amazing man. And this is how he treats people when no one is look-*

ing! It all feels so very wrong! Why? Why would he do this?

Alex's actions were out of my control. There was nothing I could do to change them. The entire situation may have been divinely conspired as a way for us to separate, but his actions weren't Pono! The only thing I could do now was continue to look at what emotions I held inside and reflect upon my own actions. Were my own actions Pono?

To my already devastated body, the way Alex had behaved was the equivalent of kicking a horse when it was already down. My health had fallen from grace so many times already, and now I had to deal with losing our relationship. It was enough to crack me into insanity, it seemed.

And yet, through it all, my housemates—strangers to me only weeks prior—embraced all of me: the funny girl, the medicine woman, the sad-alone-and-scared little girl, the loving and kind woman, the strong woman, and the angry, rebellious girl. They embraced me just as I was at that moment, without expectation, and they fostered me back to my senses. In that house, we each embraced the individual journeys of our souls. Strangers became soul sisters. Beautiful.

In my mind, it was far more than coincidence that a group of strong, independent females landed in the same house together, on the same island in the middle of the Pacific Ocean. We were all on a quest for something. While I sought that which would bring me vitality, health, security, and a healed heart, Joy, one of my housemates, sought her authentic self-expression. Her beloved, Ahava, was on her journey to find the source of her power, her own Mana, which I knew could only be found within. The fourth traveler, Kerry, a strong, independent, capable woman was still learning how to love and to embrace her own feminine power, and free herself from the emotions that tangled her heart. Like all of us, her pursuit was an inner quest. One thing I learned from those women was that all journeys ultimately took place from within; and the fates had us colliding together on that island, each on her own quest, but united together in solidarity.

Wintery nights on the beaches of Maui were warm, gentle, breezy, and starry. Living only blocks away from the beach, that house and the women inside of it held magic, frivolity, and the seeds to create something amazing. I was sure that the ancestral spirits of Hawaii, the 'Aumakuas, were with me the entire time I lived there. The 'Aumakuas walked around us, played with us, and showed us huge sign-posts in our lives to guide us to our next destination.

One night while playing with a deck of tarot cards, we discovered key pieces to each of our individual journeys. We each felt the individual meanings the 'Aumakuas were wielding in the messages of tarot: expect change, be grounded, and all of the nourishment you seek will come. Awe inspiring magic filled the room that night.

Beyond that divine reminder and much-needed encouragement, we sang songs that night, told stories, and opened our hearts to one another. As we discovered with the tarot cards, we realized that our stories paralleled; our hearts and lives shared similarities. And yet, each synchronicity we discovered was met with enough awe, amazement, and wonder to fill the room with our exorbitant laughter.

"Oh, I...I will survive! As long as I know how to love I know I'm still alive!" Joy's karaoke machine, set to random, divinely picked songs that empowered us. Mixed with some wine and whiskey, Joy's leftover birthday cake, and Indian food, we created an amazing concoction of passion, exuberance, and terrible singing. Together we chanted: *"I've got all my life to live! I've got all my love to give! I will survive! I will survive! Hey Hey Hey!"*

Following the singing, we told more stories.

"I can't show up like I have in the past." It was Ahava, lamenting her story as we cuddled together on the old, now familiar, cracked leather couch on the porch. "I need to free myself from the life I've created. No one knows the real me. Joy is the closest person who sees me, but I haven't even really shown the real me to her. I feel like my heart is going to explode from trying to hold it all together. My arms hurt and ache, I'm exhausted all the time, and I know it's because I'm not living my truth. My shoulders continually hurt, as if I had angel wings fighting against me to open."

The epic girls' night lingered into the wee hours talking, sharing our hearts, our shadow sides, and our stories that connected and echoed to one another.

"I lost myself back in Seattle," I admitted. "I was so consumed with work and trying to keep it all together, even while I was sick. I lost me in the process. I forgot how to be in joy and live from my heart. I forgot how to feel free. I put myself in my own cage! I have felt so oppressed and I did it to myself. This is my time to reclaim all of me again." I shared my own story and realized as I shared with the girls, though Alex's actions may not have been Pono, the way I treated myself wasn't Pono either. I hadn't been living my authentic self.

"I understand," Joy chimed in. "I spent years in the corporate world, living the 9-5 work week. I look back now and I have no idea how I functioned or got anything done. I was totally consumed with work." Joy had quit her big job to explore healing modalities and, in turn, also embarked on her own Pono journey to live free in her heart.

"Well, I feel like I'm never going to find that special someone." It was Kerry's turn to share the wounds in her heart. "I'm so used to being in Alaska for the summer and in Hawaii for the winter I don't really give myself any time to get to know people. I really want to experience being somewhere long-term so I have the chance to meet someone, to be part of a community."

The couch held the energy of our words as we hunkered down with each other, arms folded, with legs on top of one another like little girls at a slumber party. It was bonding at its best. The words of our conversation traveled up to the stars, where I felt confident that the Universe could hear them.

"Ah, I love you guys." I said, touching each one as if I had known them for years instead of weeks.

"I love you, too," Ahava said. "I love each and every one of you. I am so profoundly and deeply touched to have met you. This is so special, what we have here. There is no coincidence we all landed in this house." Her sentiment echoed mine as I watched Ahava's tight, curly, blonde hair express the passion and love she gave so freely: wild, untamed, and bold, just like her.

Then I turned to Joy and said, "You had me at Kahuna!" We all laughed hysterically, at my words but also at the serendipitous way we connected. I hadn't intended on coming to Maui; I thought I was heading to Kauai. In fact, I had been looking for a room to rent in Kauai for months prior to that fated day when a plane carried me out of the rain and clouds and into the Maui sun. That was my agenda, anyway, until one day I read this online ad:

Room for rent in a nice Kihei home, walking distance to the beach. This home has been blessed by a Hawaiian Kahuna and is intended to be a house for healing. It is with this intention that I am renting a room, for someone who needs to heal.

A house designed especially for healing: that was exactly what I needed! The nudge from my guides and intuition trumped my agenda to go to Kauai. I was being guided, I felt it as such, and immediately surrendered myself to the musings of the Universe and what it had in store for me. I didn't really want to go to Maui, but I felt the pull to go there and I followed it. Maui was the island of the heart, and as I responded to the ad, I knew that I would be going to the land that I needed most. I was on a journey to heal my heart and I didn't even know it yet!

"I had her at Kahuna!" Joy repeated, and we all found humor again over the synchronistic musings of the Universe. "Oh, that is so awesome!"

Throughout that night, we each served to remind the other that our quests were dependent upon surrendering to the adventure. Maui's tender heart was speaking to all of us. Because our stories paralleled, because we were all on an inner quest, I believed that the Hawaiian Islands divinely conspired the encounter between us. I was without Alex, but instead, I was living with a group of women who didn't need men to live. It was this group of women who helped me through my transplant shock. Meeting them, living with them, sharing our stories and songs and laughter—this was the first of many blessings throughout my journey.

For those brief moments when our paths mixed and mingled, our lives would be forever changed. At least, I was sure my journey would be forever changed. Now, more than ever, my journey was a Pono journey. I was in alignment with something greater than myself. The oasis where we gathered for connection, inspiration, healing, and hope was

Pono, too. We were all connected, one, and sacred. A simple realization, really, but a dose of medicine I so desperately needed prescribed.

At the end of that auspicious night, I vowed with every breath in my body to take heed the lessons before me. I thought of that wooden plaque which greeted me when I first stepped through the house's threshold, of the word Ahunui, which was inscribed on the plaque's surface.

I thought about what that word meant: "patience with perseverance to heal with every breath."

There were no coincidences in that house. That much I knew. The meaning of Ahunui, how this concept could help me to heal, resounded through my body.

I needed patience for my journey, patience to wait for the new seeds to start sprouting; and I needed perseverance to stay the course of the path that was being laid out before me.

"Ahunui has a way of bringing people together right when we need it most." Joy spoke in her soft, yet stable way of holding the deep presence of her heart. When she spoke, it was with such intention that I immediately felt centered, as if listening to her was the most important thing I could do in that moment. "We are a tribe now, *Ohana*, a spiritual family. It is a beautiful thing. And I am so honored to have each of you here."

Solar Medicine

All beings of this world revere the sun. Trees reach their arms to the sun. We need the sun for food, warmth, and peace of mind. The spiritual connotation of the sun is likened to God, the Father of all beings. The sun is a life force beaming down upon this earth. Without it, we could not exist; none of the earth or the life on it would exist. The sun reminds us to shine our own light. When all is dark, we look to the East where new beginnings emerge at the dawn of each new day. The cyclic pattern of the sun reminds us to allow our own rhythms in life to wax and wane like it does. We rise, we peak and we summit, and then descend in our lives like the setting sun in the West. All of life cycles with the sun's cycle. It is this solar cycle of the dawn and dusk, winter and summer, that we understand that our life has moments of shining bright and moments that are dark as night. Yet, it is always darkest before the dawn. The little things that trouble us shall pass, just as darkness passes before the sun rises. The sun is our medicine, our guide, and a healing presence, which reminds us that we are merely beings on a huge rock, hurling through space. *What new beginnings in your life need to be embraced? What things in your life need to set with the sun? Where are you not shining your own light in the world? What blocks your light from shining? Are you shining too much in the spotlight? Do you need to explore your dark side to understand your own identity better?* Solar Medicine is here to teach us to find the light within.

CHAPTER 8

Psychic Download

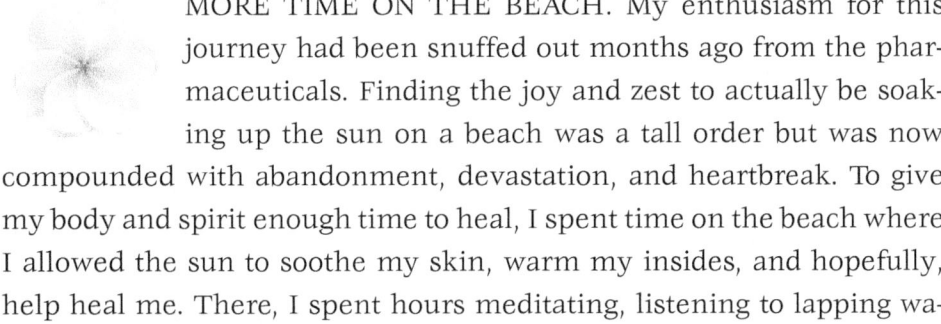MORE TIME ON THE BEACH. My enthusiasm for this journey had been snuffed out months ago from the pharmaceuticals. Finding the joy and zest to actually be soaking up the sun on a beach was a tall order but was now compounded with abandonment, devastation, and heartbreak. To give my body and spirit enough time to heal, I spent time on the beach where I allowed the sun to soothe my skin, warm my insides, and hopefully, help heal me. There, I spent hours meditating, listening to lapping water and laughing children, and focusing simply, but not easily, on staying calm and soothing the frantic energy of my tattered nervous system.

Since birth I'd been connected spiritually to the world around me. Tapping into the spirit world was as easy for me as opening the curtains in a darkened room. I was terrified of this ability at first, but over time I came to understand that it was something I couldn't ignore. I had learned the hard way over time that if I did ignore this connection it would be at a great cost to my soul and likely the planet. But now that I had so many physical stirrings in my body from sickness and heartache, I worried that the shock had severed this intuitive connection. Like phone lines downed and damaged in a storm, I wasn't getting a signal from the spirit world.

But when I tried to consciously channel energy, meditate, and open the curtains to that otherworldly realm, I realized my connection hadn't been severed, but rather, had changed. What I was seeing changed. Instead of looking out into the world for the answers, now my mind was turning inward, to my own energy body, to see what lingered there.

The sounds of the beach lulled me into a meditative state that guided me on this inward journey daily. Sometimes, there was nothing I could do except lie in a catatonic state and let my spirit guides run their energy through me in the form of telepathic messages, visual images, and scenarios played out in my mind as vividly as a movie. I listened deeply to my cells, noticing the physical and emotional sensations in my body responding to these incoming messages. And while I listened, they spoke:

"Allow yourself to be here now."

"You are capable of creating an amazing life."

"Everything that has happened is all divinely timed."

"Love this path, for it is in your greatest and highest good."

"Alex did you a favor."

Once I started listening, I realized that these and many more messages came to me through the ocean, the wind, the palm trees, and even through waves of energy I felt coursing through my body.

On one particular day at the beach, I felt charged up by the Hawaiian sun as I floated in the salty, warm, healing waters. As the gentle current held me, I imagined all the pangs of grief that I had buried so deep within me flowing out of my heart and into the hand of one being, the nurturing Mother Ocean. When my tears merged with the salty ocean waves, I knew I had been cleansed, baptized, by the ocean. I had experienced the sacred Ho'oponopono cleansing.

"Ladies, I'm home!" I announced amusingly, as I traipsed into the house loaded down with sandy towels, wet disheveled hair, and backpack. My time with the ocean and the cleansing Ho'oponopono ritual left me invigorated and at the same time totally exhausted.

Although I wanted to spend time with my new Ohana and see how their day was, I knew I needed to lay quietly in bed to recover. I always felt it as such the conundrum, how can someone be so completely exhausted from really doing nothing?

The Lyme disease was not something I openly talked about, still, and it was my visceral reaction to appear normal and healthy to new friends. Even though the room was spinning, my legs could barely walk my body to bed, no one in the house ever really knew I was in such physical misery. It took everything in me to take a shower and get into bed. So, without really seeing anyone, I quietly slipped into my bedroom hoping to go unnoticed for a little while.

I think I got too much sun today, I thought. I felt overly exhausted and wanted nothing more than to be comatose for a while. There, tucked into my cozy nook of the house, I saw a stream of pure white light come at me from above, down through the top of my head and into the crown chakra, where I connected to my intuition, the guardian angels that spoke to me, and to the divine wisdom of God.

Though I heard Joy shuffling around outside my bedroom, she had no idea of my physical state, nor the amount of energy that was channeling through me with information. As I lay there, an intense beam of light poured through me, trickling into all the recesses of my cells, which soaked these messages in like soil quenching its thirst. Light streamed into me until I was completely encased within it.

Taking account of what was happening in my body, I realized that my observation of "too much sun" was actually an experience I took to calling, "psychic download." Though this was the first time this experience happened to me since I landed on Maui, I was as comfortable with it as I was connecting to the spirit world. Through my training and practice as a holistic healer, I knew that every cell in my body was being tuned, as if my body were an antenna, until I was hyper-aware of the messages of the Universe. In that meditative state, I recollected the sights and sounds I saw and heard on the beach earlier that day. I knew that if I was ever going to heal from my many wounds, I would have to surrender to the guidance of the Universe.

Like a veil lifting before my eyes, I saw into another dimension. I saw my guides working on me as if I were a patient on their surgical table. This, too, was a familiar sensation to me. At times I felt the spirits working on my heart, my lungs, my brain. But that day, I felt my pelvis fill with their presence; I felt their love stream into my uterus, home to the second chakra—the location of all creative fire and personal power.

In that light, I was transported to the creative fires of my life, tapping into me like the tree of life would tap into the ground in an endless stream of life force. The light felt as if it carried sage wisdom. Then I heard a voice say:

"Everything you ever ask we grant you. Anything is possible, as long as you trust us."

Then, *Bang!* The bedroom door slammed shut, abruptly halting the repetitive clanking of the door against the blue geode rock propping it open. The sound had been distracting, but I felt paralyzed in my meditative state; moving felt virtually impossible with my weakened body. Yet, the door kept banging, kept distracting me.

I wish the door was shut, I had thought only moments prior.

An array of images flashed before my eyes: images of things I had manifested in similar ways, images of the amazing synchronistic encounters that led me to that moment, right then and there in that bed.

Through those flashing images came a revelation. The 'Aumakuas were working on my second chakra because I was being asked to take account of my womanhood. *This is why the spirits are focusing on my uterus*, I thought.

Again, I recollected the synchronicity of landing in that house, in a coven of lesbians who were self-sufficient and successful in their own rights, loving, beautiful, and free. I had felt their freedom from the very first time I met them. Yes, there were feelings of loneliness, isolation, and other emotions that their souls endured, but they had so much more. And I was taking notice.

So many days prior in my life were spent crying, pining, and grieving over the male relationships of my life. I had already given so many of my tears to the ocean during the Ho'oponopono baptism earlier that day. Yet, like the layers of an onion, my self-awareness was being peeled back one layer at a time so that I could see what needed to change.

With loving light filling my uterus, I saw my womanhood; I understood how I had perceived it. Up until recently, I needed male relationships to feel valued. But days prior, sitting, sharing, laughing on the cracked couch with my housemates, I summoned an inner strength that contrasted sharply to the abysmal feelings of worthlessness because Alex no longer wanted me. My higher self knew I was worthy of many great things in my life, but during my meditative state, my lesser self was being exposed like a rat in a spotlight.

With the previous distraction of the clanging door now silenced, I was sustained in my trance-like state. The ceiling fan kept its rhythmic beat in time, providing the necessary cool breeze to keep me focused on the white light inside of me. Through this light, I realized how I had compromised my own feminine power by holding onto the energy of the dutiful housewife. I understood, suddenly, that I had upheld the idea that I was not complete without a male in my life.

But now, I lived in a home where that dynamic didn't exist. The need for male presence wasn't even in the conscious thoughts of my female housemates; if anything, their actions and words showed me the complete opposite. They were light and free, to think for themselves, and make decisions for themselves without the careful consideration of their male counterpart. The stark contrast reminded me of how much I changed when the 'token male' in my life would come into a room. My needs went to the side, while his needs became forefront. I realized I had lost myself ingratiating Alex, instead of finding myself by listening to me.

Still, this newly found rat inside of me carried with it a palpable energy that expressed itself with heart-wrenching, gut-tearing sensations. Its symptoms crawling on my skin like scarab beetles escaping from the sarcophagus.

My organs shrieked at the now-exposed truth: I had relied on men for my own self-worth and validation. *Was I pretty enough, smart enough, sexy enough? Did I wear the right clothes to meet the approval of the man*

I was with? Should I cook the right meal to please him? Does a clean house gain his approval? Did I do it to please the man I was with? Should I do what he wants instead of what I want in order to keep him happy? If he isn't happy, then would he leave?

These thoughts, which had surged in the undertow of my mind, were now at the surface, where they swept me into a sea of accountability for my actions. This epiphany seemed like such a subtle thing on the surface, but removing men completely and sharing time with these capable women showed me how deeply entrained in my own cells it had become. With no male to seek approval, my body felt like it had been in withdrawal from some strange addiction.

My spiritual guides removed this rat I saw inside, in the form of a dark, sticky cloud. I saw it swirl with the ceiling fan and dissipate into the ethers. My cells were reprogrammed with the white light to remember the energy of the Divine Feminine. It was what I did in the healing work and now I was doing it to myself. Emerging from that psychic download, my body, mind, and consciousness were reunited once again with a single breath.

Suddenly I was back in my body, but unlike when I first climbed into bed, I felt myself holding a deep presence. Gratitude spilled from my being. I felt strong, I felt present, and I felt confident that all of what I had lived and experienced was all divinely in order, flowing, manifesting, and creating. They had done their job to show me the next place of my inner work. Inside of me was a powerful woman trapped inside a body with Lyme disease. But she was still in there! I wondered if I could free her from her entombment.

Have I been dimming my own light so that the man in my life can shine more brightly? Would my light have been too threatening? Is that why I stayed in the dark?

I'm sorry. Please forgive me. I love you. Thank you.

With this prayer, I blessed even my shame for my actions and I washed the negativity away in a Pono way. I knew I had to love all of me, even the bad stuff, before more healing would come.

Energy continued to pour through my head and into my body as it had done time and time before. I returned my awareness to my uterus, which was overflowing with light like the chalice of life.

All the energy inside of me bubbled up into each of my chakras. I gently massaged the places on my body that held my second chakra, my third, my fourth, and my fifth and so on. As I did so, each chakra revealed to me a vision of the life I sought; I began to feel my way into that reality, into my most authentic life. Suddenly I knew, I was sure that everything I hoped for was possible.

It was possible to manifest that life, to bring the Divine Feminine within me out of the darkness and into the light, it was possible to be healthy in my body and mind, and it was possible for all this to occur as suddenly as my bedroom door slamming shut.

Aloha Medicine

Aloha is a Hawaiian word often thought of as a salutatory expression meaning hello and goodbye. However, this word represents a very deep spiritual concept for life. "Alo" translates into English to mean "presence," and "ha" refers to "the breath of God." *Ha* is a sacred sound found in the names of almost all beings of enlightenment: Yeshua (Jesus), Allah, Buddha, Yahweh, Krishna, Amma. The "ah" sound is what summons the divine in all living things so that everything living contains the spirit of God. When two people greet one another with the word "Aloha," they are honoring the divine presence within each other. Whenever I say, "Aloha," I am actually saying in my mind, *I honor the breath of God that is within you.* I say it and mean it with my full heart. With one word, we can share a little bit of love and light with each other. Aloha also represents a moral code to live by, which is founded first in self-love and then overflows out to the rest of the world. When the spirit of Aloha is present in a person, beauty, grace, and authentic love are palpable. The concept of Aloha becomes medicine when it prompts us to ask important questions of ourselves. *Where in life could you share your self-love more authentically? Can you see the beauty of another's soul? Can you see the beauty of your own soul? Do you show up for yourself everyday ready to love and be loved?* The sacred word of Aloha is medicine to help each person's divine light shine through into the world around us.

CHAPTER 9

Burnt Pizza

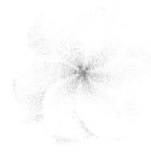 DURING MY FIRST FEW WEEKS on Maui, Aumakua of Turtle, *Honu* taught me that my home was already within me. Still, at that time, I had no physical home. I also had none of the familiarity and security associated with home. Yet, I hoped that all would be well, eventually.

The night before Christmas, I attended a Christmas Eve service full of singing, hula, jokes, and all the energy that I had come to expect around the holiday season. The unique Christmas gift that differed from all other Christmases that had come before was the Aloha spirit.

I went to the service alone. I was without Alex, without my animals, without a home or family to share Christmas with, but I made myself get dressed up and ready to celebrate. Still, with no tree in our house, and no presents, self-pity threatened to ruin my evening at any second. But I was determined to embrace the night.

My thoughts inevitably turned to Alex. That night would've been our five-year anniversary, and he was supposed to be on the island by now to celebrate. But instead I was on my own. The shock of our breakup was eventually receding like the waves I had watched so many times on the beach, slowly but surely. Finally, I had come to accept this journey of mine. *This is where I am in the world,* I thought that night, *and this is how it is to be.* Instead of turning the energy inside toward feelings of sadness, I quietly accepted the place where I was in the world, on that

Christmas Eve.

During the service I attended, a woman named Auntie Margaret led a group of hula dancers onto the stage. Ranging in age and size, the dancers wore traditional-style hula dresses that native Hawaiians adorned after the Christian colonization of their land instead of the stereotypical grass skirts. Their shiny evergreen dresses and giant, white orchid leis reminded me of a field of flowers blowing in the breeze as they flowed and swayed to the music that Auntie Margaret led.

It was she who saved me from toppling over into further despair on that night. This woman held the stage with her large, rotund body and thick, ample hair adorned with a crown of flowers. Although these features enhanced her solid presence, it was the Aloha spirit she brought forth that captivated me and everyone else in the room.

It wasn't often that I had an opportunity like this—to see and feel what it means to live Aloha. But there on stage was this woman, Auntie Margaret, who lived it with every hand gesture, every facial expression and every smile she offered. This type of Aloha spirit was so much more than the simple "Aloha" greeting I had heard so many times in Hawaii; this spirit was connected to the *Mana*, the One, Divine source that I believed flowed through all beings.

Watching Auntie Margaret dance on stage, seeing her bring the room into her bosom with a grand Aloha gesture, I felt her Aloha spirit embody unconditional love. It was this kind of deep, expansive, all-encompassing love that reached out through her hula dance and touched my heart deeply.

The Aloha spirit did more than merely touch my heart, though. It washed over me like a healing mist, taking with it any residual sadness I was holding inside. Auntie Margaret's face emanated such true, authentic love and joy that tears overflowed from the magnificent genuineness of this woman. She wasn't performing; she understood with every cell in her body what authentic love meant, what Aloha spirit meant, and she understood how to share this energy freely.

Watching her dance, I felt like I had stumbled upon a rare gem, that I was blessed to be witness to her beauty and grace.

Auntie Margaret was honoring the light that Christ brought to the world, the same light that she possessed in her own soul. She used her light to honor the light in each person watching her in the theatre. *Aloha*, I meditated through my steady gaze on her, *I see the light of God in you.*

I had felt this same light within me only days prior, when, during my deep meditation, I downloaded all the spiritual messages coming to me. It was a light I knew was within each one of us. Instead of feeling a lack—a lack of a place to call "home," a lack of a significant other, a lack of a healthy, working body—my heart was blossoming with a feeling of abundance for all that I had in that moment.

In that one moment of feeling her beaming heart my idea of what unconditional love meant completely changed. I realized, how I *receive* unconditional love is just as important as how I *give* unconditional love. The epiphany made my eyes widen as I continued to watch Auntie Margaret sway her hips and weave her arms into a story of days past. Before seeing Auntie Margaret, I thought that I needed love to be given to me in a certain way in order for me to feel loved. To feel validated. To not feel alone. But it was this conditioned way of thinking that left me feeling loveless and alone.

Sitting alone in that dark theatre, I realized that unconditional love is not selective. It is ever-present, everywhere for everyone.

The band continued to play rounds of Christmas carols, accompanying a poet, an opera singer, a jazz singer, and children's choir, while Auntie Margaret's Aloha spirit continued to resound through my soul. She was my teacher for the night. Had I not gone to that service, had I stayed home wallowing in misery instead, I would have missed this astounding insight that she brought to me: unconditional love meant not only loving someone no matter who they are or what they did, but also *receiving* love any way it is given.

My heart grew seven sizes that night, like the Grinch who stole Christmas when he realized what authentic love meant. The revelations expanded my perception of the world, and the blinders that once bound me from receiving love conditionally, soon fell away.

Love poured out through my tears as I thought of all the people that were not there physically with me, but were present in my soul. Surrounded by strangers who were watching the stage, I closed my eyes in the dark theatre and imagined all the people I could think of that had ever touched my heart.

I recalled teachers since kindergarten, old priests and nuns that were kind to me, old friends from childhood; I remembered my first boss, my soccer coach, every classmate, every patient, every friend. I saw my mother's face, my father's, my sisters and brother; I saw my nieces, nephews, aunts, uncles, and cousins. Faces, living and dead, one after the next, flashed before my closed eyes. I held in my heart and my mind's eye the eyes of each person I saw before me, each person I loved. I sent each one of them a beam of light and love from my own heart to honor them for who they were, unconditionally, as a light of God.

My gift to them was the Aloha spirit. The Christmas Eve celebration ended with a grand finale of everyone on stage singing 'We wish you a Merry Christmas'. The standing ovation and applause was to honor the entire night, but for me, my standing ovation was for Auntie Margaret. I didn't need Alex that night, I needed Auntie Margaret and the blessing she bestowed upon me. I was deeply, profoundly touched.

When I'd returned home after the Christmas celebration, Gracie, a woman who lived in a separate unit from where I lived with my housemates, asked about my night. The rest of the women were all still out enjoying Christmas Eve at their own parties, and Gracie had come over to borrow baking pans to make banana bread.

We exchanged a few words about our night while I prepared for the rest of my evening: pizza and a movie, with me all cozy on the couch. The house was quiet and empty except for the Christmas lights that shined on the Hibiscus flowers and Palm leaves outside. There was a very unfamiliar feeling inside of me, not of sadness, but of strangeness, that I was celebrating Christmas in the tropics. Instead of snow, the gentle ocean breeze brushed against me on the porch, along with a feeling of contentment and peace as I recounted my evening to Gracie.

After saying goodnight to Gracie, I stepped inside the house only to find smoke billowing in the kitchen. I opened the oven door and saw that my pizza had burned completely black! This was the first time in my life that I burnt a pizza to the point of being inedible, and it happened on Christmas Eve. It was a simple mistake, but it triggered a barrage of emotions in me. I had no Christmas dinner, no turkey, no ham, and no prime rib. I had no mashed potatoes, pumpkin pie, Christmas candy, dinner rolls, stuffing, or hot cider. I had no real Christmas meal to share with family or friends, and all the warmth I felt earlier that night went up in the same acrid smoke billowing from the oven. What I had was a burnt pizza, an empty belly, and nothing else to eat.

Tears threatened to erupt from my eyes, but somehow, the self-pity and sadness that washed through me changed into something entirely different. Overwhelming gratitude filled my being. I had something to eat, after all—I had burnt cheese. I had an oven where I burned that cheese in. And maybe most important of all, I was physically capable and strong enough to turn the oven on, slide the pizza on the rack, turn the nobs and set the temperature; and I was strong enough to stand outside, soaking in the night air while my pizza continued to cook into a crispy burnt mess.

Many times in my life I was too sick to even stand up. Now, at that moment, I was not only standing, but I had just attended a Christmas event, and came home with enough energy to slide a pizza into an oven. Thinking of my health, once again I was filled with a surge of that Aloha love. My life was perfect just as it was, burnt pizza and all.

It was a rainy Christmas day on the desert side of Maui. Rain quietly blanketed the normal sounds of mourning doves, while everything else was still tucked away from the rain. The entire island seemed quiet, sleepy, and still. With the familiar sound of falling rain, remembrances of my previous home on Lost Lake filled my mind.

I wonder what all my animals and Alex are doing right now, I thought. Images of that misty lake and the reflection of cloudy hues of morning sunlight sent me into a nostalgic grief, momentarily. *Grandmother Cedar, was she covered in snow? The geese, were they talking on the lake right now? Did Alex bother to put up a Christmas tree, or anything? How is he spending his Christmas?*

There had been Christmases in the past where I have wept and sobbed, wishing things were different, resisting where I was at that time in my life, when all I could see were things I didn't have, things I thought I needed in order to be okay. During those times, I had a closed, shut-down heart, and it was a terribly lonely place to be, especially on Christmas. And now I was on Maui, alone on Christmas, but I felt something different than other Christmas' spent alone. I understood that focusing on what I lacked created more fear.

But this Christmas morning, sitting under the covered porch and watching the rain fall softly, gently, peacefully, I felt content. I remembered the lessons of Auntie Margaret, I brought my awareness to the here and now, and I felt connected to the plants and animals outside. The mourning doves were cooing sweetly in a tree nearby. I felt connected to them in that moment. Just as the sky was sharing the rain with the doves and me, the doves were sharing the gifts they wanted to teach to me; I found myself receiving love unconditionally from the mourning doves, the trees, the rain, and the land of Hawaii. I remember thinking, *this shift in me is refreshing!*

I was selective about love before, in seeing it and in receiving it. I don't need to be on Lost Lake to feel loved. Love is all around me. I reflected that to celebrate the light that Christ brought to this world, I needed to celebrate the flowers, the plants, the sky, the rain, the garbage man, the nasty neighbor, and myself. Though I already knew that love was everywhere, this was the first time I genuinely and freely received it since coming to Maui.

*I would need to continually surrender
my own personal desires to embrace
the intentions of greater humanity.*

Storm Medicine

When positive and negative charges begin to counter one another in the air, their energy takes on a tinge of electrical intensity. The wind begins to blow and things seem unsettled, rattled by the disturbance. When a storm blows through, it brings change and the stirrings within it. We are not always aware that the power of this energy has the potential to create stirrings in our personal lives. Storms often bring change on levels that are not noticed in the mainstream, modern world. Emotions flare, arguments happen, discomfort in our lives serves as opportunity for great clearing. Winds blow change. Lightning brings power. Clouds show us our own inner clouds, and the wind reveals our inner turmoil. Often, we cannot move through a phase where we are stuck until something clears it for us. Storm Medicine brings just that: movement into our own lives. It happens in ways we couldn't have fathomed in the undercurrent of daily life, but it moves and shapes our destinies, our souls, and our healing. After a storm is over, the world feels fresh and clean again. The return of the sun enlivens hope for a brighter future. Everything seems clearer on the earth and within ourselves after a storm. Sometimes we need these inner storms in our lives to bring us out of the clouds and into light; sometimes we need storms to wash away that which doesn't serve us. *Are there storms in your life that you've been sucked into, and now you are spinning out of control? Can you see the light breaking through the clouds? Do you have emotions, attitudes and perspectives that are negative, which may counter the positive energy you could be expressing? Is this battle between negative and positive emotions creating a storm inside of you?* When storms blow in, they blow in change. Brace yourself, ride the storm and allow it to pass. The sun will shine again.

CHAPTER 10

The Hermitage

"I'M SORRY," I SPOKE INTO MY CELL PHONE, "could you please remind me of the house you're talking about?"

A moment before, my phone rang and a man who introduced himself as Alfred greeted me.

"It's the studio up in Kula with the big view and Tahitian furniture. My wife and I usually rent it as a nightly vacation rental, but for some reason the entire month of January cleared. It was the strangest thing," he said. "I've never rented it for an entire month before, but when I saw your email looking for a month rental, I thought we should give it a try. Saves me all the time of finding new people for the whole month."

Very strange, indeed. The month I had reserved to live in the Ahunui house was coming to an end, and fast. The magic of living with my housemates would soon be over. Already two of the women had scattered to other parts of the globe, while the other women had become busy with life. And now, I had three days to find a place to live.

But I felt myself holding back on other potential properties because nothing felt right—and I was growing more nervous about where I would go. I wondered if I should even stay in Hawaii. I was still so sick, and had no idea how I would find help. I knew I wanted to start a new healing practice when I finally settled into my new home, but I wondered how that was even possible while still feeling like I did. And I missed my animals so much. How would I get them back from Alex?

Initially, I had planned to stay three months in Hawaii where I could devote myself entirely to recuperating from Lyme disease. After that, I'd intended to begin making my many decisions for the future. Now, one month had already floated by, and in that month a lot had been lost, gained, and transitioned. But it wasn't time yet to be pondering decisions about my future; first I needed to find the next place to lay my head. And until I found that place, I remembered the lesson of Ahunui, of patience. *You need to persevere in order to heal. You need to breathe.*

I had no memory of emailing Alfred with an inquiry about the property he mentioned, nor did I remember a studio with Tahitian furniture. Considering that my memory was just one of so many things affected by the Lyme disease, I knew it was entirely plausible that I simply forgot what I'd done. But there was something more, something auspicious that I felt about the entire thing.

I asked Alfred if I could see the space in person. Already I felt energy around our phone call, those subtle nudges in my gut and heart that offered me telltale signs that my intuition and instinct were guiding me toward my next decision.

Through Alfred's description, I learned that the apartment was twelve miles from the top of Haleakalā Mountain. Alfred assured me that the view was incredible, as if I needed the extra push. Every time I left the ocean waters near Kihei, Haleakalā and the nearby misty hills of Kula beckoned me. The green swaths of land, Rainbow Eucalyptus, and cooler temperatures waved to me in the higher elevation. For weeks, its beauty had been luring me up, up, up to the clouds and dormant volcano. Now I had my chance, not just to go there, but to actually live there.

Stranger still. Not only was I in need of a new place to live, but Alfred called me during Hawaii's busy season. I'd heard many stories about the local housing shortage, and the difficulty that people had in finding available property. These stories usually involved professional people, who had careers and a life, but out of desperation, had resorted to sleeping on the beach and living out of their cars. I'd heard that rental properties made more money on vacationers than locals, leaving many temporary visitors scrambling for any place to lay their head.

Every day, it seemed, I met someone in the same predicament. These stories brought horror to my already rattled solar plexus. That I could wind up like these people, sleeping on the beach heavily weighed me down. Normally, I would look at living on the beach as a fun experience, but my body couldn't handle roughing it right then. It would have fallen apart, and I knew it.

Besides my health, being homeless in Hawaii wouldn't have felt so scary if I was there as a traveler. On previous trips, I'd slept on a few beaches in Hawaii, but that was when I had a home to fly back to and all the recognizable securities that surrounded a home. Now I didn't have a home anymore. I didn't have a job, either. Hearing the stories of adversity and the housing crisis, I was ever grateful to explore Alfred's place in Kula.

Along with my gratitude for Alfred's call came hope. *A month on a hill, alone with my thoughts, my body resting deeply—perhaps this is what I needed to help get me through this hump and transition. A month of total rest*, I mused. *Yes, this is what I need to feel better. I can sleep, be still and calm, and I'll be good as new, ready to start my new life! Healthy!*

It felt like more than just coincidence. It felt like divine intervention. *Why had I inquired about a property, which was normally rented for $280 per night and never offered as a monthly rental?* It was a total joke that I could even remotely afford a house at that price. I kept asking myself: *Why did I do that? And the entire month of January just opened up? How bizarre is that?*

Alfred's asking price for the month was far less than he could have got, at $1200 for the month of January, and though it was more money than I could really afford, I had no other options. I knew this was where I was being guided.

Aware of Haleakalā's reputation for being the quietest place on the planet, I summoned old memories where I had walked over its crumbling red rock, feeling like I was on another planet. Something was being wielded by the Universe and these islands. They wanted me up there in the mist of Haleakalā, close to the House of the Rising Sun.

The drive up, up, up through winding roads, twists and turns of lush farmland filled my senses with memories of the countryside on the mainland. Ah, the countryside. It felt so good to get out and away from the tourist-filled city, hot pavement, and into the cooler, greener landscape. Instead of beachgoers, I saw swaths of bikers riding down from Haleakalā. Driving required extra awareness with so many bikers, hairpin turns, and blind spots; and still, it took me a full hour to reach Alfred's place from sea level.

During the drive, along with the rainbows and rain outside, I was very conscious of the lack of oxygen in the ascending altitudes. The oxygen deprivation carried potential havoc on my already suffering body, where I knew bacteria thrived on low oxygen environments. I wondered if I was setting myself up for trouble.

But my ascent up Haleakalā seemed symbolic of the work I had set out to do. My real intention was to begin deep meditative work in order to heal and get clear with what I would do next.

In the meantime, I found a home—at least for the next thirty days.

I soon took to calling the apartment my "hermitage," for its isolated location in the hills of Kula. The little Tahitian shack seemed to teeter on a steep hillside where rooftops of other houses dotted the landscape below. The boasted expansive vista of West Maui did not disappoint. I breathed in the boundless view, and looked out toward the region where I knew the Ahunui house sat. From here, the whole area below me seemed tiny, a world away.

I had driven only an hour, and yet, this small degree of change completely shifted the way everything looked. From that height, I saw the area where the Ahunui house was, the nearby beach where I meditated, my old life, all from a bird's eye perspective. I understood that this was the first lesson on the mountainside.

What else does this sleeping volcano have to teach me?

Three days later, I arrived at my hermitage with Rupert stuffed with my belongings. The previous month I lived in a house with the Divine Feminine surrounding me in the form of independent, strong women; now, with an hour's drive, I had none of that.

I noticed that each transition already was exposing new layers to my healing journey, revealing more and more truths of what is being asked to let go. When I left the Ahunui house, my new Ohana (spiritual family), nostalgic moments recalled all the 'last times' while there. I heard my thoughts holding onto every moment and memory.

Oh, this is the last time I'll use Joy's beach chair. This is the last time I'll get gas at this gas station. This is the last time I'll get to sleep in this bed. This is the last walk on this beach. This is the last time I'll get to use the Vitamix. This is the last cup of coffee on the couch.

The nostalgic list was endless, serving as the poster child for the level of grief that was still bound in my cells. As much as I wanted to believe that I was moving on, my broken heart was still releasing layer upon layer of emotional bedrock, embedded deep in the crevices of my heart.

Holding on only creates resistance, I said to myself on the drive up. *All things will change. There is no permanent security in life. Best you learn this now*. I yearned for things to last and I grieved them when they are were gone. My nostalgia was serving resistance instead of acceptance.

There were no longer any distractions from *me*. The holidays were over and so was the security I had fostered living in the Ahunui house. Now, it was time to look at what I was holding onto and what I was resisting.

"You don't want to leave anything outside tonight," Alfred cautioned me that first night as I unloaded my few precious belongings from my car. He was securing the hatches down on his hilltop home, *my* hilltop home. "There's a massive storm coming in tonight. They say it's the biggest one to come this way in 30 years." Already the winds were picking up, and by the time he said, "One hundred mile per hour winds!" he was practically shouting.

I looked out into the horizon to see the sun descending into the ocean, already settling down to sleep. No clouds were in sight, but the wind foretold what was to come.

Another storm, I thought. *Just like down at Ho`okena. My initiation has begun.*

The spirits of Haleakalā were preparing me for yet another rites of passage. The swelling energy around me was powerful and fierce, just as the energies that percolated inside me.

The island and the 'Aumakuas wanted me here. The Universe wielded circumstances so I could find this hermitage, even as so many other people were struggling to find a home on the same island. So, here I was, living on top of the summit, with the ocean in the distance. A thirty day hermitage into the depths of my soul.

Knowing from previous experience that it took me about three days to adjust to this type of transition, I reminded myself to be gentle to my body and mind, to embrace the feeling of being alone, and to let myself surrender to the next chapter in my life. But with that surrender came the gnawing ache of homesickness, missing my friends down at the beach, and insecurity about where I had landed.

The abandoned little girl woke up inside me as the winds picked up force that night. I didn't consciously intend to put myself into a place of suffering, but pondering those times, I felt that I was teetering on the border of a very dark place, only this time I was alone, on a mountain in a storm.

Fear began to brew inside of me, and the inner charge of positive and negative thoughts became electric. The little girl inside of me was scared, needed love, and I was the only one who could supply those things to her.

As night approached, the winds howled and shrieked through the holes and unsealed cracks in the hermitage's roof and walls. Alfred had placed several buckets inside the house to catch the torrential rains that were bound to seep through the cracks in the old wood, already recycled once from a Hawaiian church. The power was out before nightfall, so any chance of a hot meal was long gone. Resorting to cheese, crackers and some fruit, I hunkered down in my new home for the ride to come.

The storm swirled around the little Tahitian shack, threatening to rip off the roof at any minute. It came from the stars, not from the sea. It came through whatever portal existed up at the top of Haleakalā. The blackness that surrounded me only exacerbated the intensity of the storm.

This is going to be one hell of a night, I thought, and with that thought came the sudden harsh reality of my decision. In essence, I had put myself willingly in solitary confinement for the next month.

I wondered, *Is this some form of strange subconscious torture? No,* I told myself. *No, it's not.* I had chosen to face everything that previously kept me from healing, and this was what that challenge looked like. My metamorphosis awaited me, I was sure of it.

Owl Medicine

Owls have the ability to turn their heads almost entirely around. This ability reminds us humans to look around in our lives in all directions. *Is there some area of your life that you are not seeing? Is there some area of your life that needs to change so you can move through your present situation? Are you seeking the things that will bring you happiness?* Owls also have the ability to see in the dark, an ability that reminds us of our own need to navigate into the dark recesses of our shadow side. If an owl comes into your life, it is there to guide you through the darkness, and to look at your life from new directions. Owls' wings are silent in flight, which allows them to swoop on prey without detection. *What is going on undetected inside of you?* Owl Medicine invites us to look for the truth within ourselves silently. They are the wise creatures capable of showing us many things that are buried deep within our own lives by teaching us to keep our eyes wide open in the dark. In order to find the light, we must know darkness.

CHAPTER 11

Aftermath

MORNING SUN ROSE over Haleakalā and bewitched the land with rainbows and golden rays of light. The storm was over, but the aftermath resulted in blocked roads, power outages, and no food to eat. The storm left an aftermath in me as well. Natural beauty was everywhere, yet I awoke with fear of my own survival.

I didn't have enough energetic reserves to go to the grocery in addition to moving my things on my own the day before. There was little food in the cupboards. There wasn't even power to heat up an old can of soup. I needed food, and fast. My body hadn't responded well to the storm, the severe change in altitude, and the physical exertion of moving my few belongings into the hermitage. I was having what I called, a "Lyme flare," and it was ascending into nervous shaking, weakness, flu-like symptoms, fuzzy thinking, and pain. But as I set off on the hour-long drive down the mountain in search of some creature comforts, I was confronted with downed trees, power lines, and cars in ditches. The storm that raged in the night caused a mess, and it seemed to have caused a mess in me. The grief and turmoil that flooded through my body left me in such a dark place from which I feared I would never find reprieve.

Though the wind and storm occurred only last night, the emotional storm within me had started days before my move to the hermitage.

And like pressure building in a volcano, I was finally starting to erupt. Haleakalā once released her strength eons ago in the form of a volcanic steam, venting and spewing lava onto the earth below. I reflected on how that must have felt: to be a mountain with the deep pressure building inside, ready to explode. The same was true for me. My insides were rumbling with so many unprocessed emotions. I suffered incredible grief over the loss of my family in Washington—my animals, Alex, my friends.

Is this the pressure building inside of me? Is this what I have to release in order to heal?

A believer in Karma, I felt that the suffering I endured in my breakup with Alex had cleared Karmic debt I had accrued over lifetimes. Still I wondered, *how much of this did I ask for? How much of this did I draw to me? How much of this did I manifest from my own thoughts?*

I watched my thoughts passing by in my mind and I was horrified at how much despair was in there. No one could possibly see all that I suffered by looking at me. Even in pain, I was always smiling, loving, hugging, inspiring. But now I was alone, with no one to smile at or love or hug except me. I was alone with my Tahitian furniture and marvelous view.

When my second night at the hermitage approached, I felt the negative thoughts encroach, feasting on all the positive things that I built up during the day. I was so accustomed to being in some form of bodily or emotional pain that I hadn't realized I was conjuring up enough pain for both Alex and me.

There wasn't any way I could have stopped any of this. This illness has ruined everything I've held dear. No wonder Alex doesn't want anything to do with me.

"You just need some time to find you," Alex had said this to me many times in conversation over our five years together. "It is the only way you're going to get well and have a good life. YOU need to find YOU." I resented him for this statement; although I knew it was true in many ways, I didn't want to hear him say it. What I wanted was for him to want me.

This was the vantage point I now faced, and it made me uncomfortable in my own skin. I didn't want to be with me. But I had no choice. Now, ready in the isolation of this hermitage, I was determined to face all of me. I was living on the mountain of Haleakalā, faced only with ME.

But whenever I looked inside of me, all I found was pain, fear, worry, and doubt about my path. The scared, wounded little girl inside reared her head in constant complaint. Like a homesick girl stuck at summer camp, all I wanted to do was go home.

What did *home* even mean? To my little girl it meant returning to my childhood home in Kentucky like a broken animal licking its wounds. I wanted to put my wounds behind me, but how could I do that?

How is it possible that I'm tucking my tail already, wanting to go home already to lick my wounds?

Home was within me. I understood that. I learned it from the turtles, but was it a lesson that I authentically embodied? The resistance I felt to my circumstances made me realize that I would need to learn this lesson over and over again.

Sun broke through the clouds above Haleakalā. Powerful rays hit swaths of ocean below, like beams of light from the heavens, as far as my eyes could see. In that moment, I saw myself as a mere ant on a basketball hurling through space. This giant galaxy was full of so much magic and wonder, and it was far beyond the comprehension and power of this simple-minded ant. A bird soared close to my head, gliding far above the rooftops dotting the hillside below. It was an owl. It circled around again, this time in a new direction. And again. Four times it circled above, in four different directions: East, South, West, and North.

This was a powerful sign to me: a different life was emerging for me now. But as the owl showed me, I would have to look in all directions to find it. I had to look for my life.

Emotions filled my little Kula cottage, my hermitage. I walked inside and I was there. Me. I was the only thing in that space, the only thing to fill it energetically. There were no animals, no distractions, nothing but my own shadow, my light, and something churning inside of me that felt very yucky and purgative. The only person that could lick my wounds, I realized, was me.

That night, and for many nights thereafter, my own sobs woke me from my dreams. It was my subconscious purging itself in my sleep. I'd learned that in Chinese Medicine, the time for the body's display of grief was strongest between 3-5 a.m. Considering that five short weeks ago, I slept with three dogs, three cats, and a large man, it was no wonder that now I was waking up in sobs for a life lost. Now when I woke up, my bed felt ginormous, cold, and alone.

It was supposed to be different, I thought. *Alex was supposed to come and rescue me, bring me home and tell me he wanted to be together. It wasn't supposed to end like this.* The grief inside of me clung to my old perceptions like a tree refusing to lose its leaves in autumn. Though I knew that acceptance was both the challenge and the trigger for release from my suffering, frustration wove into my grief, and my thoughts were consumed with condemnation.

Look at you! You are living in the closest thing to paradise on the planet and yet you are still swirling in your own personal hell. There are thousands of people who would love to be in your shoes. Look how pathetic you are. You can't even wake up happy for being in Hawaii. What is the matter with you?! There is magic everywhere and you can't see it or appreciate it.

The owl had reminded me that I had to look for my life, but whenever I looked, all I saw was a huge mess to clean up. I didn't even know where to start.

My path wasn't nearly as clear as the expansive blue sky or the ocean. The lenses of my perception were still focused on a life that should have been, could have been, but wasn't. I knew that the toxic energy I was putting out would stop the force of miracles waiting to sprout in my new life. I was so very aware of what I was doing, and yet, I couldn't stop the grief and pain. I had to embrace it and love it like I did with my broken heart. But I couldn't get passed the past. It haunted me and shrouded my experience of the island everywhere I went.

Mountain Medicine

The Inca Empire throughout Peru, Ecuador, and Bolivia referred to the spirits of the mountains as *Apus*. Translated into English Apu means "mountain." The Apus around the world serve to represent the strength and wisdom that they have to offer. These solid, sentinel beings reach up toward the heavens for a chance to be in the stars. They symbolize the ascent of our own personal healing and the strength that is required to do so. Around the world, Apus are connected through bedrock, tectonic plates, and other deep communication systems to the core of the earth. Sacred, spiritual, and strong, Mountain Medicine summons within us our own strength and the interconnectedness with the very core of the earth. Like the crown chakra, the tops of mountains bring forth heavenly energy into this earth, where it guides and shapes humanity in the undercurrents of our world. Mountain Medicine teaches us to stand strong, fiercely strong, and to not waiver. It teaches us to find that solidity of a mountain within ourselves. *Where in your life are you feeling unstable? Is there a part of you that feels like crumbling? What do you need to summon inside of yourself to stand tall with unwavering strength? Is movement too much, do you require some stillness to solidify?* Mountain Medicine summons us to point our own psychic antennae toward the heavens for internal guidance and wisdom. It embodies strength and the reminder that in standing tall within our own identity, like a mountain does, we cannot be shaken.

CHAPTER 12

The House of the Rising Sun

CRUMBLING VOLCANIC EARTH CRUNCHED under my feet, and this was the only sound I could hear in the silent mist. Silver swords, a plant that only grows on top of Haleakalā Mountain, glistened with dew along its shiny, silvery, slender leaves. The subtle grey-green leaves were a stark contrast to the red earth below them. Remnants of the thick lava that once flowed eons ago gave me the impression of being on another planet.

Haleakalā, which translates into English as "the house of the rising sun," carried with it a vortex of energy that pulled my mind out of the mundane and straight into another dimension where sights and sounds once familiar to me became foreign. Time and other dimensions I knew at lower altitudes all stood still, and with its stillness carried the intense feeling of other-worldliness. I felt pulled into the heavens.

This was not my first time walking up this mountain, and as I walked, memories from five years ago came alive. As part of a two-week training for spiritual healing using sacred geometry and shamanic cranio-sacral, my teacher and friend, Ram Ji, took our group on a very long hike into the crater.

The expansive, listless earth where lava once flowed became our place to meditate and connect with the potent energy that lived in its caverns. It turned out to be a very important day for me, but not only because it was the first time had I walked within that crater. That was the day I received my spiritual name, Sahara Sun, which I eventually adopted in place of my birth name, Jenny.

Ram Ji and I had broken off from the group and were walking quietly together. He broke the silence when he said to me, "I couldn't sleep all night. And it was because of you." When I looked over at him, I saw that Ram Ji's long braided hair and Peruvian hat were both adorned with glistening droplets of dew from the settling mist. The crunching sounds of the volcanic earth continued to echo into the silence of the fog as we walked along.

"Me?" I asked. "Why?"

"I kept hearing a name over and over and over again for you, all night long. Like a mantra. Sa-Ha-Ra."

During a period of my childhood that coincided with puberty, I often woke in the mornings with my face covered in blood from nosebleeds and my head filled with visions of the future. The sight of my dried blood was always shocking to my sister, Sarah, who woke me for school. Until adulthood, I did not understand these visions as premonitions, nor that they could have been associated with my hemorrhagic nosebleeds. Those premonitions showed me the world, my life, and the importance of what was to come, most of which I did not fully understand until adulthood.

Within these visions, prophetic, descriptive, and sometimes dire messages were also communicated. One of these messages told me that I would receive a new name. I didn't know when I would receive it, but I knew even then, at the tender age of ten, that the offering of my new name would be from a male, and it would come when I least expected it. For the next thirty years, I carried that inner knowledge, quietly waiting for it to arrive.

And when it did, I was standing on a dormant volcano, known as the House of the Rising Sun.

"SaHaRa?" I asked, wondering at the meaning of this word. Of all the names I could have received, why this name?

Ram Ji explained that the name SaHaRa had ancient Sanskrit roots: *Sa* meant "divine healing," *Ha* meant "from the breath of god," and *Ra* meant "in the form of the sun." Put together, the name *Sahara* meant a divine healing from the breath of god in the form of the sun.

From that day forward, I carried a deep knowing inside of me that when I did finally embrace the name Sahara, it would change the vibration of my cells. This new vibration would create a cascading effect that would shape and change me, and thus change my world. That it did.

Five years later, standing in the middle of the Haleakalā Crater for the second time in my life, finally embodying the name Sahara, I felt my identity circling back to this alien volcanic rock once again. The power there felt the same as it had during the hike with my retreat group and Ram Ji. And it reminded me of the power I was trying so desperately to resurrect in my own body. It was as if anything that resonated with the energy of my old life was being painfully and arduously released from my being: Alex was part of my old life, Lost Lake was part of my old life, and the illness still inside of me was part of that old life, too.

Five years ago, my new spiritual name had catapulted me out of my longstanding life and into a new one, where I still didn't feel comfortable in. Not yet anyway. The strength of Haleakalā beneath my feet showed me how the pain and grief of the old was shrouding the potential of my new path being laid out before me. Being there again on that mountain—it was all divinely conspired for my soul's journey. Later, when the cold of night settled onto my red down jacket and white hat, I sat undisturbed in meditation on top of Haleakalā. I prayed as the sun went down, and when it did, the temperature change was a stark contrast to the scorching heat I knew would still be at sea level. Still, I continued to pray: expressing gratitude for my life, for help to embrace my journey fully, and for guidance when I took the next step, the next journey. Where would I go, what would I do? I was untethered, uncertain, and alone.

After climbing out of the crater and eventually under the bedcovers in my hermitage, I could see the same stars from my window that I saw from the crater. I prayed once again: *Haleakalā, please show me the way. Give me a sign where I am meant to go, what I am meant to do. Where do you want me on this planet?* It was a prayer of desperation. Sleep soon carried me into a much-needed mental reprieve, only to be halted again in the early morning hours.

Ring, ring! Ring, ring!

Islands may have their own sense of time, but at that moment, it was 5:30 in the morning when my phone woke me. It was my sister Sarah. The ringing itself was a sign I recognized, since I usually kept my phone's ringer set to silent while I slept. That night, for some reason, I had left the ringer on.

"Good morning," Sarah said.

"Morning."

"I'm sorry to wake you, but I saw Mom today."

At that point, my mom had been suffering from Alzheimer's for at least ten years, though we never knew for sure because my father went to great lengths to keep her sickness secret. To me, I felt that I had already lost my mother years ago, the mother I once knew anyway, into the darkness that takes a person with this illness. I missed her terribly and many tears have been shed longing to be with her in the last days of her life.

"I found her sitting with a card you had sent her," Sarah said. "Mom said, 'Look, Jenny sent me some sunshine.' Then she started crying and went on about how much she missed you. After that, I knew it didn't matter how early it was where you are. I needed to call you, so you could talk to her."

I was so stunned and shocked that the guidance of this mountain produced a direct sign of a phone call, my mother, still such an intuitive person even in the cloud of Alzheimer's. She was the catalyst behind this message; I was so sure of it that I started to cry.

Did this mean Haleakalā was guiding me back to Kentucky? Was this an answer to my prayer? Was my soul's path to return home? Or was this phone call a random event that had nothing to do with my prayer?

Immediately the memory of my mother's singing flooded my mind.

"You are my sunshine, my only sunshine. You make me happy, when skies are grey. You'll never know dear, how much I love you. Oh please, don't take my sunshine away."

My mother had sung this song to me for as long as I can remember, and it summons tears from me anytime I hear it. The memories of her voice were rooted deep within me before the Alzheimer's took her mind, and even after, when her illness never touched her childlike heart.

Though at times she could not remember how to tie her shoes or use a fork, she could still summon that song, from her heart, not her head, and sing it with me. Along with these memories came the more recent ones, of us singing the song together in the nursing home where she lives—mother and her youngest child. During those times, I savored her mothering energy for all of the times I could no longer communicate with her through phone conversations, or ask for advice. I savored her loving presence that only a mother can give.

Through all of those times, she referred to me as her sunshine.

"You are the sunshine of the family." She would say many times over. "You just bring a light that we need."

I knew that my idea, my hope, my intention of living a grand life in an exotic place like Maui was merely my own dreams, my own ego's desire to experience a life worth bragging about. But I also had made a vow in my early twenties of unconditional and universal service to whoever was listening in the heavens. This vow happened during a Shamanic Initiation ceremony, I pledged that if I was meant to live a life of service, I would need to continually surrender my own personal desires to embrace the intentions of greater humanity.

I also knew, even at that moment at 5:30 in the morning, despite my sleep-filled mind that I would need to humbly surrender my control to embrace a path I knew nothing about. Even though I felt like I was drifting aimlessly, always searching for the next step, I'd known since my childhood days of nosebleeds always what I needed to do. I needed to listen to every single message, both subtle and obvious, that was revealed to me. These were the signs that would guide me down the path of my life's journey.

I have run out of excuses, I thought, still cradling the phone to my ear, still hearing my mother's voice through the receiver. *I can't control my destiny. I can't assume that I know what's in store for me. The only thing I can do is let each stepping-stone guide me forward.*

Now, more than ever before, as I lay in bed in my hermitage on the mountain, I knew I had already begun to surrender. *If I am to continue to leap into the unknown, into what the Universe wants my soul to do, then I need to get my body better! How am I going to do anything if my body is constantly suffering?*

My sister's phone call had rattled me from my sleep, but also from the cage I had put myself in. Suddenly I felt pulled back to the mainland. That much was clear to me. I wasn't sure where yet, but this was a sign. I needed a home, *my* home, to get better physically. I understood with one phone call that Maui wasn't my home, not at that time.

I wasn't meant to stay on Maui, after all.

*Healing runs deeper than a pill
and can be more profound than
an epiphany from the mind.*

Mana Medicine

The Hawaiian word *Mana* translates into English to mean "power." This isn't the kind that can be acquired from material society where success, money, land, achievement or talent is recognized as power. This kind of power is from the earth, the stars, and the Universe. Mana is a force that we all possess, which can be summoned within us when we are walking Pono in the world. Finding a way to be in service, to be helpful, will build Mana in your life. It will come forth in food, flower, and abundance for your world. A person who has great Mana is one who lets their light shine to the world. Mana is the sparkle in a person's eyes, the joy emanating from a baby, the love and compassion felt in an elder. The Mana of the land, the Mana of the soul, the Mana of a relationship are all one in the same. It is the light of the god/goddess, masculine and feminine energy, and the infinite power shining through all matter. *Have you found your mana, your own personal power? Is there some way you are living that disconnects you from the powerful life force that flows through all things?* Your own journey to heal and thrive is a summoning of the Mana that is within you. *Have you been on a quest for another kind of power that steals energy from your mana?* The quest for achievement, the perfect house, the perfect partner, the perfect job, the perfect body are all examples of goals that have the potential to dim your light, stifling the Mana that flows through you. Mana Medicine teaches us to find the power within, our personal truth, so we can live Pono from the heart.

CHAPTER 13

Star Beings

DAY AND NIGHT, THE SUN CIRCLED above Haleakalā then down into the deep blue ocean. Its return the following morning was the only constant, the only thing I felt I could trust in the midst of my despair.

Days passed in my Kula hermitage, where, even though I was in paradise, I suffered at such a deep level that even the sight of the sunset lost its inspiration. I knew my time on Maui would end at some point. My sister's phone call and talking to my mother had made that clear in my heart. But before I left, I needed to understand more fully what I was being asked to do. I didn't feel called to return to Kentucky, not yet anyway, and I was still combating the little bacteria in my body every day.

I pleaded with my guides and any divine being that would hear me:

Please, show me the easiest and gentlest path to take. Help me see clearly what I need to do. I can't do this without you. I don't know what to do. I am overwhelmed by fear that I cannot acknowledge. Please, help me. Show me the way.

Relentless tears poured down my tanned cheeks. Would my tears ever stop? Would my suffering ever stop? I needed guidance; I needed help. I knew I couldn't do this on my own.

"I'm going to this workshop to learn to *'Fly'* today. Want to come?"

Another phone call, divinely placed with my prayers. This time on the other end was Rose, my already dear friend whom I met weeks prior at a communal dinner full of wine and crepes, sweet and savory. Though we were little more than strangers then, in an instant I felt a deep connection with her. I felt we had been cut from the same cloth in the cosmos, and because of this, I felt she deeply understood the hidden energies of this world and beyond.

There was no need to explain ourselves or prove ourselves to one another; we both recognized our connection to the spirit world and we both appreciated that all things speak messages of guidance, grace, and wisdom. Stones, seashells, birds, plants, water, clouds, whales, words, stars, and moon: all things were connected in our minds. All things in the spirit world spoke to both her and me.

We spoke the same language and our fated paths embraced one another like two Russians, sloshy with vodka, who hadn't spoken their native tongue in many years. We reveled in laughter, appreciation and love for the kindred soul connection. She was another member of the Ahunui family and our kindred spirits felt each other's love instantly.

So when Rose called me, I didn't need to ask what *Flying* was; I already knew that I would find out. An answer to my prayers, however small, another stepping-stone on my journey. I only had to say yes.

On that quiet Saturday morning, we met at the Montessori school in Upcountry, which was still *down* from the mountainside where I lived in my hermitage, in Haleakalā country. As I headed down, down, down, the rolling hills and waving sugar cane danced and sang along the roadside at me and my little Subaru, Rupert. By now, Rupert had become not only my trusted steed, but also my best friend, going everywhere with me.

A small, yet mighty woman who seemed ageless to me led the workshop. Her tool belt of healing and teaching came from the ancient healing art of Kahuna bodywork, which was rich with indigenous Hawaiian medicine. Having my own experiences with Hawaiian healing traditions already, I deeply respected this woman and the energetic presence she held for the honor of this bestowed medicine she carried. She led our group to an area where huge banyan trees grew and the land overflowed with their supporting root structures. It was here, with these trees, that we would learn to *Fly*.

Rhythmic Hawaiian chants that summoned the 'Aumakuas, the Mana, and the healing energy of the land, accompanied the leader's ancient prayer chants in preparation for our initiation to this ritual. Her small stature only seemed to amplify the power of her words as she spoke.

"Flying is sacred dance that has been passed down for generations, before any other cultural influence came to Hawaii," she announced. "It is a sacred movement meditation taken from the essence of pre-Polynesian Hawaii, from the original inhabitants of this land who are identified now as the mystical Manahune. It is the essence of this ancient work that allows modern people to access a state of being where they are open to the infinite source inside them, communicating with the vibration of our cellular memory, our consciousness, and every aspect of our being."

I would later discover that the Manahune (later called Menehune as a derogatory term for lowly status and small in stature) were mystical people that lived in deep harmony and reverence for the 'Āina, the land that provides. Their connection to the stars were the seeds of their own consciousness and it resounded through everything they did. The Manahune were responsible for many of the ancient structures of Hawaii that existed today, such as the amazing walls constructed out of lava to make fish ponds, aqueducts, and more. I wondered if the gripping marks made in the birthing chair I was shown years prior down at Ho`okena on the Big Island was used by the Manahune women.

"This dance generates the healing energy of the infinity symbol inside each of you. Infinite movement with the cosmos. We are always in motion, even when still." Our teacher's dark skin and hair flowed along with her seemingly endless arms and legs as she demonstrated the simple steps that became complex when integrated all together into one fluid movement.

I watched her swirling steps and arms fly in a graceful act of ebbing and flowing into the shape of the infinity symbol. Some members of our group already seemed to understand its magic and settled into a meditative trance while moving their bodies as if in flight. Others stumbled over their feet, stirring frustration, but the energy of the dance held their focus. I found myself fall into the grace of the movement, but as soon as I started thinking, I would lose the steps.

"Whatever is coming up inside of you while you dance is what you need to work on," our teacher continued. "This movement offers you a reflection of what is held inside your soul. Go with it. Keep going."

I still found my flow, even if I was getting the steps only as best as my nervous system would allow. As I continued, I felt this movement open up my energy to reveal the limitless Universe inside of me.

I saw how my own daily rhythms of life were held in this infinity symbol. The infinite flowed through *me* with each graceful step (at least it was trying to). I felt carried into another dimension where this immeasurable connection and potential began to unfurl in front of me. As we moved into this trancelike dance, light and shadow were held arm in arm. I saw the Taoist symbol in the collective shape of our bodies, the circular yin yang, as it opened and stretched flat to depict the light and dark in that mysterious and swirling figure-eight symbol.

It was through this pattern of light and dark within me that I recognized how I was disconnected with that infinite flow of the Universe, all because of my resistance to change. There the message was again: I was *holding* instead of *allowing*.

"Don't stop no matter what comes," the teacher encouraged. The power of her words were building with the summoning energy of the dance. "Let yourself feel into this movement. Let it show you what you need to see."

I felt it, we all felt the power, the *Mana*, grow with our steps, her words, and the drumbeat of the music. The pace of our dance intensified with the rhythm, and its intensity carried me deeper and deeper into my own internal connection (or disconnection for that matter) with the Universe.

I can't do this. It's too hard. I'm afraid.

These were the thoughts that arose in my body during the dance, but they were the same thoughts I held about my life in general. All the fears I'd held onto so tightly were being summoned in the dance. I was being stirred and splattered all over the place, so I could finally see the big mess that was me.

I am too weak to do it alone. I don't want to do it alone.

These thoughts reverberated through me. Doubt around my choices and my resistance all surfaced during my graceful flight. The energy coursing around me, through me, and into the cosmos was so revealing and powerful and intense. I saw the chains that bound my energy from flying gracefully through my life, but my continuous movement beckoned me to release those shackles of perception that had enslaved my soul.

I could fly free if I only freed myself.

Impressive pain surged through my legs as I continued to dance. The urge to humbly fall to my knees in front of everyone was paramount, but my own stubbornness kept my arms flying and legs twirling. Eventually I felt my fluid movements intertwined around those shackles, straining all that I had to release. The pressure was building and swelling inside of me, and my desire to continue and my desire to quit lived simultaneously inside of me. The experience became a brutally honest mirror as to how I was showing up in my own life.

When we finally stopped and stood in the swirling infinite space under the banyan trees, the aching pain in my legs amplified. It was the onset of another Lyme flare, of which I was very familiar. But I held it together, ignoring the pain like I had done time and time again.

Later, alone again in my little Kula hermitage, I could barely walk. My legs seemed to carry the weight of all the wounds of my misperceptions. I felt that I had been cut off at my knees from the infinite source of all of creation. The ancient medicine of *flying* revealed how disconnected I was from living authentically in my body. Healthy.

What I held in my soul, in my heart, and in my own illusions created my world. I was sick from a bug, but I was also sick from me.

I ended my day with more prayers and meditation releasing them into the West, with the setting sun, the cosmos, to God, and the stars. It was all I could do.

Settling in after my prayers, I realized that none of my electronics in my hermitage worked. Just as the pain in my legs, this too was an issue that I was familiar with. I had spent most of my day silently connecting to others and myself while *flying* under the banyan trees, and now I yearned for the simple pleasure of watching TV after the sun set. But the cable connection was not working. Then I tried to turn on some music on my computer to listen to while I knit, but the Internet connection wasn't working either. I tried to play music on my phone instead; it kept shutting down.

Finally I deciphered this as a sign that I was not meant to connect to the world through electronic means at that moment.

So, in sighing acquiescence, I relinquished what I wanted and surrendered to what I was being asked to do. I laid there in silence, listening to the white noise of stillness in my hermitage. For the rest of the evening I did not think on other matters. I did not plan. I had no agenda other than simply to live.

And then, a light flashed. Then, more bright flashes. I saw little flecks of light descending through the ceiling. The humming of the refrigerator took on a deeper tone and shifted from one sound wave into another, resounding in my ears until the falsetto toning and humming sounded like music from angels. I couldn't believe my ears. Reflexively, I thought that the music I was hearing was coming from my computer, but my ears told me that the sound wasn't coming from the other side of the room. It was coming from the refrigerator, a simple household appliance.

The moments that followed are difficult for me to convey. It may be difficult for you to comprehend, but healing is often beyond our comprehension. Healing runs deeper than a pill and can be more profound than an epiphany from the mind.

As I allowed myself to sink deeper into this experience, I realized the seemingly possessed refrigerator was carrying the angelic sounds from another dimension. Time did not exist as it existed for most of my life. I was still swirling in the infinite Mana that coursed through me and around me. A veil lifted, and the seen and unseen merged.

Accompanying the noise, I watched flecks of light twinkle like stars. *Am I really seeing this? Or is this just the neurotoxins from the Lyme bacteria causing me to hallucinate? Is this really happening? Am I hearing things?*

I honestly didn't know. But I knew that the answer didn't even matter. I was in a deep meditative state, having another psychic download, and to my ears, to my eyes, I was in another dimension. It was a certainty that resounded through every cell in my body. Later, I realized that hours had passed, but in those moments in my hyperawareness, it seemed like only minutes.

Everything inside of me tingled and juddered. The sound in my ears was healing, gentle, heavenly, and it continued to carry me deeper and deeper into my trance. Lying motionless, yet feeling full of life and movement, I followed the energy coursing through me as it led me into an altered state of consciousness. I understood.

I was in the presence of far more than light and sound; I was in the presence of spirit guides, of messengers from the stars. Though I would not learn for another year that the ancient ritual of *flying* translated to mean "pathway to the stars," I felt the connection to those celestial beings. I saw myself standing on a bridge between dimensions, where humans and star beings once gathered together. Were the Manahune with me, too?

Whoever was present, they were there to help me, to see all the emotional wounds that had, up to that point, locked my heart and blinded me from living authentically. With their help, I saw very clearly the areas in my life where I was resisting change, resisting the evolution of my soul.

They showed me the reasons why I resisted and how that kept me sick. It happened so fast, but somehow I understood perfectly. The star beings were showing me the holding pattern: resistance. Then they showed me how to free myself: acceptance.

Suddenly, the shackles that I'd seen while *flying* earlier that day released! I felt an emancipation of my soul! So very aware of the shackles from my old thinking, I had asked for help, and help came. It came in all the synchronistic encounters that brought me to this very point, on a bridge, staring off into the heavens with beings from another dimension. These beings surrounded me in a cloak of light, which began to pull out the suffering I held in my body. They surrounded me in love, light, music, and healing energy until I finally felt free to fly.

The entire day of Flying and the visit with Star Beings held an alchemical medicine that would continue to work on me through the night. My cells tingled like one of those fizzy candies I ate as a child. Infinite movement coursed through my blood. I felt Mana like I had never known before. Then the portal closed, the light faded, and the music stopped. The energy of the room was still and not so still. The humming of the refrigerator was back to normal, the angelic toning was gone and the quiet of my hermitage held me in space and time. In what felt like a single moment, I breathed as if for the first time into a new body, reborn.

We all belonged to the same, single deep experience channeling Mana in all things.

Whale Medicine

Imagine having an eyeball the size of a bowling ball, a body weight five times that of an elephant's, and all the abilities to speak, play, sing, love, and live while floating in the ocean. Whales are these creatures. They are communal by nature, and are considered to be enlightened beings originating from the days of Lemuria, the lost island in the Pacific and Indian Oceans. Once considered an enchanted city, Lemuria is now believed to be a magical land in another dimension. Both the islands of Hawaii and the San Juan archipelago in Washington are considered to be remnants of this ancient land, capable of wielding Lemuria's magic. Whales are thought to be the reincarnated beings of Lemuria, holding deep wisdom to teach us about our own magical potential, alchemy, and love. They are considered the record keepers of the earth, protecting the memory of a time before greed, power, and fear dominated the planet. Whale medicine teaches us to seek our inner truth and to summon our inner voice. They help us to account for the emotions that affect our daily lives and surrender them to something greater, like the ocean or God. When one sees a whale, it is time to take account of the emotional unrest that affects your life. Is there a holding in your life that hinders your joy? What emotions are causing turbulent waters inside of you? What old wounds and perceptions shackle you to a falsehood about your life? What is your personal truth? Whales summon accountability for manifesting our own peace within. The experience of seeing a whale in the ocean can be deeply healing and awe-inspiring. Living in authentic joy from their soul is what whales emanate. Divine joy springs forth in a child and it can become a quest to find that joy again as adults. Whale medicine reminds us what it feels like to live in childlike wonder.

CHAPTER 14

Flesh, Bone, and Being

"TODAY IS GOING TO BE A GREAT DAY!" I exclaimed upon waking the next morning. I felt the hope of my utterance ring through my body. Last night's experience produced such a euphoria that I jumped out of bed and felt a lightness in my step, despite the pain in my legs I felt only the day before. I was ready to embrace the day: I would now choose freedom. No longer would I dwell in sadness over my past. I *was* being guided, after all, and I trusted that my next step would be revealed.

My mind felt free and light and open from what I thought it *needed to be, should be, or could have been.*

In the sweet surrender of communicating with the infinite Universe, I had allowed the winds of heaven to carry my soul; and in that flight, all the beauty and magic of this world sang its chorus with me.

Later that morning, I drove down from my misty, cold, mountain home into the warmth of the sun on the roads and beaches below Haleakalā. I picked up Rose to head to a special little beach that I'd held in my heart for special occasions, both for its remote location and because of the magic I felt every time I went. It was also a nude beach, so it was a place where I felt completely free. How auspicious was it for me to be on that beach that day, to fly free?

I had *wanted* to go to that beach for several weeks, but circumstances always intruded and it never happened. And at those times, I was frustrated because I was resisting what was unfolding for the day and controlling what I wanted. But I began that particular morning by surrendering to any outcome the day held; with that surrender within me and with Rose by my side, I felt that I was meant to finally experience that sacred area of sand once again.

In spite of my surrender, it still took a small pilgrimage to get to the beach: first, we took a long walk from my car on scorching pavement, which seemed to radiate a heat like no other on the island. Then, we trudged with our sandaled feet and backpacks loaded with supplies through deep sand that made my calves burn. After wading the deep, hot sand, we climbed over a small mountain covered in sun scorched, jagged lava and crumbling rock. To someone else this may not have been a big deal, but to me, in my state of health, this was a very large feat.

Finally we arrived, and the reward was worth every difficult step.

Spilling out in front of us was a small cove of blue water that held soft, white sand and a sand break that tamed the waves into a playful rather than fierce pattern. Beachgoers played in the water, rode waves with boogie boards, practiced yoga on the rocks, played music, and tossed a Frisbee. They did all of this naked. The freeing energy that surged through us with our nakedness inspired memories from an earlier time when material things didn't matter. All that remained on that beach was flesh, bone, and being.

"Let's go to the far end of the beach," Rose suggested, lured as I was by the drumbeats from a small group of djembe drummers. Approaching them, the many beach umbrellas, and families with naked children, that same primal energy was summoned in me again.

We found a lovely shady spot along the tree line and immediately stripped down to our skin.

"Ahhh, this feels so good!" I said, giddy to finally be here. My nipples hardened with the exposure to unfamiliar breezes, and as my naked body settled into the soft sand, I received the warm energy of the beach. The sun could finally kiss the places that were usually kept hidden on me.

Whatever physical insecurities previously shrouded in clothing were now lovingly exposed. I may have felt fat, sick, pale, and less than ideal compared to the stereotypical female body idolized in mainstream culture, but on that beach, I was a body just like everyone else.

Looking around, watching people come in and out of the water, breasts heaving in flight with the catch of a Frisbee and penises bouncing in the return toss, I exulted in the notion that I was just like everyone else. I had flesh and bone like everyone else. I remembered that all skin sagged, got old, wrinkled, and eventually became dust on this earth. But in spite of that realization, I could still find beauty in the imperfections in every physical form I watched that day. It didn't matter what they looked like. My nudity embraced and accepted their nudity, no matter their body type, scars, warts, lumps, bumps, bones, tattoos, or color. Being naked in front of all those other people, I had no choice to accept the body I was born. Either that, or I could cover it up.

When Rose and I were ready to cool off, we headed to the water, naked and free, ready to embrace the ocean and offer gratitude for this day. The cool water was invigorating, and the feeling of weightlessness, like a baby swimming in the womb, was intoxicating. Everyone in the water was smiling, buoyant, free, and delighted to be unshackled from clothing. Playful energy reverberated from us and the other beachgoers, who unknowingly sent their energy into the world. It was a call, like a radio signal that went out to any beings that wished to be a part of the naked freedom we felt. I sensed this energy, and I felt it was our way of summoning something great.

"Can you feel the whales?" Rose asked, taking account of the large waves that were now breaking along the shore. "They're here."

I nodded my understanding, feeling the same energetic presence building in the waters.

"Look! Oh my gosh!" A woman squealed at the close breach of a humpback whale not even a football field in length from the shore. Like a stadium of fan's waving together, we filled the air with collective murmurs of excitement.

"Rose! Look!" I shouted with glee. We both stopped our playful banter in the water to give all our focus to those divine creatures who answered out primal energetic call. "Dive down under the water, Rose, you can hear them talking! They're so close it sounds like we're right next to them!"

I was so excited to hear the sonar sounds of our whale friends talking to one another beneath the water's surface, and to think that they were quite possibly talking to us. As I listened to their peaceful call, carried not by air but by water instead, a sense of wonderment and calm settled over me: everything would be alright; everything was already alright. I received their message and took it into my heart as my medicine for the day.

Shouts along the beach ranged from, "Ohhhh!!" and "Yayyy!" to "Wooohooo!" and "This is so amazing!!"

We were completely captivated by the whales. There were at least a dozen of them, babies and adults together, flapping their tails and breaching fully from the water. The sight of it all was awe-inspiring. These creatures were so at ease in their watery home. I pondered their medicine even as I watched them: I had been looking so deeply into my dark, shadow side, but now it was time to breech myself back into the light.

"Thank you, God." Rose announced.

I held my arms and heart open wide to feel the energy of the whales. I poured gratitude from my heart onto theirs.

"Can you feel them leave, Rose? Their energy is receding." I conveyed to her and she responded with a nod, deeply holding prayer with her whale friends. "It is as if they came in for a moment to play, share their wisdom and love, and now they are leaving."

"Bye, bye," I said to the whales, "We love you. Thank you. Bless you.

Aloha." My heart was full of grace, gratitude, wonder, and bliss.

The last breech felt conclusive as if their own goodbye. They swam on to other waters leaving us enchanted.

Time felt irrelevant. What was happening in the rest of the world seemed to wash away in the tide. I witnessed a glimpse of peace for humanity in that moment with the whales. Visions of life in joy without worry of material things or superficial ideals flashed before my third eye, which carries inner sight.

The whales summoned us humans into re-remembering the delightful expansion of hearts when we were young. The vibrant energy it produced in every person was palpable to me. That day on the nude beach marked six weeks since I first came to the magical islands of Hawaii, though the challenges and twists and turns I had experienced made it feel like six years. I felt so alive that day, and I was determined to continue to live that way regardless of the circumstances.

No remnant of self-consciousness existed in me with the whales there. We all belonged to the same, single deep experience channeling Mana in all things. We were humans *being*.

At the day's end, I felt certain that the magic on that beach would not have manifested if I was in my previous, stuck state of holding out for something different. I would have sat on the beach and watched the whales, disconnected from all sense of joy. I would have wished Alex were with me. I would have wished that my life were different, instead of embracing what it was at that moment—a magical gift to share. I would not have felt that deep sense of calm had I not *flown* the night before, had I not fell into a deep trance state in my hermitage and heard the angelic messages the star beings offered me.

I basked in the gratitude that my prayers were being heard. Finally I was beginning to move through the muck, finally I was choosing to embrace my most authentic life.

Dream Medicine

The subconscious realm is connected to our spirit. In Chinese Medicine, while one sleeps, the soul slips into the spirit world to explore the lessons and freedom that linger in that realm. The spirit could be living in many different worlds simultaneously. Anything is possible in the dream world, but one thing is for certain: dreams are information for your waking reality on this earth. Making sense of some dreams is complicated, vague, strange, and otherworldly. Other times it is clear as a picture, almost as if it is real. Dreams are a way for the guardian angels and the soul to relay cryptic messages on our path to health, happiness, purpose, and destiny. When we remember our dreams clearly, it is important to take note. These are messages for your journey. *Are you sleeping well enough to dream? Do you ignore repetitive dreams that carry a hidden message for healing? Do you nurture your sleep as much as your waking life? Are you approaching what you are dreaming with fear?* Dreams are merely information, the more vivid, the more informative. Dreams, and even nightmares, are messages from our guides and our soul. They are the shouts from the soul to look at something that is held deep within. If Dream Medicine is working on you, pay attention.

CHAPTER 15

The Flare

"I AM REALLY SICK OVER HERE," I texted Alex the next day. In spite of the epiphanies and miraculous encounters, in spite of *flying* and the naked frivolity with Rose the day before, my body wasn't equipped to live life like a healthy person and it fell apart the next day. Another Lyme flare hit. The glaring reminder that I am far from well, and I panicked.

With Lyme disease, I could go about my daily life and play, acting and looking seemingly healthy. It's the next day, and the days following when the symptoms and bacteria rear their ugly heads behind closed doors. Friends often misunderstood my panic and pain. To them, I seemed healthy enough to play, so they couldn't understand why it would take me sometimes weeks to recover from a day of normal activity.

The previous days of *flying* and playing with Rose and the whales caused my body to flare up and totally fall apart. Not only that, but the high altitude of my Kula hermitage had put an added strain on my body; the lack of oxygen sent my cells swirling in a Lyme flare for over a week.

Unable to walk or think clearly, I knew that traversing the winding roads down Haleakalā Mountain to a grocery store for food and supplies would be too difficult to endure. The neurotoxin confused me so that nothing seemed right. Even my own thoughts seemed distorted. Feeling desperate, lonely, and scared, I needed Alex.

But there was no response.

I sent another text message: "I really need to talk to my best friend. I miss you and I need help."

No word came all day. Only stillness, rest, and the unshakable pensiveness of what I was doing—starting a new life—sick and alone. Doubt shrouded me like a cloud that had rolled in overnight.

In spite of myself, in spite of my growing inner strength, I still wondered how Alex could leave me like he did. *How could he just walk away after all we had built together, especially knowing how sick I was? How could he encourage me to go to Hawaii on a personal quest, and then leave me here to rot?*

Just a few weeks prior, still living in Washington State, I believed Alex was beloved, my lifesaver. But now, it seemed that he had tossed me aside and forgot about me. I needed saving, desperately, and as the hours passed by with no response from him, it became more and more apparent that he was not going to be a part of my life in any way anymore, not even as a friend. It was a heart-wrenching realization that only added to my panic.

Fear poured through my veins: I was utterly alone. I was on a mountain with no home, no health, and no income.

What am I going to do? I agonized. *You have gotten yourself into quite the predicament, haven't you!*

Torrents of detestation for my actions and my circumstances trumped any amount of self-love I could offer, though this was the same love and compassion I could easily have given to a patient or friend in a similar circumstance. Losing all compassion for myself, for Alex, and my situation, survival mode set in. I was desperate to heal.

You can't live like this anymore. This disease has destroyed your life. You aren't going to last another ten years, not if the bacteria lives in you that long.

I was huddled under layers of blankets, freezing, shivering in pain. Even my muscle convulsions hurt. Missing the creature comforts of my dogs and cats, a loving embrace, someone to make me a cup of tea, I held onto the sides of my bed hoping the darkened skies of Lyme disease and pain would pass quickly.

Fourteen hours later, I received a much-awaited text from Alex.

"I hope you feel better." That was it. I had reached out to him, shown my most vulnerable emotion to him, and after fourteen hours of waiting, that was the response I got.

Alex wasn't my lifesaver; he was a rock that was very close to sinking my ship even quicker than I felt it already was. Once again, the familiar but still startling realization came to me: I was on my own.

Lying in bed, realizing that Alex was no longer willing to even be a listening ear or friend, the echoes of my mother's voice resounded in me:

"You are my sunshine, my only sunshine. You make me happy, when skies are grey. You'll never know dear, how much I love you. Oh, please don't take my sunshine away."

I sang quietly to myself, tears and snot coating my vocal chords into a febrile intone. Clinging to the pillow like it was a teddy bear, I whispered this song, wanting my mother. She was so very far away, thousands of miles both on the planet and in her mind. An ocean, a continent and Alzheimer's separated us now.

She has no idea the peril I'm in. I don't want her to know. I miss her so much, but I couldn't get there even if I wanted to. I'm too sick.

My heart wept for my mother, and for my father, my family. I wished I had someone to help me. Anyone.

Too weak to get out of bed, I watched the Maui sun move across the vast sky until it descended into the ocean below yet again. Another day spent in bed, unable to even drive my car. There were no whales and glees of laughter that day; there were only tears, loneliness, pain and despair. Hummus and carrots, a bit of chocolate, and a cup of tea were the foods I managed to prepare and get down.

The next day, still in bed, still weak and in pain, I stewed in thought as to what was next on this journey. *I have to do something. My month at this Kula hermitage will be over in two weeks. What am I going to do? I need to let Alex go. It's too painful holding onto him like this. Maybe I need to be*

with my mom. She isn't there anymore, so what good would it do? Her mind may not be there, but her heart is still there. What am I going to do?

The worrying anguish I was wallowing in under the covers only made matters worse until it felt like an unstoppable force. The Lyme bacteria were messing with my mind now. I was losing my senses, yet again. Darkening feelings of suicide started to distort my thinking. It all felt too hard. I couldn't see a way out of my predicament. Yet, the growing light within, my newly rediscovered life-force, my mana, fought hard to keep me from slipping into further obscurity.

I can't just crawl in a hole and die.

I resolved to get myself out of bed regardless of how I felt, and live the day as best as I could. Many moans and groans slipped past my pressed lips during the simple act of getting dressed. I couldn't see straight and the fatigue of walking to the bathroom left me gasping for air. But I was determined to stay in the light.

Finally I made it out of the house, into my car, and down the winding road to the closest store. It wasn't even a store really, just a tourist trap for visitors to buy trinkets, sweatshirts, post cards, and jewelry. But there was a small section of groceries. Some boxed soup was all that I could muster to purchase. And that was the extent of my activity for the day.

Reflecting back, I became aware of so many times that I should have said, "I'm not feeling well."

This mystery illness has raised many skeptical looks over my twenty-four year battle. So many times I'd been camping, playing, socializing until suddenly the room started spinning and I was overcome with the fear of passing out. My legs screamed with pain, my body shook, my ears rung. But I pushed aside all of it. I continued to converse, play, and socialize even as my heart palpitated inside my chest. No one had any clue of my pain, my shaking nervous system, or my fatigue. I always did such a marvelous job at keeping me from the authenticity of what was happening, that many times I even tricked myself.

How long had I lived in a body that contained this foreign Lyme bacteria? How long has this bacteria ravaged my identity, my dreams, my relationships, my life?

First showing symptoms of this mysterious illness at age sixteen, I had no idea what it was like to have a normal body anymore. What I recalled before that time, when I felt healthy, was the feeling of weightlessness. I had no aches, no pains, and no relentless exhaustion. Any fatigue I felt as a child was nothing compared to the suffering I endured after contracting Lyme disease.

I haven't been well for over half of my life. How can I even begin to comprehend such a thing? How can I continue to reach for my dreams and live a full life with this illness? How can I get the strength to keep going?

It was never an option to give up. Instead, sheer will, fortitude, and perseverance allowed me to live without actually ever living. My mask was a healthy body; my truth was that tiny bacteria were having a feast with my flesh.

Besides the physical suffering, besides the pain, disorientation, fatigue, I suffered deep emotional pain. I suffered from a lack of trust. After contracting Lyme disease, even before I had a name for it, I could not trust my own body. The simplest things set it off—an emotional reaction, too long of a walk, too much food, or too little sleep. With this loss of trust, I also lost my freedom.

If I were healthy, I thought, *I would not need to think about my health. I could just live.*

I managed to get down some carrot-ginger soup that day, drinking it from a teacup because using a spoon felt like too much effort. My empty stomach devoured the nutrients as well as the continued thoughts. Something was brewing inside of me. Something was beginning to change.

The elation coursing through my body woke me from my dream.

"Sampson!!!" I'd cried in my dream only a moment before. My arms had been outstretched as my black-and-tan dachshund ran into my arms for a reuniting embrace. I'd called out to him, saying, *"I love you so much! I've missed you!!"* My short-legged friend clung to my face, pressing his black-and-tan cheeks against mine, licking me with kisses and whining in joyful exuberance for this reunion with his mama.

I woke feeling empowered. I had reclaimed my babies from Alex, even if it was only in a dream. Righteous vindication rode along my waves of delight as I listened to the mourning doves coo outside my window. As I brushed away the last of my sleep, I made a decision. My dream had revealed the next step in the journey. I would go to the mainland and get my babies back!

By that time, the sun had already risen over Haleakalā and the early morning light had warmed my room. The warmth pulled me from bed, which, to someone with Lyme disease, was like summoning a series of tortures on the body. Groans and moans couldn't help but slip past my lips yet again. My heart felt heavy but clear. My time in Hawaii was coming to an end. It was time.

I'd already realized that no life I created would ever matter if my health did not improve. But now I had another realization: having the companionship I needed from my animals was just as important to my quality of life as my health.

Reluctant in this admonition, I realized that I had wanted to leave Hawaii on some level since the moment I arrived. Still, while I lived in the quagmire of grief, shock, sadness, and fear during most of this time in Hawaii, I learned much about my own shadows. Moments of ecstasy, peace, and joyous splendor also abounded. Yet, through the good times and bad times, the undercurrents of my disease stirred.

I realized after this last flare the severity of my illness. I could no longer ignore the warning sirens screaming from my cells. The bringer of destruction, this illness had ravaged every part of me: physically, emotionally and spiritually.

It's finally time to show up for me! All of me! No life will be worth living if this illness is in charge of me.

Leaving would be bittersweet. It meant that I was actually turning down living in paradise. But my spirit was strong and the message in my heart was clear: I needed to get help in order to heal from Lyme disease. Real help. I needed to go to Reno, Nevada to receive the holistic treatment that I had learned about. I needed to go to Sierra Integrative Medicine.

But first, I needed to get my babies back, and to do that I needed to face Alex.

Pachamama Medicine

Pachamama, a word used by indigenous people of the Andes, is the sacred name of our Earth Mother. As a goddess, Pachamama offers all living beings unconditional love, support, nourishment, stability, and strength. Embodying the energy of the Divine Feminine, Pachamama emanates pure love, a security and constancy that teaches us to surrender our fear and preconceived notions for outcomes; instead, she teaches us to stay centered in our hearts regardless of what wind blows through our lives. At the same time, Pachamama is a fierce goddess, powerful, and unwavering. These qualities encourage us to find that same steadfastness and power in our own lives. Pachamama teaches us that we are home, no matter where we walk. We, her children, are surrounded by her love. She—Mother Earth—is our home. She is the mother of us all. She possesses the creativity and life force to help us create our best lives, and to nurture our healing when we need it most. She is the ultimate mother. Pachamama Medicine asks us to look where life is stable and where it is not. *Where in your life do you look for support outside of yourself instead of finding it from within? Are you nourishing yourself? Do you take care of the earth that you walk upon? Do you have a Pono relationship with our earth mother? Do you take care of yourself? Can you muster up the courage to stand in your own power with deep presence and love?* Pachamama beckons us to change like her own seasons. But she will always welcome us back to her bosom, where we will be held in her beauty, grace, and the sweet surrender to her limitless abundance of love.

CHAPTER 16

Closure Through Prayer

THE SETTING SUN REFLECTED its ethereal grace in pink hues all over the ocean and sky around Maui. It was the last Aloha sunset before I left, and it did not let me down. In my mind, there was nothing quite like a Hawaii sunset. Whatever energy that emanates from that place seems to turn the air into some kind of found medicine. It touches the skin, you breathe it in and you are bewitched by paradise.

For my last get-together with my friend Rose, we met at a manicured beach, full of soft grass that spanned the shoreline where we would pray together for the last time. Picnic benches and picturesque views were abundant. The soft grass was lovely under my bare feet, and I was very aware of my connection to Pachamama, our Earth Mother, and her land, 'Āina. I felt that all of it—the lush grass, the wide-open ocean views, even Rose and myself—was connected within Pachamama.

Though I was saddened that Rose and I were parting ways, the collected nature of Pachamama reminded me that no matter where my feet took me, I would be home.

"I think we should walk over that way," I said to Rose, pointing towards a small wooded area that was sparse with people. Barefoot, holding each other arm in arm, we walked toward the trees.

She and I had spent many days together on the beaches, laughing, crying, and expanding our horizons with each other as the witness. We helped each other connect to wounds from our childhood to understand how they impacted our lives now. We explored our heartbreaks, fears, frustrations, epiphanies, and perspectives. We were mother, daughter, sister, friend, healer, listener, and consoler. We sang to the whales, prayed to the ocean, and prayed with each other.

The irony of our deep bond and love for one another was that we were both sick. We both had bugs eating away at our insides. Rose had spent over twenty years of her life traveling as a spiritual healer, where countless trips to Malaysia, India, Japan, and Europe had exposed her to parasites. So many parasites, in fact, that they were eating her brain along with the rest of her body. Her healing journey summoned the same courage in her that I was hoping to summon for my journey. How was it that two people walking the same soul path, with the same capacity for deep, compassionate love, doing similar work in the world would meet on an island in the Pacific with maladies that produced eerily similar symptoms, now standing on the same beach walking arm in arm?

"It looks like a pergola," Rose said to me, her eyes sparkling as she pointed to the bow-shape tree limbs over our heads. Scenes of brides saying, 'I do', flashed before my eyes.

Sitting under this archway of trees, heart to heart and hand to hand, we breathed. We breathed with the trees, the ocean tides, and with each other. Centering and grounding ourselves, we conjured energy to set the space around us as sacred ground. We prayed.

I began by sending out a most powerful prayer for both of us to every divine being I knew.

"Dear Great Creator of this earth, this Universe. Dear great spirits of this 'Āina, the 'Aumakuas, the ocean, trees, water, and Mana. Dear angels, guides, ancestors, and energy that are here to protect and guide us in love and light. I thank you. Mahalo nui loa. Mahalo. Mahalo. Mahalo. I am so very grateful for this time on Maui. Thank you God!"

I expressed my gratitude for all the divine encounters, the blessings, and the people who showed me the way here on Maui. As I summoned energy from all four directions, tears flowed freely, my heart expanded beyond our sacred circle with the trees and into the cosmos. The wind picked up strength and I felt the Mana coursing through me.

I squeezed Rose's hands and continued to pray. "Help me to let go of the pain I've held in my heart. Help me to surrender my fear, so I can face this path I must walk. I call to you now, those that have walked before me, to stand with me, guide me, and help me on this road."

As I prayed, I felt the sensation of hands being placed on my shoulders—the hands of my grandparents, aunts, uncles, great grandparents, my ancestors all joined together, connecting their love, their courage and support one by one so that I could receive their blessing on my journey. I breathed in the Mana of this prayer and the communal breath I shared with Rose.

"I am in service to You, Great Creator. My heart is opened and I am ready and willing to walk this unknown road stretched out before me."

My words flowed like my tears as I continued to thank the heavens for all of the gifts shared with me.

"Thank you for this time on Maui, for the chance to swim with the whales in her sacred waters. Thank for your teaching me how to be. I love you." To end my prayer, I offered up one final sentiment in native Hawaiian, "Aloha and A hui ho!" which translated to mean 'until we meet again.'

Feeling full of prayer and thanksgiving, I marveled at Rose's beauty and how the wind blew through her silvery hair, her luxurious mauve-pink shawl, and white skirt. Though she had her own journey toward healing, she prayed not for herself, but for me. It was a prayer of protection for my journey and my reclaimed health. Her tears equally flowed as she said in closing, "May we continue to stay connected in this lifetime and the next. Thank you, God."

I felt her sendoff through every one of my cells.

PART TWO

THE HEALING GAUNTLET

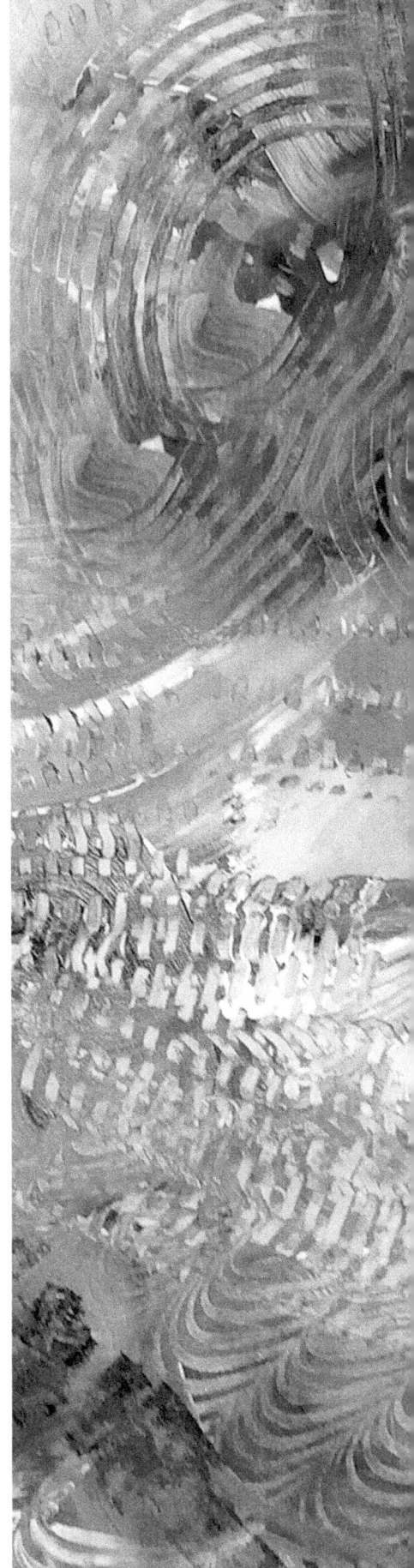

Ghost Medicine

The saying, 'ghosts in the closet' can drum up the secretive image of something we don't want to face inside. Those ghosts that still linger in our inner closets are our teachers, ready to help us achieve healing on our journeys through life. They indicate where in our lives we harbor negative emotions that may affect our health and overall ability to thrive in the world. If we try to run away from the ghosts inside of us, they will usually come back to haunt us. If we refuse to turn and face our ghosts, our ghosts will continually rear their heads especially when we least expect it. Ghost Medicine comes to us in our dreams, showing us where the subconscious is trying to heal us. They also come to us in life, whenever we face situations that resonate with our old wounds. Ghost Medicine allows us to revisit old traumas so that we can finally allow them to transcend into a place of peace. *Do you ignore your old wounds and avoid looking at areas in your life that are too painful? Do you skirt around certain circumstances that may summon your own ghosts? Is it time to face your inner ghosts and release them from your body and into another world?* Ghosts return in life, not to haunt us, but to heal us. Whatever memory or emotion haunts a person reveals the places that need healing. In following these ghost guides, we can summon parts of ourselves we thought were dead. We must face our ghosts to understand they are an illusion of the past. They no longer exist in our world now. What does exist is who you are becoming. If we bring the ghosts of our past with us, we are constantly being haunted by what needs to be resolved. Aspects of our old selves we thought were lost can finally return after we set our ghosts free.

CHAPTER 17

Facing Ghosts

ON THE NIGHT OF THE NEW MOON, which fell auspiciously on the eve of Chinese New Year, I was about to get a bird's eye view of Maui. The island where I called home for three months was about to be nothing more than a spec of land surrounded by the wide blue ocean. Many times the Hawaiian Islands have served as my place of spiritual refuge, healing, and rejuvenation. It was in my final moments on Maui, however, that I realized this latest adventure there was truly the most arduous.

In the course of a few weeks, I'd purged every negative emotion that I held so steadfast in my heart, my solar plexus, and my perspective on life. I had listened to the messages of my guides and acted accordingly, to leave Maui. Still, I knew even then, moments before takeoff that I was holding fast to so much that still needed to be released. And as the plane ascended and I looked out through the tiny window on that vast ocean, I felt baptized by its waters. Maui had prepared me for the next phase on my journey: healing my body.

The ease with which I left Maui gave me further confirmation that I was finally, after such a long hiatus, on the right path.

On the way to the airport, I'd sold my car, Rupert, to a beautiful family who seemed to love him as much as I did. I'd had Rupert shipped over from the mainland when I first arrived on Maui three months prior. I reasoned that if I stayed, at least I would have a car. If I left, I would sell him. In an easy flow of energy in alignment, I met Rupert's future owners at a coffee shop just before my flight to make the exchange.

After a brief conversation, the family paid cash and happily took me to the Kahului airport. Turning over the car keys, kissing Rupert on the hood in gratitude for taking such good care of me, a strange realization emerged. After all these years of holding keys—car keys, house keys, office keys, storage keys, keys for filing cabinets, keys for bike locks, keys for post office boxes—this was the first time in my life that I no longer held any keys. I was free of them.

With that realization, I left Rupert in the hands of strangers, and all that remained in my hands was a small figurine of a turtle key chain. I held in my grip the small reminder from Honu that no matter where I went, I was already home.

Now, with paradise quickly fading into the backdrop of the plane and the backdrop of my life, I was heading toward the next unknown experience in my life at five hundred miles an hour. Ahead of me was the clinic in Reno, Nevada, where I would soon undergo treatment to heal by body. But before I made it to Reno, before I began that part of my life's journey, I would make a short stop with my past to face my ghosts—Lost Lake, Alex—to reclaim my animals.

The noise of the plane's engine and compressed cabin air had merged into a quiet hum around me. The pain from sitting so long in one position, crammed and unmoving in my airplane seat, sent my cells screaming with trouble. If only I could readjust, or lie horizontal: what a simple request!

My legs were sweaty and shaking with pain, my heart rate was fluttering, my kidneys shot out twinges of pain, and my breathing was shallow. The long list of symptoms, all of which I was familiar with after years of dealing with Lyme disease, created such an out-of-body experience that I felt it was a miracle I was conscious and able to move at all.

The week prior to leaving Maui, I received a phone call from my ex-husband, John.

"I heard you're coming back to Seattle?" When he heard about my troubles in Maui, being sick and heartbroken, he reached out as the supportive friend he'd become after our divorce.

"Yes," I'd told John. "I'm coming to Seattle."

"How are you getting to Lost Lake?"

"Well," I began, and explained the details of my plan. "I have to rent a car and I have five pieces of luggage, so I don't know how I am going to juggle all the logistics to get me there."

Although I knew I needed to get to Reno, I had used every last drop of energetic reserves over the last few weeks on Maui. My body didn't have anything left to give and I had no idea how I was going to get myself there. The only information I had was the next step, revealed to me through a dream: get my dogs from Alex. The worries of *how* I was going to do this in my physical state wanted to take my mind down into a torrent of despair. The "How" was always in constant question in my life.

How am I going to do this by myself? God, help me, please.

Then John called, only days prior to leaving Maui, with an answer.

"No," John said adamantly when I'd mentioned my plan. "You aren't renting a car. I'll come and get you and you can drive my truck." It was as if he'd had it all figured out, and knowing him, he did; I knew I didn't have any room to argue.

The relief was an understatement.

At the tender age of twenty-two, John and I fell deeply in love and married. The uncertainty around my strange illness left us ill equipped to handle the emotional and financial strain it produced. In the end, it destroyed our marriage.

Over the course of my eleven-year marriage to John, I was bedridden for two years with a still-undiagnosed disease. It was an experience that was harrowing for me and overwhelming to John. He saw me at my worst. He saw me experience excruciating pain and fatigue, crawling on the floor, unable to cook food, go to the grocery, or visit with friends. He witnessed my struggle to attend a friend's baby shower once—a simple outing that lasted no more than an afternoon—but which left me bed bound for three weeks. He would help me walk from our house to the nearest stop sign and back, a distance of a mere 50 feet, only to then watch me collapse afterward in a heap on the bed, my prison. I was unable to move or talk for hours from the exhaustion of simply walking. He had lost his wife, best friend, and lover in that bed.

John lost me to an illness that left countless doctors scratching their heads in perplexity. It took every ounce of strength for me to scramble from a place of near death to even walk again.

But walk again I did.

I consider that two-year time when I was bedbound to be my first spiritual awakening, my first understanding of the depths that one must traverse to heal. It took me ten months to walk around the block, and a full year before I could walk a mile. But slowly, over time and with sheer determination, I began to heal, gain my strength and reclaim my life.

But by then, the damage was done. My physical collapse from an unknown malady, coupled with the pressures of John holding down three jobs, taking care of his sick wife, doing all the household chores with no family support, was too much for either one of us to bear.

We had been divorced for some time when he announced his engagement, which was around the same time I'd finally received an official diagnosis for my mystery illness. Though I supported John in his new life and new relationship, his upcoming wedding coincided with the period of time when I underwent the pharmaceutical treatment, swallowing dozens of pills each day while living on Lost Lake with Alex. I'd known it would be too painful to watch him venture into his new life while mine was spinning out of control with sickness, again. I chose to not speak to him for over a year after I'd heard of his engagement.

Still, unlike Alex, who disappeared when I needed him most, John reached out to me when he heard about my struggles in Hawaii from his sister, my still dear friend. It had been ten years since I was shackled to that bed and seven years since our divorce. John was the one person to witness the true devastation that this disease does to a person. He knew what this unknown journey ahead to heal meant for me physically and emotionally. Even though it had been years since we even sat in the same car together, he stepped up to help me.

I believe John found relief when the proper diagnosis came to light. There was an answer to the mystery illness. And perhaps the hidden judgements he concealed in his heart as to what happened to me in that bed were given pardon with the confirmed verdict. Finally, he had an answer, too. John stepping up to help me was a miracle staring me down, but still I doubted.

"Really?" I said. "You would do that for me? Are you sure?" I desperately needed John's help, but I didn't want to create any problems between him and his new wife. The life I once had with John was gone, but I certainly didn't want my illness to destroy another relationship in his life.

"Look," John declared. "You need help. I know how you're feeling right now. You don't have to do everything by yourself."

Well, I thought, that was that. John would pick me up from the airport. It was settled then. Almost, settled.

"What else do you need help with?" I knew that his direct, curt tone was merely a reflection of the strain and worry he was carrying for me. Of all people, John understood the fine line I was walking between the living and the bedridden.

In turn, I understood how serious he was to help me. His offer seemed a miracle both in my mind and my heart. With this simple question, I felt my doubt lift and a trusting energy surface that could heal the old wounds between us.

"Well," I said, feeling myself relent to his genuine offer of support, "I could really use some help buying a good car. It's been twenty years since I bought a car by myself."

Alex should be the one to help me buy a car, I thought. *He is the one who knows about cars. I can't believe he isn't even willing to help me transition into a new life, that he could just leave me sick without a care.*

I didn't share my thoughts with John, but I observed them floating by, without attachment to them or their meaning. I was meant to heal everything that seeped out of my broken heart, to transform the pain and suffering into forgiveness, compassion and grace.

Was this God's way of helping me to heal even deeper? A further opening of my heart was happening. I felt it as such.

"Done," John said.

It was that easy. I'd asked for help and he'd said yes.

The plane landed at the SeaTac airport before dawn. The red, yellow, and white lights of the airport reflected over the wet, rain-soaked pavement. Compared to the tropical heat of Maui, I felt the cool air through the window and hyperventilated a pensive breath. Contained in that breath was my excitement to see my animals, the power I was summoning to face Alex, and the desperate need to acquire oxygen for my starved, bacteria-ravaged cells.

I walked off the plane onto Seattle soil. The magic and mystery around Hawaii was now a memory, and pain and exhaustion from the flight had left me feeling half dead. I floated through the airport terminal like a ghost until I saw John, already there, waiting to help me take the next step on my journey.

"You didn't have to come in and get me," I said as I approached him. He was a little thinner, perhaps healthier, but he still carried a solid rigidity in his body that I felt when we hugged briefly. His long brown ponytail stuck out from under the orange and green knitted hat on his head. His big brown eyes, which I once fell into like a pool, were worried.

As he heaved my suitcases high onto a luggage cart, I was still stunned at his help. I spent the last three months living, and struggling, on my own. If something needed heaving or lifting or doing, I was the one to do it; on my own, or with very little help from someone else.

"Look, I know your energy level right now. You do not need to be hauling suitcases. I'll get them. Don't try to help me. I'll take care of it." And he did.

The crisp, misty air of a Washington morning in February greeted me when we walked through the airport doors to the parking lot. My lungs took in the familiar cool, moist air, noticing the contrast with the hot, humid air of Hawaii. With every step I took towards John's car, I felt one step closer to my old life, my old home, and the lake house cottage where my animals still lived.

John drove toward Sammamish, the little lumber town where Lost Lake and my little cottage sat tucked away on its outskirts like a secret hideaway waiting to be stumbled upon.

I stared through the window at all the cedars interspersed with the morning fog. How they shone in the grey-lavender light of the misty morning sunshine!

It was all so surreal. Seeing John after so long, riding in his truck, about to face the man who banished me from the life I once had. Reclaiming my animals. How sick I felt, the shock of leaving Hawaii still inside of me. But I kept it inside me, quiet and contained.

The hour drive from the airport carried us northeast into Sammamish, where John's truck climbed the forested foothills of the Cascade Mountains. There we arrived at my temporary home, at least for the next week: a hide-a-bed couch in the small, detached home of a friend's property. I knew this space well, as I'd rented it for my healing center when I was healthy enough to practice holistic healing. For two years, that space had served as a place of healing and surrender for my patients.

"You going to be okay?" John asked as he supportively placed his hand on my shoulder. Bringing the last of my luggage into my temporary home, he found me staring out the window. The window glass and

500 hundred yards down the hill separated me from my old home, my animals, my own bed and pillows and sheets. And Alex.

My tired eyes and sad smile likely said it all, but keeping my chin up I said, "Yes, I'll be alright. Thank you for bringing all the luggage inside."

The shingles, Grandmother Cedar, and the huge deck appeared as slices through the densely needled trees. The surface of Lost Lake sparkled amongst the leaves. The little cottage remained nestled on the lake, right where I had left it three months before. I welcomed the sight, even as deep sadness stirred inside of me. I knew that part of that home would not welcome me. It existed there, dead, it seemed, like a headstone of my old life.

*I would have to surrender, continually
surrender, into a journey I did not expect
or fully choose, all on the basis that
it was* my *journey.*

Dog Medicine

Our four-legged friends have been dedicated to their human companions for hundreds of years. They are our guardians and loyal servants who protect those to whom they have bonded. Their level of love and devotion often brings a sense of trust and solace in a world where humans have difficulty sharing authentic love. To the wounded soul, a dog's companionship is medicine like no other. We can trust them to be there for us, to love us even if we don't love them in return. They are our best friends, a listening ear, and often serve as an intuitive presence, detecting subtle energy shifts in people around them. Dog Medicine teaches us to love without expectation. It teaches us about loyalty and honoring those closest to us. Dogs teach us how to go with the flow, and to be willing to embrace a new adventure. Their playful spirits also remind us to enjoy life and not take things too seriously. *Is there a resistance in your life to loving and honoring your four-legged friends? Is this resistance closing you off to a greater love? Do you love someone only when certain conditions are met? Is there a person or circumstance where you could love without expectation? Even yourself? Are you playing enough in your life? Have you lost the ability to find joy in the little things?* Dog Medicine is here to remind us how to be loyal to others in our pack as well as loyal to ourselves. Dogs have the capacity to forgive without resentment and love with all of their being. Dog Medicine feeds the soul and serves as a reminder of how to love unconditionally and without fear, from the place of the divine child that is within each one of us.

CHAPTER 18

Banished Queen

CHOOSING TO APPROACH THE SITUATION before me in a *Pono* way, I decided to call Alex to let him know I would be arriving. I could have surprised him, but I wanted to know that at least I maintained a level of integrity through this painful transition. Instead of returning my call, Alex responded with a curt message in an email: he did not want me to come see the animals until the following day.

Whether he would choose to show integrity, to show responsibility for his actions was entirely up to him. The only person that I could control was me and how I showed up.

Alex's car was visible through the trees from the windows of my temporary shelter. He was down there. He was in that cottage home, which I still considered mine, sharing the space with my three dogs, four cats, 12 chickens and a duck, all of my furniture and housewares, and a closet full of my clothes. Not being able to see my family of animals for three months, with the possibility that I would never see them again, had been torturous. And now I was so close to them! The pining energy of a mother seethed inside of me. *Be strong*, I told myself. Choosing my battles and reserving my energy, I acquiesced.

I tried to sleep, but painful, angry thoughts continued to haunt my mind. I felt angry and resentful—not toward Alex, but toward myself. *How had I allowed Alex to manipulate me to leave my home, my animals, and all of my belongings?* It was still a quandary to me. *I chose to leave for Hawaii with hope and desperation. I chose. This was the consequence,* I supposed. My entire existence felt so surreal.

Would my life have been better if I'd kicked Alex out months ago? Would my body still have been so sick if my heart wasn't confined in a relationship that was sick and undernourished? Should I have kicked him out and given myself enough space and support to figure out my next move? What could I have done differently? I didn't see this coming. I was too sick to see it coming.

There were so many questions that arose that day, and none of them had answers. Once again, I was faced with the same lesson: I would have to surrender, continually surrender, into a journey I did not expect or fully choose, all on the basis that it was *my* journey.

Night had finally come and the pain of staring out the window to see the lakehouse cottage, knowing I had to wait until the morning to go down there, finally abated with the dark.

With a full day of rest for my body, I woke up early the next morning, full of anticipation and excitement. To prepare for the day ahead, I sat in my old healing space and meditated quietly. I rooted myself back to this land that was once my home and I listened to the wisdom of my spiritual guides, allowing my heart to remain open and hear their messages. They told me that I should approach the cottage house at 9:20 am.

Shortly before the appointed time, I descended the familiar, winding trail down, down, down to the lake through a small patch of woods. It was the same trail I used to walk every day from the cottage to work, to that same space where I slept last night on a simple hide-a-bed. Traversing the familiar trail through the foggy morning made me feel like a ghost, haunting a life that was not mine anymore.

Ready or not, here I come, I thought, *the unwelcome dead.*

This was Alex's claimed home now, a little sanctuary just for him, in the midst of big leaf maples and cedars. The first glimpse I caught of

Alex was of him sitting in his usual morning spot, in his favorite chair, feet propped up, writing and drinking coffee. His initial face spoke of uncomfortable surprise as if he'd seen a ghost, my ghost.

French doors separated me from my animals, and him, but I opened those doors as if they were still mine.

"My BABIES!!!!" I cried out, collapsing on the ground with my three wiener dogs, cats darting about wildly from the excitement. My anticipation was exactly what I'd expected. My animals were as elated to see me as I was to see them. Licks, kisses, whining, jumping all about, barking, and exuberant embraces with my four legged children were medicine for my weary heart.

It felt like I had never left them, and from their reactions to my return, I knew that they didn't care I'd been gone for so long, only that I had returned. All of us—the animals and me—sunk into a deep comfort that we were with one other again. Finally, I looked over to Alex, who sat stoic and alone on the couch.

"Hi," I said meekly, feeling so dejected, abandoned, and shunned.

There I was, sitting on the ground with the dogs, looking up to him like a banished queen who had committed treason and he was debating what to do with my head. As I moved up onto the couch to be eye-to-eye and heart-to-heart with him, I centered myself, hoping to see some shred of love still in his eyes. But there was none.

I looked around me, taking in the space, noticing the little changes Alex had done here to move the energy of the room. The house still contained the furniture I bought and acquired on my own, but now it was arranged to his liking. He had claimed my possessions as his own. He had made the space his own. The dream catcher I made him still hung in the corner window. The drums we had made together for his birthday hung on the opposite facing wall.

If he wanted me out of his life so much, why would he keep such sentimental gifts on display? It made no sense to me. The only answer I could find at that moment was that he just took over the life I had made here—my life—and claimed it as his own.

I didn't have the strength to fight him for things that didn't matter.

I didn't care about the couch, the dishes, the rugs, the bedding or the outdoor furniture. I didn't have the strength to move it, deal with the emotional upset, or where I would put it. I only wanted to be with my animals. I loved them so.

Our conversation did not come easily. I was nervous and guarded, and from his stoic posture on the couch, I knew he was too. He didn't ask me how I was doing or how my trip was. He merely watched me embrace and play with my animals.

"Well," he said finally, "I didn't think that you were coming down so early. I'm not really ready to have a conversation with you." I realized then that his morning routine was not complete. Alex had been a creature of habit when I left for Hawaii, and though I felt I had changed during the past three months, I could see that he had not. He usually devoted his mornings to writing, which, by his comment, I understood meant more to him than talking to me. It was the first time we had seen each other in three months, and still, his routine was more important to him.

My heart sank at this realization. A feeling of hopelessness poured over me as I felt with certainty that there was no love left in him for me, not even enough for a peaceful separation.

Choose your battles, I thought. *Keep it business. Do not emotionally engage him. He isn't capable of talking this out with you. He has already made that clear. Your mission is to get your babies back; nothing else.* My body did not have the energy for such a draining action as arguing.

Speaking clearly the terms I'd decided, I said, "This is what I want. I'd like to have all three dogs to spend time with, and then tomorrow morning we can meet and discuss what we'll do about the animals and my things. I'd like to come down here while you're gone to see the cats. You know they aren't going to come sit with me until the house is quiet."

But Alex sat rigid as stone. He didn't want me "unchaperoned" in his home, in the new energetic space he'd created there. Alex made it clear that this was *his* sanctuary now and I was only a guest.

But I saw a small crack in his stoned façade. He was afraid of me. He was afraid of feeling into his heart. He was afraid that I would change the home he had created in these past three months. His heart was so hurt by me leaving for Hawaii that even his self-proclaimed home couldn't bear to have me in it. So hurt, so afraid to look at his own broken heart, he was protecting his life from me.

Was I that big of a threat to him? Had I become the representation of all the other women who have hurt him on some level? He had encouraged me to go to Hawaii, but had my leaving triggered abandonment issues that eluded my mind and emotions?

He didn't push me out because of me; he pushed me out because he couldn't look at his own emotions around our relationship. Removing me altogether was safer and easier than being accountable for his actions. He took my life and made it his own, dream catcher, furniture, lake, and even setting the energetic space inside our home. The subterfuge of my life astounded my broken heart and bewildered my senses.

My head was spinning with Lyme disease, heartache, and a slurry of emotions that I saw in him and felt in me. This was a gigantic mess and he wanted it swept under the rug, with me swept out of his life. I didn't have the strength to fight him or the ability to convince him of another way. This was survival mode, operation get my animals and get me to Reno! My resolve to stay the course gushed through me and I responded to his comment with rigor in my voice.

"I see, well, since you are so good at setting energetic space, you can just go ahead and redo it once I'm gone," I retorted.

"So, you'll bring the dogs back around 5:00?" He asked, ignoring my comment. He wasn't going to bite.

Was he joking!? I haven't seen them in three months and he thinks I'm going to spend one day with them, returning them "home" like children of a divorce? Anger started to boil my blood, my patience was running thin, but I held my cool. *Pick your battles, this isn't one of them. Stay calm.*

"No," I said. "I'm going to keep them for the night. Sampson stays with me from here on out. You're not getting him back. I'm going to make my decision whether I keep Delilah or not. I'm assuming Franklin isn't an option."

"No, Franklin is not an option. You want to meet for coffee in the morning, say around 10:00?"

"Sure," I replied, sunken, defeated, beat down from everything that was happening even as I felt warmed from the love of my animals. It was all so confusing.

The coldness that came through me made my own heart sad. This was not at all how I wanted to part ways with Alex. I tried to remain friends with my exes, parting as amicably as possible, so I thought. But this was cold, cruel, and so not in alignment with how I choose to live life. He portrayed himself as so kind and open-hearted to the rest of the world, but it was a different story with me. How had it come down to this? There was no way to break through this impasse with him; it stopped me dead in its tracks.

There was no fork in the road; there was only a dead end. This was the transition, reclaiming what I choose to take with me and what I choose to leave behind. It was time for me to embrace a fresh start.

Later that night, too exhausted to move from my temporary bed, I rested deeply, meditating on the journey at hand. My three precious wiener dogs surrounded me, burrowing under the covers, trying to touch any part of my skin that they could. I was with my babies, finally. Franklin clung to me, like a toddler who didn't want his mother to leave him ever again. With his head nuzzled into my armpit, he curled up to get the mama love he missed while I was in Hawaii. They all had missed me, and yet, there was nothing for them to forgive. I was with them now, and they savored in the cuddling, love, and warmth just as much as I did. The unconditional love of my four-legged friends was the lesson I was trying desperately to give to Alex.

I had done it though. I faced Alex and savored my animals, but I was still in the midst of a fight for my life. My physical suffering—the pain, the fatigue, the weakness—constantly reminded me that if I didn't do something quick, soon there would be nothing left of me. Alex's wounded heart could shut me out, but I wasn't going to let that stop me from healing myself—body, mind and spirit.

I stayed in my former healing sanctuary for a week. During that time, I focused on getting my animals and my belongings from the lake house, and finding a car that would get me to Reno for treatment. Alex and I agreed that I would take two of the three dogs with me, though after that first day in the house, he refused to let me inside again. I never even got to hold the cats.

Not stepping inside again meant that I had to rely solely on my memory (already weakened and unreliable from my illness) to decide which of my belongings I wanted from the cottage house. Then I had to try to estimate how many of these items would fit together in a car, which would be my only transport on my unknown journey. I had no idea where I would go after I'd completed treatment in Reno, but I knew that I could salvage some of my belongings to take with me. Some of the few things that I managed to reclaim from my old life included enough clothes to partially fill a closet, a large houseplant that was my grandfather's, two pet carriers, my juicer, and a bicycle. But even these items I had to rescue from the stoop where Alex had dumped them in the rain.

I was about to go into treatment for the next two months and Alex showed no concern of my wellbeing. He just wanted me gone.

"You look really tired. What's up with that?" He asked in the middle of our negotiations.

My look likely said it all. No words could summon the level of disgust I flashed before him. Emotions overtook reason and I spoke. "You know, I promised myself I would not emotionally engage with you. But I need you to hear this so that I know it is at least on your conscience."

He shut the back of his big SUV and stood there with his muscled arms folded, waiting for the rest of it.

Alex had watched his dear friend, David, slowly die of cancer a few months prior. But his partner Julie was with him every step of the way. Steps away from leaving, I still felt that Alex needed to see what he was doing to me. Franklin was in the car, alone.

"I look at what you are doing to me as the equivalent of Julie walking out on David in the middle of his cancer treatment. Isn't there any shred of you that cares about that, about what I'm going through?"

Alex sighed, looked at the ground and made his way towards the driver's seat of his truck.

"I'm a broken man. You're just going to have to forgive me."

He was already gone in mind and spirit, his attention already occupied with his list of to do's even before his body got in the car.

And that was it. Our family was officially split up. I had two dogs, Alex had one. My belongings—my clothes, my houseplant—all of it lay in a wet heap, and I stood next to it, my body in a bigger heap. Before he'd driven off and left me there alone, Alex proclaimed himself as a broken man. Hearing those words from him, I knew that my wish to honor each other's paths in a pono way would not happen. Neither one of us could summon the love in our hearts to honor that. The vision of us staying friends was for naught. I realized then that Alex had left me the moment I stepped on that plane for Hawaii. When I left for Reno, I would never see or speak to him again.

*I took her words as confirmation that
I was right where I was supposed to be.*

Angel Medicine

Angels are often an archetype depicted in the Bible, metaphysical realms, and even cartoons as ethereal beings with wings and halos. Angels, however, come in many disguises. They resonate with the light of the soul and feel the struggles in a person's heart. Although there may be guardian angels of the heavenly realm, earthly angels can take form in the most unassuming places. If we allow ourselves to listen to the subtle messages that even a total stranger can convey, we will find that angels are everywhere, even in the least likely circumstances. Getting delayed five minutes before leaving for work could very well have been the work of an angel interceding to stop a horrible accident from happening. A random person who offers words of encouragement can also be an angel by gently giving healing advice when we least expect it. *Are you open to receiving messages from anyone you come in contact with? Is your heart open to listening for guidance without expectation for the source? Or is your mind too stuck in this reality, with bills, home life, work, childrearing or healing? Where in your life do you need to open your perspective that a guiding angel may be right before you?* We often look back on a past experience and see someone as an angel, but in the moment, we may be too preoccupied to notice the guiding presence of these beings. Angel Medicine teaches us that divine assistance often comes in mysterious ways. We are always protected and loved when we allow ourselves to receive that love and support from anyone or anything, for it is all God.

CHAPTER 19

Divine Assistance

FINALLY I WAS IN RENO, arriving much later than expected, but I was there.

"We made it!" Mikayla exclaimed as she pulled my new car into the driveway of the old, run down duplex in the heart of gambling town, Reno, Nevada.

Mikayla was John's sister, my ex-sister-in-law, though now I referred to as my sister-friend. She also had witnessed the extreme level of suffering I endured from my illness, and she also knew I needed help. Days prior, Mikayla had flown across the country from her home in Miami, Florida to drive me to Reno in the car that her brother helped me buy.

It took us two days to make the trek from Seattle to the treatment center, but even after we arrived, she stayed to hold my hand while my treatment began the following day. If the first miracle on my healing journey was John showing up to help me when I least expected it, then Mikayla was the second.

The brown, arid region was an unaccustomed site for me after I'd grown accustomed to the palm trees and blue waters of Hawaii and the tall cedars and moss-covered logs of the Pacific Northwest. When the three-bedroom duplex I found to rent came into sight, our shouts of glee were met with squeals of Sampson and Delilah, now my road dogs. Treatment would start the next day, and I would be living in this unfamiliar city for sixty days and nights. It felt like I was starting a pilgrimage into the desert.

Inside my new home, Mikayla was already turning up her nose at the old furniture and gaudy fabrics. The mismatched, pastel flowered curtains that looked like they were from the eighties glared against contemporary black and white lamps on the nightstands. The bedspreads were equally garish, reminiscent of a hotel from the same decade as the curtains. We couldn't help but to laugh at the decorator's expense.

It may have been outdated, strangely decorated, and in need of proper maintenance, but I was grateful for the duplex nonetheless. All my needs were met there: I was in close proximity to the clinic; there was a fenced backyard where my dogs could play without supervision; and there were three bedrooms, which I'd anticipated would soon be filled with people who had agreed to help me through treatment. Though Mikayla was staying only temporarily, I was indebted to her.

"I love you Mikayla, it really means a lot that you are here. I don't know how I would have gotten down here without you." I didn't know how I could ever repay her.

Collapsing on the couch, grateful to be horizontal after so long sitting upright in the car, I sighed another breath full of emotions, physical ailments, and nervous apprehension about tomorrow's appointment. Finally, I would get some help. A lot was riding on it. But already I felt like I had made a long journey in my heart to get me to this point on this strange couch. I had faced Alex and reclaimed my animals. But now, I had another journey ahead of, and this one was for healing my body.

Mikayla began her routine of humming like a little bird while she prepared our late dinner of boxed soup and grilled cheese. I smiled, listening to her operatic voice coming from the kitchen. I loved her so. In that moment, I realized that even though, by law, I was no longer family to her and John, my heart disagreed. We were still family, bound by the love we shared for one another. I realized that the hurt of my past did not need to live on in my present.

If I'd tried to fix my broken heart weeks ago, my healing with Mikayla and John would never have manifested. My healing experience continued to transcend beyond a war with bacteria and into healing any unresolved emotion, wound, heartache, and misperception that still lingered in my soul.

⁂

It was the morning of my first of many appointments at the clinic in Reno. Walking out of the duplex I breathed a good morning breath to the wintry azure blue sky. The cold, dry air was so refreshing on my skin and in my lungs. The high sierra desert had left a film of frost in the night on every window where the sun hadn't touched in the morning. I sipped tea in the cold car while I nervously waited for Makayla to finish getting ready (she was always running late).

I felt clear about my path ahead. Although I was focusing on positivity, the sheer exhaustion was ever present with each exertion of my energy. Even speaking, even keeping my eyes open was difficult.

After our short drive, we arrived at the clinic and Mikayla took my picture standing at the front doors, where the sign for Sierra Integrative Medicine welcomed us. Going to treatment was a big step for me, and she wanted to document my healing journey.

Inside, the frosted glass doors opened into the cathedral ceilings of the reception area where my eyes immediately noticed the huge sign that hung on the wall that read:

> No success can compensate for the
> premature failure of our bodies.

At the sight of those words, pangs of overwhelming emotions stirred in my heart. Though I felt too weak to express what was in my heart, I understood those words deeply. In Hawaii, I'd already come to realize that no life I could ever create for myself, no success that I could ever achieve would matter if I were sick. This copper-colored sign in the reception area was the first of many reminders that I was in the right place.

The building was modern, with a pretty tiled floor and an opened staircase that led up to the dispensary and administration offices overlooking the waiting area below. Although the floor to ceiling windows would have brought the pretty blue sky indoors, the blinds hanging from the windows were drawn closed to keep out the sunlight, which I knew was for the benefit of photophobic patients like myself. But the walls were painted a horrid neon green, which seemed to singe my eyes with pain, firing my ocular nerves into a quaking frenzy. Meanwhile, the acrid smells of alcohol, sterilization and medication overwhelmed my olfactory nerves.

After checking in, the friendly and busy receptionist handed me a clipboard with several pages of forms to fill out. *Here we go,* I thought.

Plopping down on the white sectional leather couch, I attempted to read and take in the questions on the forms:

What other treatments have you done?

What pharmaceutical drugs have you taken in the last year?

Now it had been six months since I swallowed my last pill. But even after that interim period, the damaging chemicals still felt lodged in my body, damaging my brain. Though the antibiotics, antimalarial, and antifungal medication I had taken the previous year had killed some of the bugs inside of me, in doing so they unleashed a flood of neurotoxins into me. Once unleashed, the neurotoxin continued to do its job, damaging anything it touched. Eventually, such a high level of toxins had built up inside of me that every one of my organs was screaming for help.

My symptoms had worsened physically even after I stopped the meds; and cognitively, my senses were distorted so much so that reality was not discernable for me anymore. Instead of living my life as I should have been, I was living as a spectator, watching the world go by through a television set with a bad signal. My damaged neurotransmitters left a fuzzy screen for me to view the world, and it was a lens that created much confusion, misunderstandings, and pensive emotions for me.

"Honey, you look so tired," Mikayla whispered in my ear. I was doing my best to comprehend the eight forms in front of me, but the task was useless with a ravaged brain like mine. At that point, I didn't care about the risks or stipulations. I just needed help.

Looking up from the paperwork, I saw people of all ages, ethnicities, and walks of life in the waiting room, shuffling slowly to and fro with IV bags attached to poles. Before that morning, I'd always thought this illness was disguised. I had always disguised it, so I'd assumed that other Lyme patients would look like I had—normal. But being in the same room with these fellow Lyme patients, our disease was glaring. It was a busy clinic and it seemed obvious to me who was sick and who was there for support.

The one's who were sick held a dim energetic light around them, whereas the others, like Mikayla, were full of color, life force, and Mana. But for us with Lyme disease, our Mana was being sucked out of us, eaten away by bacteria. Only the fierce will to live seemed to keep us breathing and moving.

As I was watching these people, I noticed an older woman with dyed red hair take a seat near me. I could feel her assessing me as I tried once again to fill out the paperwork.

"You in for Lyme disease?" she asked.

"I am," I said, too exhausted to embrace this stranger with my sunny disposition, which had seeped out of my body weeks ago. The simple exertion from answering the questions on the forms brought on lassitude, so I set down the clipboard and closed my heavy eyes.

Apparently the woman who had sat down had been watching me closer than I thought. From behind my closed eyes, I heard her say to me:

"Honey, you came to the right place. I was here twenty years ago and I've been better ever since. I'm just here for a tune up now, but overall I got my life back. It was such a miracle and a blessing. You'll make it through the treatment. It's tough, but it will be the best thing you could possibly do for yourself."

When I opened my eyes to look at her, I noticed her kind green eyes first; they shined brightly, contrasting with her pale but rouged skin and red hair. I wanted to reach out to her, to thank her, to shed a tear of gratitude over her encouraging words. But I couldn't. There was not enough energy left in me to summon even a single teardrop.

It was a tall order to believe this woman's words, and the ones that followed—about her treatment, about my treatment—especially through the thick fog hanging over my brain. But her words were my last shred of hope. Maybe it was possible to heal my body after all, maybe this treatment could help me regain what had been lost by Lyme disease over the past twenty-four years.

After that morning, I never saw that woman again, but I thought of her often during my treatment—my red-haired angel. I took her words as confirmation that I was right where I was supposed to be. I held onto the hope in her words as I ventured down the gauntlet of needles, IV bags, and unbelievable agony, as I waited for the bacteria inside of me to die. They had to die; it was the only way that I could live.

Twenty cold, maroon vinyl chairs that reclined along the perimeter of the large treatment room had become the familiar place to land for another day's treatment. The same sickening neon green paint color I had seen that first day in the waiting area still glared at me from the backdrop of the treatment room every day.

A beautiful model, a preacher, an Amish girl, and a Vegas girl were becoming familiar faces and they too were readying themselves for another day of killing bugs. So was the college student, the old farmer, the soccer mom, and the marathon runner, all of whom I had met by the end of my first week at the clinic thus far. Outside the clinic we were so different from each other, but here, all of our arms were bruised from IVs and injections. Blankets, hats, sunglasses, and scarves adorned most of the patients. I saw these items as evidence of what I already knew about them: their nervous systems were as sensitive to light, temperature, smells, and sound as mine was.

Tears welled up in my eyes unexpectedly throughout those first few days of treatment. Though I had suffered for decades from this illness, now I was actually seeing other people whom I knew suffered from the same disease. My heart ached for them. It was going to be a long two months.

A now familiar patient, Ryan, set his things down next to me.

"Are you ready for another day of battle, Ryan?" I joked with a new friend and fellow patient, though even as I joked, I put my hand on his to connect to him with love. He had been bedridden for two years before coming to the clinic, just like I was ten years ago. At the vital age of 27, Ryan should have been out on dates, building his career, and having fun. Even though I was sick at that age too, I ached to watch his body and his spirit suffer.

"Morning, Sarah. How are you today?" Ryan had gotten my name wrong, again. I was getting names wrong, too, so I compassionately smiled and ignored the error.

"I'm doing okay. I'm just hoping they get a good vein today. My veins don't seem to want to cooperate." I showed him my beat up forearms, which had begun to show huge hematomas of blood under the skin as a result of my consistently low blood pressure and weakened state. My veins were failing me, and eventually it wouldn't be long before the clinic insisted that I have a common outpatient surgery for patients with veins like mine, to get a more permanent IV, known as a Picc line. The procedure inserted a catheter into the brachial vein of my arm and was then shunted into my heart where it would remain for the duration of my treatment.

Ryan sympathized with me even though he was dealing with another problem.

"I feel like I eat and eat, and I keep dwindling away. I wish I could put on some weight." The heaviness of his emotions were written all over his sad eyes and tired smile as he spoke. His sallow complexion indicated to me that his blood was much depleted.

While my brain seemed damaged, Ryan's enteric nervous system, which ruled the body's digestion, was suffering from the bacteria's neurotoxin. And the more people I met, the more I realized how differently Lyme disease can affect a person. These bacteria inflicted their evil on a person in varying degrees, ranging from cognition and fatigue issues all the way to paralysis, inability to swallow, talk or move until, eventually the body expired in death.

While Ryan was in a chair on one side of me, a woman in her 50s received treatment from the chair on my other side. She seemed possessed with the illness as if it were a demon. She had already lost her ability to talk, swallow, and move years ago. But through it all, her husband dedicated his life to caring for the living corpse that his wife had become. My heart wept for him as it did for her; he lost his life just as she did, the moment when a tick drank her blood and infected her with Lyme disease. Even though she was unable to communicate with the world around her, I knew this woman was still inside her body, trapped unable to communicate to the rest of the world. *At least I never got that bad*, I thought, counting my blessings. Yet, we were all trapped, trapped in a world of bacteria that were eating us away.

And our fighting chance to free ourselves was eight to twelve hours of treatment per day, six days a week. Every day our bodies were hooked to IVs containing concoctions to reawaken our immune systems and prepare our bodies for war—not against the Lyme bacteria, but against the neurotoxin that would unleash into our bodies when it began to die. It was our chance to heal, and, I learned that for many of the other patients, this was our last chance to survive.

*You can't help another person
until you can heal yourself....*

Death Medicine

Death usually stirs a level of discomfort in a person with images of the Grim Reaper, the personified harbinger of something to fear. In death, we face mortality, an end to our bodies. Naturally one might consider what comes next, what comes after death. Without our bodies' five senses of perception to feel what death would be like, it is difficult to have faith and trust that something beautiful might happen after death. Or that perhaps there is no end, but rather a continuation of life in another form. If we can embrace that all of life cycles, then death is an equally important part of life as birth. By working with the spirit world, I have come to understand that a baby's birth is considered a death on the other side; in contrast, a person's death is considered a birth on the other side. In life, we are merely a transference of energy into another dimension, which rides on the current of love. It is this omnipotent love that becomes clear in the literal and symbolic death. Death Medicine summons our courage to let go of the life we once knew so that a new life can be born. If one resists this dying process due to fear, then a little bit of the evolving spirit will die too. Resistance to this kind of spiritual death and rebirth will choke the vitality and Mana from us so that our spirits are stuck in ennui: they cannot die, but they can no longer live either. *Is there an aspect of your spirit that is yearning for a peaceful death? If you are on your own healing journey, what personality traits, outlooks on your life, and self-made labels need to die so you can thrive? Are there relationships that need to die so you can live?* The Law of Impermanence in Buddhist philosophy helps one to embrace the certainty that all things come to an end. There is no permanence in life, not even the rocks of the earth are everlasting. Although a rock may sit in one place for thousands of years, eventually it will shift or crumble or change. The flowers on the trees will die, but fruit will come again. In all death, literal and symbolic, there is rebirth.

CHAPTER 20

Unmarked Grave

A WEEK HAD PASSED since Mikayla left, and the three-bedroom duplex felt empty as I walked to the front door.

"Stay here. Mama will be back. You guys be good." I said to Sampson and Delilah, leaving them alone in the duplex for the day. I hated leaving them alone all day, but when I'd eventually return, their unconditional love was unwavering.

Mikayla had stayed with me and held my hand for three days, long enough to get me settled, attend my first doctor's appointment and help me to communicate what I couldn't. She was there for my first day of treatment and she made sure that I was in good spirits. But once she left, the only thing in my awareness was Lyme disease. I was in the thick of it now. Alone.

Nothing existed for me outside that clinic and the duplex less than two miles down the road. Although short, the distance felt like a very tall order for me to drive, and I prayed every day that I would get home safely from the clinic. After each day's treatment, nothing of me lingered. I was a walking corpse going to and fro, hoping for reprieve. But I continued to linger in this dead-like realm in the high Sierra desert for eight weeks.

During those first few days, I was still adjusting to being a patient. I endured lab tests and more visits with the doctor and nurses, all of which confirmed how sick I really was. As IVs were administered into my veins to begin a course of treatment, relief washed over me. I felt the understanding and empathy of the healthcare team and the other patients. Finally, I had validation for what I had suffered for so long in silence. No more hiding under a façade of my smile, pushing my body, or overlooking my pain. The invisible symptoms I was experiencing were real, and they were taken as such by the healthcare team and other patients. Finally, I was in a place that allowed me to authentically show the way I felt, which was sick—so sick that I felt dead.

The three bedrooms were originally intended for all the people who said they were going to come. The clinic staff had advised that someone be there to help me endure the treatment and the effects of the raging neurotoxin. Many of the friends and family I'd asked indicated interest, but their plans fell through. My niece, Amelia, only two years younger than me, intended to come from Kentucky during the most intense part of my treatment, but two hours before her flight, she suffered a massive panic attack that changed her mind. She so wanted to be there to help me, but as a result from her fear of flying, she was flooded with guilt and frustration. I was scrambling for support to no avail.

"Can anyone come?" I asked Anne, one of my three sisters, during one of our phone conversations. I'd already known that my friends couldn't leave work, didn't have the money to travel to Reno, or were drowning in their own lives and couldn't stop what they were doing. I couldn't tell my parents what I was going through, not in the mental state they were both in, fighting for their own lives in a nursing home in Kentucky. Although I wished it to be so, they didn't have the faculties to be of any consolation, comfort, or care.

There was a long pause on the other end of the line when I asked the question.

"No, I don't think so," Anne replied heavily.

How many times had I flown to Kentucky to help my family when my parent's health fell apart? I sacrificed my health over and over again to be there, getting sicker every time I flew. How much money and time away from work had I spent to be there for my family?

My family had helped me the best they could, financially, so that I could pay for treatment. And that was a godsend. But in all other ways, I was on my own. None of my large family could come support me during treatment. Not one. Their energy was sapped from their own families, their overly taxed work or school schedule, along with the burden of taking care of my parents. My heart sank.

Instead of feeling stranded on a deserted isle by Alex, now I felt stranded in the desert by my family. Abandoned yet again.

I was walking through the desert, praying for an oasis and a miracle.

Try as I might to find support from my friends and family, I was the only patient in the clinic at the time to have no one by my side after Mikayla left. Once again, I found myself alone in a city I didn't know, having to figure out how to survive on my own, and with no home to return to when treatment was done.

Amelia and Mikayla would call me every day. I needed them, but often making a phone call seemed like too much effort for my body. My lifelines became the company of my precious wiener dogs and the advice of my guardian angels. The perceived lack of support summoned my biggest fear—facing death alone. It tore down my strength of spirit each day. But I had no choice but to surrender to my fate: endure treatment alone, or die.

As my own internal battle ensued with weeks of treatment, every cell in my body felt the damage of the neurotoxins. An invisible war was occurring inside of me, with my body as the battlefield. And few fuzzy memories of needles, bruises, and pain accompanied the darkness I felt inside. Fevers, convulsions, vomiting, and drastic changes in body temperature, blood pressure and appetite were only a few of the symptoms I experienced. Horrendous pain coming from inside my bones made me cry out in agony many times. I wished for death to take me. It took some divine power greater than my own strength to win over my wish for mortality. The war consumed whatever Mana remained inside me.

Too weak to continue at the duplex by myself, with no choice left, I was assigned a hospital bed in the back of the clinic, which was reserved for seriously ill in need of close monitoring. I would stay in that bed all day and often into the evenings, until I eventually could muster the strength to drive myself home.

"Are you sure the electric blanket is working, Frank?" I feebly called the head nurse over to my bed. Even with my layers of clothes, my hat, and a blanket, I was shivering with no reprieve. I felt like I was being buried under an avalanche of ice. Frank assessed my bed, the blankets, and the outlet plug.

"Honey, your blanket is on high and you have, one, two, three, four.....nine blankets on you. I can't give you anymore blankets." We chuckled together at the mounded blankets on top of me. "You are just going to have to ride this through."

Even though I felt consumed in my own misery, with my heightened senses, I could almost smell the devastation that the Lyme bacteria had caused to the other patients. There were many that came through those doors during my eight weeks of treatment. I made a point to connect to each one of them with my heart. Although I was too sick to deliver healing work as I once did, I could still offer healing in other ways, like holding someone's hand or listening to someone's story, getting someone a drink when they couldn't, or just laughing with another patient.

Reassurance and positivity from fellow patients went a long way. Just as we all gave to each other, we all received through the mere act of giving what little strength we had to one another.

"How is it going with the kids and their father?" I asked Tami, a fellow patient who came back to the bed next to mine, exasperated after a phone call with her lawyer. It was early morning still, but already she was battling with the knowledge that her ex-husband had filed a court order to declare her incompetent to parent her children. He'd thought what so many of my own friends and family had thought of my pain—that it was all made up, that it wasn't real, or understood.

"It's a total nightmare," she replied, angst clutched her vocal chords and hands. The strain in her face made Tami look older than her forty-five years. "I just can't believe he would do this to me. He knows how sick I've been and he knows I'm a good mother. I don't know what I'm going to do. I can't afford the lawyer fees on top of these medical bills, just to prove that I'm a good mother." Tears threatened to pour over her huge hazel eyes when she spoke.

I could see her spirit was determined to fight, but the blow of this threatening news pushed her close to the edge. And six hours later, a siege of emotional and physical pain swelled inside of her that she could no longer bare.

"Oh my God!!" she screamed. "It hurts! It hurts so bad!! Oh, God! I can't breathe...I can't ...I can't breathe!" Tami gasped and screamed, gripping the rails of the hospital bed. Silhouetted against the red vision lamp that provided light for the nurses in the darkened room, I watched her scream and howl, sob, and cuss. Her body writhed in pain like a soul trapped in hell.

I, and the entire clinic, listened to her writhe in agonizing pain for several days. Even though I was in my own hell, it was heart wrenching to see someone suffering like that, and left me feeling helpless.

"Oh....help me.....oh, God. I can't handle this anymore! I can't do this." Her cries weighted on everyone's shoulders in the clinic. But what could we do?

Finally a nurse yelled from the hallway: "Frank, you need to come help me calm down the patients up front. They're getting freaked out about her screaming." Frank moved through the clinic like a bull, and as soon as the nurse spoke he was out the door to calm the distressed patients.

This left Tami and me in the room, alone together. Maddened with fever and pain, she whimpered with her back to me. I could hear the staff down the hall discussing what to do about Tami's screaming, which was rightfully upsetting the other patients. But I was right next to her, tethered to my own IVs, fighting my own battle.

Yet, the part of me that wanted to help another ailing soul couldn't ignore her suffering. Even though I was combating my own fever, too weak to stand, and in pain I slithered down from the bed and onto

Frank's nearby medical stool. With the IV pole as my support, I scooted myself over to her bed.

"Tami," I whispered. "Tami."

"Hmmm," she whined.

"I'm going to put my hand on your belly. Okay?"

"Okay," she whimpered, but she continued to moan and groan. I gently and lovingly placed my hand on her solar plexus and attempted to channel healing energy into her body, as best I could.

"Tami, I know you are going through so much right now." I consoled, "It all hurts, even the emotional parts. It's the emotions that are making it seem more painful. Let's just focus on getting you through this moment. Right now, all you need to do is breathe and settle yourself into the bed. There is nothing you can do about the legal battle right now. All you can do is focus on getting better, so you can fight for your kids. Just keep breathing into my hand." I rubbed her belly, stroked her arms, and held her hand. Eventually she seemed to find consolation in my genuine touch, and steadied.

"Sahara," I heard from behind me. It was Frank, his hefty hands landed firmly on my shoulders, which made me slump from the added pressure on my weakened body. "I know it's hard to see someone else suffering. I know that you want to help, but you can't help another person until you heal yourself. I've got it from here." Then he wheeled the stool where I sat back to my own bed and helped me crawl under my mound of covers.

From there, I saw Frank administer medicine to Tami to break her fever and sedate her. As I listened to her cries lessen to the whimpers of a scared little girl hiding under the blankets, I realized that my story to heal was not unique to me. My frustration to be free of this illness was shared by Tami and every patient at the clinic, and all the other Lyme patients around the world trying to find their own way to heal. Each patient had their own heart wrenching story of how these tiny bacteria took their lives away. They too, endured similar losses, devastation and lack of support. Just like Tami's grief, all the patient's grief was palpable. They were beat down in spirit, in life, and yet still they found the strength to fight for their lives. I had felt so alone for so many years, but in walking this healing gauntlet with others, I realized I was a classic Lyme case. At some point, each one of us had felt the same slow approach of death. We had suffered alone, behind closed doors, and we had been too sick to reach out. My story was just one of many. All of us were dying from the same illness which was unseen and misunderstood by society; we were all teetering on the brink of the same unmarked grave.

Eagle Medicine

The bald eagle is a symbol of freedom to many people, but it is also a reminder about perspective. Eagles have the ability to soar to great heights, riding the thermals where the wind carries them forward. The soaring of an eagle brings expansive awareness to our minds, with the feelings of freedom in flight. This is an important lesson for humans, that there is something bigger and freer than the scope we are thinking of right now. Eagle Medicine is here to teach us how to fly high into the stratosphere in order to gain new perspective about our current situation. A bird's eye perspective is just what one needs when one is shrouded in stale ideas. This new vantage point helps us to make new decisions, to change, and to grow. *Are you too focused on what is right in front of you? Are you stuck in one particular way of thinking or being? Do you always see things in the same way, a way that perpetuates unnecessary drama in your life?* Eagles bring the medicine necessary to broaden our points of view, allowing life to change and grow—for it is in these moments that we appreciate the beauty that is all around us. Eagle Medicine invites you to soar to greater heights, spread your wings to fly, and let the winds of heaven carry you.

CHAPTER 21

Miracles and Blessings

IN THE DAYS AND WEEKS THAT FOLLOWED, the same thick fog hung over my brain and clouded my ability to think, to understand, to remember. Daily living was a huge blur. While the clinic set out to heal my body, I focused on healing my spirit and mental attitude. I used meditation tapes and my own music to channel positive energy, to be present, and to focus solely on asking the bacteria to leave my body, mind, and spirit.

Waiting to be assigned a hospital bed for that day's treatment, I waited in the neon green treatment room, adorning my hat like a trusted friend. Unable to fold my arms because of the large hematomas that were forming from my failing veins, I sat stoic, alone and freezing. I watched mothers fetch blankets or cold drinks for their sick child, young and old alike. I watched a pair of sisters laugh together over a movie while one of them received treatment. Husbands ran errands, fetched food, and helped their loved ones walk to the bathroom.

There was support all around me, it seemed, but none of it was for me. It left me feeling even more alone than ever before. If I needed food, I had to get it. If my dogs needed to go outside, I had to move my war-torn body to let them out. If I was cold, I had to endure the pain in my legs to procure a blanket. If I needed to scrape the morning ice off my windshield in order to drive to the clinic, I had to exert the little energy I had left to do it. Every single step I took was on my own.

Finally, during the third week of treatment, one person did come: my ex-husband, John, yet again. His presence continued to atone on so many levels, healing old wounds that we both had been responsible for inflicting.

For five precious days, John stayed by my side, held my hand, and cried as he witnessed me in such extreme suffering for the second time in a decade. Even with him by my side, I wished for death. I wished for this life to be done. I didn't want this life anymore. I didn't fear the spirit world; in fact, I would have preferred to live in that realm than suffer through another day of treatment. Still, my perceived lack of support from friends or family acted like fuel to my suicidal fire. Amelia was worried and kept suicidal watch over me from afar. Each day I fought for my life, not only in my body, but also in some other dimension that the rest of the world—not even the other patients in the clinic—could see. I didn't want to be a part of this world anymore, and yet, I kept fighting. Through it all, somehow I kept fighting.

"I really need to get out of this one-and-a-half mile radius," I told John on his last day in Reno.

The neurotoxins had been flooding through me for three weeks of treatment, which had made it nearly impossible for me even to drive down the street. My world was reduced to the clinic and my nearby duplex. For three weeks I'd seen nothing but desert and sagebrush, pavement, needles, and nurses. I pleaded with him to drive me two hours southwest up into the mountains where Lake Tahoe awaited.

John was hesitant, concerned that the trip would wear me out even more than I already felt. But I was desperate for fresh air and new perspective, and for a reminder that I would not be trapped in some kind of hell forever.

"Once you leave," I told him, "I'm on my own. I won't be able to get out again. I really need this, even if it is just a car ride. Please." He was my only chance to have a much-needed escape from treatment, even if it was only temporary.

"Alright," he finally consented, "I'll drive you up there."

The two-hour drive led us through windy roads, pine forests, higher elevation and snow. Now nearing the end of March, the ski slopes were reserved for the diehards hoping for one last ride down the mountainside. Through the car window, I saw that the pristine, white, powdery snow had been replaced with grey, filthy snow clods from plows and road dirt. Melting mounds of it held onto their existence as the early spring sunshine began exposing the sleepy earth below. I could feel the difference in elevation as we drove, but the cool, crisp air and the broadening view of the Washoe Valley below us was good medicine for me. The clinic and all the despair contained inside was down there somewhere, but I was up in the mountains away from it all.

Fierce winter energy still had Lake Tahoe in its grip. When we pulled up to a public beach, I watched choppy waves rage against the shoreline in manic torrents. The snow-peaked Sierra Mountains stood enchanted, otherworldly across Lake Tahoe. If the day were foggy, I would have thought this was the River Stix, and Charon lived over in those mountains waiting to take me to my death.

"That's all you got?" John said after I plopped down on the sand. I'd walked about twenty feet from where he'd parked the car, but already my legs had given out.

"Such progress," I joked. "Twenty feet, not bad for a day's exercise." *Humor was better than judgment*, I thought. But in truth, I was happy just to watch the water and let the dogs play on the beach. I was out of breath from the short walk from the car, but I smiled in delight for the fresh air and time to contemplate all that had happened thus far, away from the clinic.

The daily physical and emotional toils of treatment and listening to other patients' hardships had taken their toll on me. Suffering shrouded my world. It coursed through me like a river threatening to sweep me and all the other Lyme patients downstream, where we would be forced to fight against the swift current. I couldn't escape the daily stories of how other patients' lives had slipped through their fingers. None of it seemed right.

Why does this country not know about the catastrophic wreckage this illness causes? Why does it seem like it is being covered up by the CDC, the insurance companies, and the government? Why is it always misdiagnosed? Why it is not covered under insurance? Why is disability status and its benefits so difficult to acquire?

My contemplation on the sandy beach unearthed a seed of anger that had sprouted inside of me over the weeks in treatment. *There is something seriously wrong when so many people lose everything to these bugs and no country, medical association, or creed has stepped up to help. This isn't right!*

I had been brooding over these thoughts every day as patients continued to share their Lyme stories with me. It became glaringly clear: Lyme disease was not just a physical illness; it was an illness that stripped us of our life, our heart, and eventually our souls. Thinking of all the loss, all the grief, all the suffering that this one single clinic contained, I realized it was an epidemic of massive destruction creeping right under our noses. It had been right under my nose for over twenty years before I could no longer ignore it.

Although the biting cold seemed to run straight into my bones, the sunshine and fresh air at Lake Tahoe gave me reprieve from the long days inside the clinic. Just as I settled into this precious time I had on the sand, a bald eagle soared overhead. The screeching cries echoed in the thin, mountain air, making it seem like the eagle was much closer than he appeared. Watching him soar above me, I felt connected to that magical creature; I felt avid and open to learn the lessons he had to offer. *Perspective*, I thought. *A bald eagle is a sign of perspective.*

I began to reflect on my journey thus far, knowing that in order to know where I was heading, I needed to know where I had been. *I did need a change of perspective and attitude*, I thought. *But how?*

"You ready to go?" With red, wind-whipped cheeks, John had approached me, still in the same spot where he'd left me on the beach to be alone with my thoughts.

"Yes," I said. "I'm ready to go." He helped me stand, shakily. I thanked him for bringing me there, and, taking one last look at the white caps rolling endlessly on the water, I thanked that eagle for the calm reflection it prompted in me.

In the days that followed, the eagle continued to guide my perceptions into a place of gratitude, strength and positivity. My brief outing with John had changed something in me. Lake Tahoe and the views from up high seemed to remind me that I was still being supported by my guides and angels. They had carried me thus far, I knew.

John's brief presence was a blessing, one of many that I experienced through the terrors of treatment. Slowly, as word got out to the other patients that I was on my own, I received a stream of kind gestures from other patients and their caretakers. People brought me soups, drinks, blankets, heating pads, essential oils, and more. One person held my hand during a convulsion, while another went to a nearby restaurant to buy me dinner; yet another person went grocery shopping for me.

What continued to unfold from the first day I stepped foot in the clinic was a deep loving connection to complete strangers who extended the simplest of kindness to a suffering soul. They didn't know me, hadn't known where or who I'd been; nor did they need to know. We came together, the other patients and me, like soldiers in a jungle fighting for their lives, watching each other's back, and helping each other laugh and stay strong.

One day I would be down and someone would bring me up; the next day I would be up and help someone who was down. The people that were mere strangers to me a few weeks ago had become guardian angels, healing wounds far deeper than those inflicted by Lyme disease.

Other angels continued to come in over the wires of communication. Many of my friends and some family, who couldn't be with me during treatment, phoned daily. They were there with me in spirit and they, too, held me up when I was so down. Daily texts, phone calls, and emails kept coming in from friends all around the world wanting to know how I was doing. Financial donations and words of encouragement were being offered by my friends and fellow patients alike. Most of the friends who supported me were ones I had met on spiritual quests throughout my life, but only then in treatment could I see the true berth of my spiritual family. Each one of them was a huge lifeline during my sixty days of treatment.

With each kind gesture, I felt the presence of my guardian angels as they continued to heal me in places beyond the physical. They helped heal the little girl deep inside of me who felt so very abandoned. I was receiving all the love that I needed through the love of strangers.

I realized that if help had come in the way I had expected, such as with a friend's or family member's company, I would never have seen the beauty of the human spirit the way I did in Reno. I was expecting help to come in one way, but instead it came through miracles and blessings. I was supported after all.

It is in that moment of nothingness that the caterpillar somehow, miraculously, redefines itself....

Butterfly Medicine

Transformative, intricately beautiful, light-filled, flitting in joy, and drinking the nectar of flowers are some of the ways we describe butterflies. Their presence evokes the mystery of how a ravenous caterpillar seeking gratification from external sources manages to go deep within to change its entire cellular structure and emerge transformed. A butterfly is not only different from a caterpillar in cellular form, but also in the way it shows up in life. Compared to the ravenous caterpillar, a graceful butterfly embodies inner peace, detachment and allowing. This is the medicine that butterflies are here to teach. *What areas of life are you struggling to change? Where do you most need inner transformation? Are you chomping at the bit for the next direction in life or are you allowing yourself to let the winds of heaven guide you?* Butterfly Medicine teaches us to release our desired outcomes and allow the guiding breath of heaven to lead our paths. Their beauty reminds us that our own beauty will shine through inner transformation. *Can you turn inward and allow yourself time within a spiritual or mental cocoon? Or do old thought patterns weigh you down? What needs to change inside so that your exterior world changes too?* Butterfly Medicine shows us opportunities to think differently about our world and about ourselves: to live from a heart-centered, divine place instead of an ego-driven, fear-based place. Butterflies are the outward expression in nature of the inner transformation necessary for true change and growth.

CHAPTER 22

Metamorphosis

"THIS WAY," I SHOUTED TO MY TWO DOGS, "come over here!"

Sampson and Delilah romped and frolicked in the green grass at the park near the clinic in Reno while I sat on a blanket and tossed a ball for them.

The beautiful spring day held the sweetness of being Easter Sunday, and it also marked the 40th day of my treatment. Forty days in the desert of Reno so far, readying myself to emerge from this healing pilgrimage and cocoon of treatment. I already felt that I underwent a pseudo-crucifixion during my treatment when I surrendered all that had happened thus far on my journey and forgave every aspect of my life, including myself. I felt as if I was ready to resurrect from my death as a Lyme patient into my new self. The fact that this day fell on Easter felt so auspicious.

The new season's dandelions were already beginning to flower in the fresh, green grass, which was truly a rarity in Reno. While the rest of Reno faced unquenched thirst from a three-year drought, this irrigated park was the only green space for miles around the clinic. It was my personal oasis in the midst of treatment, a place where I could lay on the grass, watch the clouds, work on shifting my perspective, and find gratitude for the journey I was on.

As I tossed the ball again for my two dogs, I spotted three little white butterflies flitting about, going to and fro between the early blooming flowers. Always when I saw something three times in nature, I took it as a sign for my own journey. That day, those three little butterflies danced around me, whispering hidden messages and little gems of wisdom into my intuitive mind that I began to contemplate.

My twenties were spent diving into the world of science. But at the core of my being, I knew I was meant to be a holistic healer since I was a little girl. Yet, the pressures to please my parents and society led me down a path where I pursued advanced degrees in biology, horticulture, and medicinal plants.

There is a difference between having a life and living a life, I reflected.

Even though the spirits of the butterflies spoke to me about the transformation of the soul, I reflected on the physical metamorphosis that each one of those butterflies underwent before becoming what they were on that day. In a sense, I was a caterpillar who was struggling to transform every cell in my body until it was free from Lyme disease.

The sunny day lulled me into the sweet meditation of what butterflies mean to me. I recalled my time as a biology teacher and my lectures on the magic of metamorphosis danced in my mind.

When the caterpillar begins its transformation inside the cocoon, it actually becomes a mass of liquid, gooey cells that are undifferentiated from its physiological role for the caterpillar. There is no differentiation between a cardiac cell, a muscle cell, an eye cell or a stomach cell. During this stage, the caterpillar's cells revert back to their original function, or lack of function. They have no assigned task other than to exist, take in nutrients, make energy and excrete waste.

In this moment of metamorphosis the caterpillar can no longer be defined as a caterpillar. This liquid substance of cells, with no form, function or definition of what it will be are known as *imagination cells*. It is in that moment of nothingness that the caterpillar somehow, miraculously, redefines itself into color, wings, antennae, an abdomen, thorax, and head. All parts completely reinvented to become a butterfly.

I felt like a pile of goo sitting on the grass. I wondered if it was possible to imagine my life from the caterpillar of Lyme disease into the butterfly of my new life.

I continued my daydream as the dainty white wings flitted about me tasting the sweet nectar. *White is the symbol of spirit,* I reflected. Understanding this significance, I took it to mean that Spirit was speaking to me through these butterflies summoning the light of my own spirit to come forth from my cocoon.

Inside the chrysalis of change, the cells once having a role and purpose as a caterpillar have surrendered their identity. They have become a part of a greater whole of being, nothingness, without label or form. I reflected on the similarity of how caterpillars seem to represent my own ego.

All the times my unyielding drive for an outcome was like a caterpillar with its head down, chomping at whatever is in the way for the intended conclusion. In the caterpillar's case, it may have been food. In my case, it was a degree, a relationship, or material possession that I thought I 'wanted' or 'needed'.

When the caterpillar emerges as the butterfly its personality seems completely different. It doesn't strive to be anything. It just is. Am I still chomping at the bit for an outcome or am I just being?

I wasn't sure yet, but I knew something was changing inside of me from the treatment and the way I was seeing the world, my world.

The little butterflies flitted around me and the dogs with a joy and carefree nature seeming to sing a gentle tune carried in the wind. I marveled at their carefree lightness. A sense of surrender and allowing that made these tiny creatures seem pounds lighter energetically than a caterpillar.

One seems made of matter, this earth, this reality; whereas the other seems made up of ethereal essence, soul essence, fairy essence.

I took to understand the meaning of my own metamorphosis as that caterpillar transcending this physical reality and stepping into a spiritual awareness manifested in the beauty and grace of the butterfly. A rebirth into a reality of magic, beyond the five senses for the soul.

Through the winter months, I had found myself sunken into the depths of my body to purge not only the bacteria, but also every thought, emotion, and perception that kept me from living my most authentic truth. I wasn't buried under my old life, but rather planted deep in the soil, gestating quietly under the earth. I understood that like the seeds in winter, I needed to go deep within and allow myself the time necessary to let nature and the Universe guide me through healing. I only had the small feat of making it through treatment and the rest would unfold.

Forty days had carried me through a healing gauntlet of agony in Reno thus far. I was seeing the light at the end of the tunnel, the end of treatment was in sight, my own resurrection. I had twenty days left and a big gigantic unknown was sitting before me. I began asking, *what's next?*

*This is the day, when I throw it all away
to the fire of the all loving One.*

Tree Medicine

The soul of a tree taps into the wisdom of the earth. The roots honor and symbolize the ability to dive into the depths of one's own soul and to look into one's own heart to find the answers we seek. Trees, also known as the Standing Tall People by the Lakota, help us to understand what it means to stand firmly rooted in place within ourselves. Yet, within this rootedness, our tree friends embody the lesson of surrender. When leaves fall, branches break and the fruits of their labor fall to the earth, trees accept and stay in peace. Our lives must also surrender to what must be returned to the earth. *Are you holding onto a perspective or idea that no longer serves your heart? Are you scattered and uprooted inside by trying to be so strong that it feels daunting? Are you being too rigid in your stance, unable to sway in the winds of change? Or do you need to take time to root yourself and find your center? What stability is there in your life, inside of your own heart and soul? Do you need to summon this stability now?* Tree Medicine teaches us to let go when necessary and to trust that new growth will come. It also teaches us to sway in storms, be still inside our hearts, to listen carefully, and to accept where we are right now.

CHAPTER 23

Standing Tall Being

AFTER ANOTHER DAY OF TREATMENT, after another five hours attached to an IV bag and pole, I was set free to breathe fresh air, eat lunch, and take care of my dogs. This was the time of day when I acted like a functional member of society, if only for an hour or so, to enjoy life as a normal, healthy human being.

Stepping outside, seeing the swelling buds and emerging daffodils outside the clinic, my body wanted to skip giddily from my car with carefree delight. Instead, I hobbled to my car smiling in gratitude for the spring day.

Sampson and Delilah greeted me as if I had been gone for days, with such exuberance from their little hearts my own spirit immediately lifted upon opening the door to my duplex. Playing with them in the backyard, I felt reconnected to the land, the azure sky, and the sun's sparkling array of light.

From there, I could see the tips of the snow covered Sierra Mountains, in the distance, this regions Apu. Which I took as a reminder to stay firm in myself when so much of me still yearned to be free of my body once and for all. Even the dry earth and unfamiliar smells in the backyard consoled me despite it being so different from the humus rich soil of the Pacific Northwest.

"Where's the ball? Go get it!" I taunted and teased my precious friends, and as they bounded over the uncut grass and obstacles of downed tree limbs, I sat under a seasoned old tree to rest.

Looking up into the old, worn branches, I noticed all the subtleties that made it unique: shaggy bark that was grey and weathered from the dry, harsh high-desert climate. It looked as ragged as I felt inside. But just above that ragged bark were newly emerging leaves bursting with fresh vital life-force. Perhaps this was why that tree beckoned me and captivated me as strongly as Grandmother Cedar captivated me at Lost Lake.

Even the memory of Grandmother Cedar brought forth pangs of grief, sadness and longing in my heart. But under this old, worn tree, I did not feel so alone. I felt connected to that tree, that Standing Tall Being. But it wasn't just the tree. I befriended the insects crawling up its trunk, the rocks around its base, the clouds and sky above its leaves. Suddenly I was aware of all the beings encircling me, emanating so much life, so much Mana, that I hadn't noticed before. All of the trees and plants were alive and talking to one another through their roots and branches and unseen realities that humans seldom touch.

I felt that we were a family, just as Grandmother Cedar and I were family, just as my dogs and I were family. The same reminders of interconnectedness flowed through me as when I was *flying* on Maui, swimming with the whales, hugging trees, and holding a fellow patient's hand during treatment. All of those moments were my family; all of those moments and beings were there to support each other.

Somewhere under the internal blankets of my exhaustion, I also felt a delicate new seedling of energy and potential vitality stirring inside my cells. Although I was still weak, small little surges of strength seemed to sprout, if only for a moment, into my limbs. My brain seemed to be going through the same change. I felt more stable emotionally, and more capable of making decisions. Perhaps this treatment was working after all. My own springtime would eventually come and with it the new seeds for my life.

Eventually my break from the clinic ended, and with that, my time with my dogs and tree friends in the backyard also ended. Another ending was coming into sight, too, though: the end of my treatment. The finish line was only three days away.

Although the doctor wanted me to stay another two months, I couldn't afford to spend any more money without a steady source of income or a home to return to and recover from treatment. I was not sure how I was going to do it, whatever *it* was. Considering all the unknowns ahead of me, I felt pensive and worried rather than excited.

What on earth am I going to do?

"I just don't know what I'm going to do, Frank." I said to the nurse after I'd returned to the clinic.

Frank came over and sat on the edge of my bed as he attached an IV bag to my Picc line for the afternoon treatment. He checked that my electric blanket was working properly, then placed his hand on my shin and said, "Honey, you are so pretty, I have absolutely no doubt you are going to be okay. Everything is going to be alright, you'll see."

Though I appreciated his reassurance, and the compliment, I didn't really believe him. Still, I trusted in him; he'd helped me so much during my treatment. He was in charge of the group of hospital beds where I received treatment once my symptoms became severe. To cheer me up one day he turned on a movie; another day he brought me an Italian soda. He'd picked up prescriptions, and even sent me text messages in the evenings to make sure I was okay. He was one more angel I encountered at that clinic.

In spite of the support I received, from Frank, the fellow patients, and from my friends and family (who had been supporting me from afar), I was still filled with fear, doubt, and uncertainty about what I would do after I left Reno. But at the moment, I was literally tethered to that spot, by an IV.

Okay, I thought, *stay focused*. I turned on my well-worn meditative music and listened to the words of a song I had listened many times before, but which seemed auspicious at my time of doubt.

"Now is the time that I let go of my fears and sense of dread... When I give up control and I let you hold me with no resistance in my soul... This is the day when I throw it all away to the fire of the all loving One. Now I have just what I need to be free. To feel who I really am...I surrender...I remember the beauty that I am..."

The words resounded through my ear buds as a divine message. I *was* being guided. I stayed focused in my meditation and heard my guides speak. They were the same guides that came to me in the psychic download in Haleakalā, the same ones that helped lead me to the clinic, and the same ones that helped to break open my heart.

"Listen for the 'yes'."

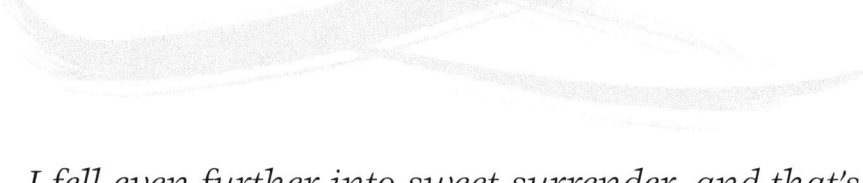

I fell even further into sweet surrender, and that's where I continued to linger.

PART THREE

DIVINE GUIDANCE

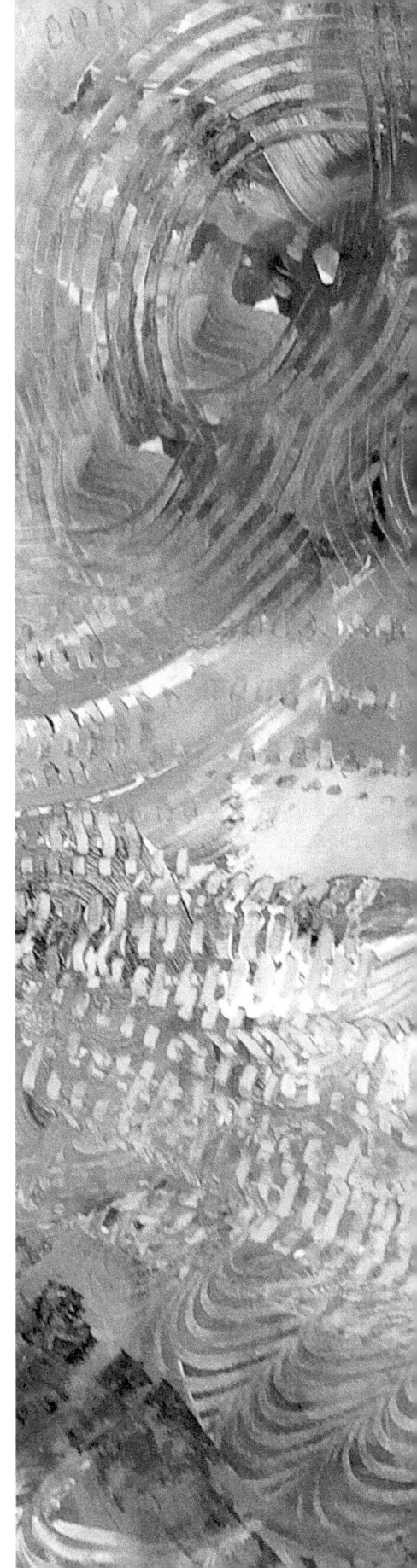

Hawk Medicine

In Native American culture, the red tail of a hawk reflects the Red Road, which stands for the spiritual path we must walk to find our soul's path. This path connects us to the great mystery of life. Red tail hawks remind us to trust in the great, universal forces at play in our lives. They also remind us to say, "Yes," to life when it calls us. Hawk Medicine teaches us to listen to our own inner guidance. *Are you listening to your own intuition? Are you listening to the signals your body is giving you? Do you give yourself enough time for introspection, meditation and journaling? Or do you spend most of your time in your head, listening to all the mind chatter?* Hawk Medicine is the reminder that we are all on a spiritual journey, and that where our journey takes us is not up to us, but rather to the greater forces of the Universe. *Do you spend too much time in fear of upcoming decisions or life choices? Do you doubt in the Universe's ability to guide you?* The soaring hawk is medicine that brings clarity and confirmation that the Red Road we walk is filled with magic, mystery, and blessings. We must spread our wings and surrender into the spiritual flight of our soul, riding the thermals that help us to fly into our best life.

CHAPTER 24

On My Knees

THE NEXT DAY I MET WITH THE DOCTOR for the last time. I only had one more day of treatment and then I would be on my own.

"You know," the doctor told me, "I tell most of my patients to go home and rest for at least a month, preferably three months." I was sitting in his office, with miles of his glossy wooden desk separating me from him. I watched him stroke his chin in a pensive, jittery gesture; he seemed truly concerned with my predicament, as if he was my concerned father. "But with you," he continued, "I don't know what to do with you. You have no home, is that correct?"

Well, that was true. I didn't know what to do with me, either. He was preaching to the choir with his concerns, and the mere fact that he brought it up was like shining a spotlight on the fear weighing on my chest. I recoiled slightly at his direct question, and scooted around in my seat, wishing I had some sort of answer.

"No," I said, looking straight at him, trying to appear strong, though I could hear my voice quiver. "I don't have a home anymore." The strain to even discuss the subject was enough to make me cry.

"Well, this is very concerning," the doctor counseled, as if I needed reminding. "I don't like the idea of sending you out on the road in the physical state you're in. I don't normally have patients in your situation. I am not sure what to do with you. I don't want this situation to compromise your recovery. It is possible to relapse," he warned me. "You still have a very long road to travel before we can say you are in remission."

After discussing my current living situation, that I would need to vacate my rented duplex in less than a week and that I didn't have anyone coming to help, the doctor suggested I stay in Reno until I was strong enough to drive. Though this option didn't feel right intuitively to me, I didn't have another answer. I hadn't heard that *yes* from the Universe yet, but I had heard my guides whispering their support and encouragement.

Remember that you are being taken care of and guided.
Trust that you will be okay.

I knew that my spiritual guides were right, but I also knew that my doctor was right. I had successfully survived treatment, but I still had a very large mess to clean up inside my body. Just because the war was over didn't mean there wasn't rubble left behind. Years of damage from bacteria boring holes into my cells still needed repair. I had liver pain, and recent blood work indicated my liver enzymes were overtaxed from treatment. Meanwhile, neurotoxins were still actively attacking my body. My short-term memory was all but gone—I would lose words in midsentence, I couldn't get them out, or they would just drift away from my grasp before I could finish my thought. And I had pain everywhere still. If I bent over too fast, stood up too quick, laughed too hard, talked too long or reflexively moved quickly my entire body would quake like the earth, shuddering pain across my flesh and bone, taking my breath away.

I didn't think it possible, but I was even weaker than when I arrived at the clinic sixty days prior. I needed time to recover.

That day of my last appointment with the doctor, I felt incredibly fragile.

"Thank you," was all I could muster to the doctor. I was more than grateful for his help, but I still felt too weak to express myself authentically.

"I think you look better than you did when you first got here," he said. "You're going to be okay."

"I'm coming to help you," my friend Laurel said to me through the phone receiver the day after my meeting with the doctor. A dear friend of mine, Laurel was a kindred sister calling to tell me about her recent dream: one of my little dogs, Delilah, fell through the cracks of the floor and Laurel couldn't save her. Upon waking, Laurel interpreted the dream as *me* falling through the cracks, and promptly booked a flight from her home in Western Washington to help me transition into the next stage of my life.

"I don't know why," she'd tell me later, "but I knew I just had to come."

It was the Universe nudging her, I knew, and Laurel had said yes. I hadn't expected her to come considering her limited income as a working single mom, but she did. She had listened to her own internal guidance system, dropped everything in her busy life and came to Reno to help me.

For five glorious days Laurel worked her little fingers to the bone cleaning up the mess that I'd made in the duplex from two months of living without energy to clean anything up. I watched her hustle around the duplex, cleaning, singing, and bee-bopping about with her exuberant, peppy personality. After she packed my clothes, she loaded them and the few other belongings into my car, then cleaned the kitchen and bathroom, and stripped the sheets off the bed. She even took my car to have new tires put on them in preparation for the unknown road ahead.

Though she had not been able to come during my treatment, she was here now. Yet another guiding angel to my rescue. I was eternally grateful for her presence and help. By the fourth day, she was exhausted. The perspiration on her brow was evidence of her tenacious spirit and hard work. Had she not come, social services would've had to help me vacate the house.

While Laurel cleaned all she could, I lay horizontal on the couch and listened to her counsel on approaching my next step. We talked about the most feasible options for hours on end.

Do I head to Kentucky to be with my family? How do I get to Kentucky? My family had suggested that I sell my car, get on a plane with my dogs in cargo, and fly across the country to stay with them.

But Laurel knew that this was impossible in my current state of health. So we toyed with the idea of me staying in Reno, of returning to Washington or Hawaii. But how? Every question only produced more questions and logistical nightmares for my invalid body and limited income. So many questions and no clear answers. I wasn't hearing a 'yes' from the Universe to go in any particular direction. I knew I had to be still until the 'yes' came.

When Laurel left, my future seemed as uncertain as when she'd arrived; I knew her departure was as hard on her as it was on me.

"I feel so horrible having to leave you. I can't believe you still don't know what to do."

"I am so sad you are leaving." I said, embracing her bouncy, 5'2" exuberant body, packed full of expression and love. Often I'd watched her as she worked and I noticed how similar her blonde hair, blue eyes, skin tone and frame were to mine; many times I felt the kindred spirit of sisterhood with Laurel.

With each moment of uncertainty when I had to explain my unknown future, surrendering became the reactionary response. I became steadfast in my conviction that the Universe was going to guide me on my path home—wherever that home now was.

Though so much was unclear, there had been way too many miracles in the past few months of my life to ignore or not trust that I was being guided. Equally so, my gratitude blossomed out from these miracles, like the lotus blossoming out of the mud and muck. The light of all these miracles was shining down so brightly I couldn't step into the dark anymore.

"Thank you," I told Laurel as best as I could. What I could emote never seemed to convey what I truly felt inside. I had dropped her off at the airport curb. "I Love you. Bless you." We hugged one last time and with that I saw her disappear through the sliding glass doors. She was gone. The silence in my car echoed the emptiness of walking alone, yet again, on this arduous journey.

I breathed a centering breath, looked over at Sampson and Delilah and said, "Well, it's just you and me kids."

In the quiet morning hours after Laurel left, my dogs and I were alone again in the duplex, lying together on the couch. The little bit of energy I exerted to help Laurel where I could resulted in a major Lyme flare. I couldn't move a muscle. My legs were so weak that I could barely lift them to walk. My head was clouded with a confusion of thoughts and neurotoxins, leaving me unable even to complete a sentence. The memory of what I ate for breakfast only that morning had already escaped my mind.

This level of forgetfulness seemed akin to Alzheimer's, except I was still aware of it all; I was very aware of what was happening to me, of what I had forgotten, of what I was unable to do.

Like the rustled stirrings of energy before a storm, a whirlwind of fear entered my mind. *What am I going to do? How am I going to get the rest of my stuff in the car? Where will I go?*

My mind was spinning with uncertainty and confusion, but through the storm, I heard the faint whispers of the Universe. *Hold steady,* they said.

And I did.

My legs and body were shaky, but my intuitive mind—the only part of me I seemed to have control of at that moment—did what my guides told it to do. It held steady.

Breathing, centering, coming into a still presence on that couch, I stepped into the same deep, healing meditation that I had practiced every day while in treatment and during my psychic downloads in Hawaii. Like summoning a different type of sleep cycle, I stepped into the world of the Spirits. I imagined being surrounded by their beautiful healing light. It was the same light that came through my divine connection to the Star Beings through the humming refrigerator and the whales on the naked beach, to Auntie Margaret's Aloha spirit on Christmas Eve. With the visualization of this light came the knowledge that every cell in my body was healing, that the Lyme bacteria were being lovingly escorted out of me and into some other dimension where they would no longer harm me.

Calm surrender lapped into me with each breath I took, and I settled in deeper, down to the very depth of my ravaged memory, where gratitude still held strong. There, I summoned all the amazing blessings that had come my way thus far on my journey, and then began to imagine the many more blessings to come. I visualized a home in the country, where I would be healthy and free, a garden, lots of love all around me, and more. I believed that more good things would come to me.

I have no recollection of how long I laid there on that couch, but the sweet feeling of surrender coursing through my body was enough medicine to put out the fires of anxiety and desperation that were waiting to burn out of control. Acceptance and trust took over my heart, and peace allowed me to embrace where I was in that moment with my body.

What is the kindest and gentlest path I could be taking right now? This question became the gauge for most decisions that were still to come.

Finally, the faint vibration of my cell phone pulled me out of my meditative state. It was a text from a fellow patient at the clinic, Carolyn. When she'd left the clinic the previous month, she had invited me to stay at her home in California. She had suggested I stay for one week. One week felt fruitless to what I needed, and considering that her house was a four-hour drive from Reno, I did not even consider her offer an option. I needed a place to rest and recover without stress. I needed time.

"Sahara," the text read, "where are you in treatment? Are you still there? Ned and I are driving into Reno tomorrow to pick up my medication. Would you like Ned to drive your car to our house and you can stay with us for a little while?"

I could not believe the words I was reading. If my soul had been walking around in a spiritual desert these past sixty days of treatment seeking reprieve, this was the first sign of an oasis capable of finally quenching my thirst.

My body, still lying immobile on the couch, couldn't move. As I felt a single tear fall down my cheek, my soul fell onto its knees in gratitude. I felt it fall. Like an out of body experience, I knew my spirit had dropped into the bliss of the divine hands of God.

There, it floated like a child kneeling before angels. My heart poured light through the cracked fissures, miraculous awe-inspiring light. My guides had told me to hold steady. They'd had a plan that I wasn't privy to, until now.

I fell even further into sweet surrender, and that's where I continued to linger. Overcome with emotions, more tears flowed from the corners of my eyes as I clutched the phone to my chest. I heard my guides speak once again. And what they said was, *"Say yes!"*

Phoenix Medicine

The Phoenix is a mythical creature recognized by cultures around the globe, but its folklore originates in Greece. It is unknown whether the phoenix ever existed or not, but its symbolism has far reaching implications surrounding rebirth. It is said that near the end of its 1000-year lifespan, the phoenix builds a funeral pyre and sets fire to itself. From its ashes, a new bird rises. Phoenix medicine is the symbol of letting go of the old so that something new can be reborn. *Have you experienced a death in your life, symbolic or literal? Do you need to summon an inner rebirth? Do you need the courage to rise again from your own ashes?* Phoenix Medicine shows us the path to rebirth when we have overcome impossible odds and now need to summon the courage to complete our transformation. It teaches us the true meaning of rebirth, to rise from the ashes of our old life so that our new life can grow. Depicted with outstretched wings, the phoenix is ready to embrace what life has in store; this is the reminder of the courage needed to step into a new life with an opened heart. When we rise, when we are reborn, the power to transcend can be profound. Phoenix Medicine asks us to step inside our heart where new seeds linger in wait until they feel enough self-love to grow new life once again.

CHAPTER 25

Paradise

THE DAY AFTER I RECEIVED THE TEXT from Carolyn, I sat in the front seat of her Subaru with my two wiener dogs on my lap, both of them as uncertain as I was to what was happening. All of us were hot inside the car, as the late spring sunshine of the Nevada desert made its way across the sky.

Through the windshield, I saw my car, which Carolyn's husband Ned was driving, leading our two-car caravan through the deeply-cut ravine propelling us onto the eastern side of the Sierra Mountain Range and into California. The road meandered along the jagged rocks of the Truckee River. The water's swift current, the steep slopes, and the forged roadways all felt so new; I felt like I was seeing the world for the first time.

We were strangers in all other ways but one—our common battle with Lyme disease—but that was enough for Carolyn to reach out to me and invite me into her home to recover. Like always, help had come when I least expected it and I had no other options. Too weak to take the next step by myself, unsure of where to go, the Universe had offered Carolyn and my only task was to say "Yes."

Small conversations about our life bantered back and forth between us during the four-hour drive to Carolyn's home, but most of me was still processing my journey since leaving Washington that previous winter. I went to Hawaii, and then I chose to leave Hawaii, knowing it would be some time before I would return.

Though the clinic was behind me now, I knew that I still had months of recovery ahead of me. I had learned in Hawaii that my home was within me and that paradise was most certainly a state of mind rather than a place. But now, I had found my way to paradise again, this time to Paradise, California, where Carolyn and her husband Ned lived.

Our caravan finally came to a stop around dusk in front of a row of towering pines. Somewhere inside these pines nestled Carolyn and Ned's home that they built over twenty years prior. The big front porch and yellow trim against the natural woodwork made their home stand cheerful tucked in deep amongst the trees.

The backyard garden immediately lured me down the stone and gravel pathway where the familiar plants I hadn't seen in so long embraced me with sights of their flowers and foliage. Lavender, violets, lemon balm, oregano, mint, thyme, and rosemary were some of the standbys I noticed dotting the rich landscape. Walking near the garden's raised beds, I saw seasonal greens and daisies popping with happiness.

It was a lovely sensory experience to my eyes, nose and heart after so long in the clinic, in wintery, dry Reno. I immediately sighed in relief. I had landed in a lovely spot with good energy and giving people. All the parts within me that held trepidation and doubt settled into the love that I felt in Carolyn's garden. I felt safe for the first time in weeks.

I broke a sprig of rosemary and inhaled deeply the piney scent. So many times before I have done the same with this plant being. Its familiar culinary delight was like coming home to an old friend. I settled into one of the chairs while Carolyn and Ned got dinner ready. The sun was just about to dip behind the tall pines, but kissed my skin briefly before saying goodnight. I was home in her garden and I was home within me

I woke the next morning to the cooing of mourning doves in the trees, their calls reminding me immediately of my mornings in Hawaii. How far away my time there seemed now. But I had no cause for complaint because my room was filled with my favorite, golden sunlight. With my morning cup of coffee, I ventured barefoot into the backyard to sit in one of the garden chairs I saw the previous day.

Only days ago, the doctor in Reno had cautioned me at my last appointment about working too soon.

"You aren't even allowed to use the 'w' word. No talking about work, thinking about work, or planning for work for at least one month." He emphasized the importance of giving my body enough time to recuperate before I exerted myself. "Or else, it's like you're giving all your treatment away!"

Most of my life, up until that point, was centered on what I was doing, and what was the next outcome, the next decision, the next thing. This next step was about *not* doing—but rather *being*.

Finally, something I desired was also the doctor's orders! Now I was at a sanctuary in Paradise with two people who were kind and good, and all I had to do was *be*. The miracle of it all was stunning.

My heart grew immeasurably as I sat in the garden and embraced the faint reminders of my time at Ho`okena. My goal there was the same: just to *be*. I had walked the lava rock around at Ho`okena and carried a feeling of surrender inside of me; I had nowhere to go, nothing to do and nothing to prove. And now for the second time in my life, my only task was to embrace what was around me. Instead of mongoose and palm trees, I took in the scent of the herbs, the flitting joy of the butterflies, the exuberance of the hummingbirds, woodpeckers, crows, and turkey buzzards. The wind brought messages of peace and stillness played in the songs of the swaying pines. I was in a new place of refuge.

Each day I took in the peaceful serenity of the garden and just as the flowers were bursting forth from their buds, I felt my own energy slowly emerging from my wintery, healing experience. Settling into deep reflection of all that had passed, all that I had gone through with my breakup with Alex and my treatment in Reno, and the courage I somehow summoned to forge this unknown path. My awareness of it surfaced like the seeds of the garden sprouting new growth through the dirt. Small inklings of strength and trust were being unearthed in my heart as I continued to recover.

Although my body was still very weak, with most days consisting of a small walk and sitting in the garden until I walked back into my bedroom and rested, I felt different. Though the foggy haze of treatment still shrouded my awareness, I could feel I wasn't the same as before. A new strength had emerged, one I hadn't known I had. The pain in my body was receding like the waters of a tsunami after its swell. My emotions felt stabilized. I felt like I was beginning to reclaim my own centered pillar of strength.

Somehow, without consciously being aware, I had placed my life on a funeral pyre and set it ablaze, like the mythical phoenix at the end of its long life. Those fires healed me from the inside out, and changed how I valued myself. I found strength to follow the compass of my own heart, patience to listen for the 'yes', and the courage to allow my path to unfold.

I had placed expectation in that fire and what was being reborn was total surrender and acceptance of what had transpired and what will become. I had fled to Hawaii trying to find that girl I left down at Ho`okena with the mongoose, who had figured out how to *be*. I found her in a different kind of paradise. The paradise that was within me. It had been there all along.

...when I allowed for the magic of the world to let things unfold everything felt alive and limitless.

Gratitude Medicine

The energy of our cells puts out a vibrational frequency that is connected to our emotions. If we are sad our cells vibrate sadness. If we are angry our cells vibrate anger and people can feel it, animals too. This vibration is what attracts and creates our reality. When we are vibrating in love and gratitude the vibrational frequency brings us beauty. It also brings forth health. The vibration of gratitude is one that creates a state of bliss in our body so that all of our cells can operate with their fullest potential. When we can say thank you for the opportunity, no matter what it is, how it transpires, or affects us is when we have found the key to our own inner paradise. *Are you focusing on the lack in your life? Do you try to control everything so you don't get hurt? Are you finding the negative in every situation instead of embracing the lessons that are there for you? Can you learn to be grateful for your life just as it is, good and bad?* Gratitude Medicine shows us the way to healing and creating a life that is rich, abundant, and healthy.

CHAPTER 26

The Bridge Man

"GOOD MORNING," I SAID TO CAROLYN and Ned when I walked into their kitchen one morning. The dogs ran into the room after me and jumped into Ned's lap, whining and squirming their loving affections onto him. He smiled through his scraggly, white beard and greeted them eagerly. Three weeks had passed since I'd first arrived at their home and all three of us, the wiener dogs and me, had become comfortable living in their little paradise. We had found our routine and I was continuing to find inner strength as my body recovered and soaked in the next phase of treatment.

My home treatment involved injecting several shots per day in my arms and derriere, that prompted a series of reactions in me ranging from a beneficial energetic boost to long, dizzy spells and extreme fatigue that left me bedbound for two days. It was all a part of my recovery, allowing my body to continue to repair the damage that these little corkscrew bacteria caused over the past two decades.

In my rebirth and rise from the ashes of my illness, I felt like I was growing up again in a new house, as the only daughter of Ned and Carolyn. I felt nurtured in the routines of their daily living and reveled in gratitude each day for their garden, good food, conversations, and peaceful sleep.

Still, I knew though it was only a matter of time that this too would pass and I would have to leave. I was a transient here, just like I was in Reno and in Hawaii. I didn't have a home to call my own; I didn't know where I would go from here. This time, though, I trusted in the Universe with my heart and soul. I knew I would be guided to the next step in my life if I could just listen for the 'yes'. I now understood that I didn't need to struggle and force a particular outcome to make it happen. I just needed to hold my intention and let the Universe do the rest.

"Have you talked to your friend yet about driving to Kentucky?" Carolyn asked while she worked on a knitting project.

"We are working on a plan, but haven't figured it out yet," I replied.

The only path that felt plausible at the moment was returning to Kentucky, to be with my family and hold vigil for my ailing parents in the nursing home where they lived. Sitting in Carolyn's garden, I spent hours on the phone conversing with my friend Daniele about possible scenarios of *how* I would get there.

Daniele was the next divine messenger to help me traverse the next lag of this journey. I trusted Daniele as a friend who also listened to Spirit and understood that the path would unfold for me. She was there in the crater of Haleakalā when I received my name, Sahara. She had trekked with me across Peru and shared in the shamanic initiations and rituals while there in the Andes Mountains. We had bonded while diving into the realms of spirit, ancient mysticism, and astrology. Her love and support became the driving force to help me on this next step into the unknown.

Daniele agreed to drive with me from California to Kansas, about half way, but the rest would be up to me. From a recent test drive to visit friends at a nearby hot springs a few days prior, I couldn't trust my energy. It varied daily. One day I'd feel strong enough to take a long walk, and the next day I was too weak to get out of bed. The unpredictability of my body on the road was too big a risk for me.

But my hope was not deterred. Something else was coming, I was certain, but had no idea what it could be.

My breakup with Alex, his treatment of me during our final interactions, and the ravages of being sick the past two years took a toll on my self-image. My circumstances had been feeding my shadow side with messages that I was unlovable, undesirable, and too unique, sick, and complicated for any man walking the mainstream world to understand me. It seemed like a hopeless task to find someone who would embrace this multifaceted soul of mine, rich with intuition, depth, and a spirit that often felt too powerful and strong for most men. And I had been sick, for a long time. Who was ever going to want me? The quest seemed daunting and hopeless. My legs had atrophied into jelly from not walking, and I was homeless and jobless. What man would ever want me?

I knew that if I let this negative self-image seep into my emotional energy, it would sabotage all the hard work I'd done to heal. So, as a way to remember that I was desirable, I forced myself to explore online dating, just to get my dating-feet wet again.

But almost every aspect of my identity was undergoing a massive metamorphosis of change. I had plenty of doubts along the way. *How could I get involved with a man while I'm still morphing into something that even I have never seen?* My values, strength, healing, and lessons were amalgamating into the new me—I was being finely tuned into a new instrument.

It seemed impossible, then, to find someone with a similar energetic resonance when my own energetic resonance was still under construction. The man I pick today may not be the man the new me wants tomorrow.

To my surprise, several men had expressed interest in me, and over the months in Hawaii and Reno, I exchanged playful banter and innocent emails with a few interested candidates. Pascal was one of these men. We first made contact a few days before I left Reno to head to Paradise.

Pascal's profile said he lived on Orcas Island, which I knew as one of the many islands in Washington State. I had camped there several times, and coincidentally, had considered moving there with Alex only a year prior because I liked the nourishing energy. Ultimately though, I'd chosen the Hawaiian Islands months prior for their warm water and sunshine.

Even talking with Pascal seemed fruitless because I didn't think I wanted to return to the grey clouds of the Pacific Northwest. But I heard the infamous 'yes' when he sent me his first message: he intrigued me, so I responded. I shared that I was the youngest of five siblings and I learned that Pascal was number 11 of 13.

"In that way, you and I are both children at heart," he'd written.

Over the next few weeks, I continued to learn that his upbringing taught him resourcefulness, initiative, and resiliency to live life according to the beat of his own drum. Sharing the kindred spirit of wanderlust, and adventurous free spirits, we connected immediately. I discovered Pascal was a kayak guide, sailor, estate manager, and builder of his own off-grid, sustainable, five-acre homestead with two cabins—these were the ways he lived his life. Curious, I asked him to share some of what his life was like on his property.

"There is much to do on the property this time of year. I have a little 16'x20' cabin I'm turning into a summer rental, and I'm plumbing in a propane refrigerator today. My big excitement is that I am gearing up to be a part of this huge boat race to Alaska....I'm not the kind of guy who is generally into racing as I kind of think competition is very overrated. That said, there is something powerful when a group of people work together for a common goal. The real reason I am wanting to do it is the desire for a little adventure in my life."

During this time, while I was sitting peacefully in Carolyn's garden, Pascal had traveled into Seattle to attend a kayak protest to stop the oil drilling in Alaska. His life sounded ambitious and fun. I admired him for living his life the way he did, instead of watching it go by from the sidelines. Hearing about what he created for himself made me appreciate him for who he was, nothing more.

Compared to some of the other men I met online, alluring men who spewed romantic prose of showering hibiscus flowers on my bed and rubbing oil all over my body, Pascal was interested in knowing my story. He had substance and authenticity that I felt I could trust. I was drawn to know this man. *What could it hurt?* I thought.

On one of my last days in Paradise, I took in the morning slowly, savoring every detail. It may have been early May, but the mornings were still cool at the foothills of the Sierra Mountains. Drinking my morning cup of coffee with the dogs burrowed under the blankets, I opened my laptop and I began writing my daily email to Pascal.

I had mentioned in an earlier message that I was a spiritual person, to which he asked if I was a "fairy worshiper." I replied the best I could, honoring the fairy worshiper inside of me, but also the grounded part of me, full of grandmother wisdom. "It is good I am so grounded otherwise I might disappear into the cosmos ;^)."

Though I was happy at Pascal's interest, and happy to share myself with him, I was curious to hear more about his property. He had five acres, I learned, which he built up while living in a bus that he fitted with a wood burning stove, bamboo flooring, and a swing.

But the view was what peaked my interest: "My place has the most amazing view," he'd written. "You can see Mount Baker and the water from my deck."

The email conversations continued on as part of my daily routine, along with the homecare shots, helping around the house, tossing ball with my dogs, and sitting in the garden. I learned that he had built a life for himself on Orcas Island after months of traveling throughout Thailand, India, Central and South America. He had many adventures living on the road as a vagabond. Pascal was becoming my friend, a friend who I was beginning to appreciate for his thoughtfulness, consideration, and wanting to know me as a person.

Though I continued to enjoy our conversations, I couldn't help wondering: *Why am I even talking to this guy?* He lived in Washington, the state I never thought I would see again. Worse, insecurities about my self-worth flooded me: I feared that I was a broken-winged bird that could not fly.

Then one day, he opened the door to a conversation about my health. It was something I hadn't even mentioned. I never told him why I was in Reno, why I landed in California, and what was wrong with me. Then the question came, but not the one I expected. He'd heard about my illness from my business website, which mentioned that I was on medical leave for Lyme disease.

"Are you okay? I hope you're feeling better." He wrote.

Far from running away from my illness, he seemed concerned. So I shared my story with him. I would likely never meet this man, ever, so I was more open with him. And the more I talked with him, the faith that someone could still desire me in spite of my health filled me with light like a sunbeam breaking through the clouds of a storm.

For the next few email exchanges, I continued to enjoy his sincerity and simplicity.

"I know what it is like to not have a home and live out of a suitcase. It is an unsettling feeling for sure," he wrote.

I reveled in this kindred spirit, for my current friends couldn't relate to what I was experiencing on the road. They were safely tucked into their own lives, with a home, a career, their health, and likely preparing their own gardens for the growing season ahead. He was the first to fully grasp the pressure I was under.

"You have to trust each day, using your wits and finding resources based on the kindness of others." It warmed my heart to have someone understand and reassured me that I wasn't totally alone in the way I felt.

I was living under someone else's roof in Paradise and soon I would have to leave. I continued to exchange emails with Pascal, hunkered in my bedroom where the mourning doves continued to coo me awake daily. Although I felt a deep sense of presence had washed over me there, the unsettled feeling that this was temporary was likened to the feeling right before a big trip.

You know you have to go, you are nervous about it, and your mind carries you into what life will be like away from the creature comforts. I had no real creature comforts of my own, except what was contained in my car. The bed was still not mine, the kitchen was someone else's and I had to adapt to another's routine of daily life.

Although I felt welcomed, I was a guest in someone else's house. It seemed Pascal was the first person who genuinely understood the plight of living on the road. There is no reassurance that one day you can plop on your bed, your own bed. There is no certainty or consistency on the road for daily routines. And any creature comforts must fall to the wayside for more practical things you need for travel. The extra variable to this vagabond equation was that I was also recovering from a major illness.

While I continued my email banters with Pascal, my friend Daniele and I continued to discuss my plans over the phone. My potential departure date to Kentucky was a few days away.

Up until then, Pascal and I had only communicated through email. Up until then, I thought of him as just another friend to swap life stories with. Then he opened the door to talk on the phone and everything changed.

Our first phone conversation occurred at 7:15 a.m. the following morning. It was now only four days before my tentative departure to Kentucky. Pascal and I were both early risers and had already been texting for close to an hour before he decided to take the leap and call me. How refreshing! Morning was my favorite time of day, with its golden light shining on the trees, and this was the first time I heard his voice through the phone receiver. Besides, I was relieved because my energy was like that of a morning glory flower, which rose with the sun and faded by high noon.

"Hi," I heard through the receiver. His voice was deep and sultry, but reasonable. Flutters expanded my heart, and I felt it fill with tinges of nervous energy.

We talked for three hours that day. It was surprisingly easy, open, and with a level of intimate honesty to transition from our email conversations.

After we said our goodbyes I sat still in the recliner chair and listened to the world in deep presence. The embers of the morning fire in the fireplace had crackled their way into ash, but the embers in my heart were glowing. I had felt this sensation many times over the past several months and this morning was no different. In the stillness of my contemplation, I felt light where I'd previously felt heavy and weighted-down with expectations. Recounting my conversation with Pascal, it had become apparent to me that when I allowed for the magic of this world to let things unfold everything felt alive and limitless.

Meeting Pascal was significant, and even though I didn't know why yet, I knew somehow this man would help me cross the bridge from Paradise to whatever came next. My life was in transition, and just as during the other transition moments these past months, someone had come to guide me across the bridge. Regardless of how our relationship would blossom, if it would turn intimate or not, I knew that Pascal was my bridge man.

The possibility of the Divine at work...mustered a confidence in me to take this next leap of faith.

Trust Medicine

Even though we may find resolve to make decisions for our best life, the movement through the change requires trust. Trust Medicine is the reminder that we are not alone. Trust that if you ask for help through intention, prayer, or your words it will be given. It may come from the most unexpected places or ways we may not want, but when we have faith in the medicine of trusting something greater than ourselves an opening into further healing is possible. *Are you having a hard time moving through a decision because you are afraid to trust that help will be there when you need it? Do you hold firmly in the way something needs to happen because you can't trust that another way is possible?* The places that we need to heal inside usually carries wounds of the past. We would rather not acknowledge those feelings, lying dormant within us, waiting for the right moment to reemerge. But when we set the intention to grow, to heal, to love we must also set the intention to trust that what comes down the pike is meant to help us with our intentions. Trust is often the missing ingredient that prevents us from taking that leap of faith. *Are you clear in your heart with what you need to do, but can't seem to bring it into fruition?* Trust is more important than action. *Can you trust that even if something seems painful, awkward, or pride swallowing, it is an opportunity for you to create your best life?* Trust Medicine teaches us to hold steady, for when we get to the other side of our obstacles we may just say thank you.

CHAPTER 27

The Invitation

"I FIGURE AT OUR AGE there is no need for pleasant chitchat when we can just get down to the nitty gritty of things," Pascal joked in one of our phone conversations.

It was now three days before my scheduled departure to Kentucky and Pascal and I were having another three-hour conversation. I laughed easily with him and embraced the camaraderie. I also felt invigorated to have a man's attention. But in spite of our ease of conversation, I hesitated to answer his question about whether I was still going to Kentucky.

"There aren't really any other options," I said. Even as I said it though, even though I would have liked to be with my parents, I still couldn't see myself heading east. I didn't understand why, but I had learned by that point to trust in my intuition. Pascal's intuition seemed to be aligned with mine.

"What you need is a place where you can rest and won't feel like you are living out of your car. Are you sure you want to go to Kentucky to recover? Would that be truly supportive for you?" With his usual logic, he reasoned that I may not be strong enough to handle the emotional toll of seeing my parents.

I appreciated his concern, knowing I had not yet regained my cognitive ability to discern the choices and make logical sense of my situation. I still needed help in that department and I reveled in gratitude for the guidance of this man.

"You know, you don't have to leave just yet," Carolyn said as she swabbed an alcohol pad over her deltoid muscle, "You are welcome to stay as long as you like. Ned and I love having you here, the dogs are so great, and it's nice to have someone else to help around the kitchen." She injected herself with the shot, grimaced slightly in pain, groaned and took it out of her arm. "Gosh, I tell you, I feel like my entire arm is just one big knot of scar tissue."

I, too, was preparing my scarred arms for my daily shots. The misery of our shots loved the company we gave to one another every morning. It was nearing the end of May and the clock felt like it was ticking towards my fated departure out of Paradise. Carolyn and I talked about many subjects over needles both medical and knitting, alcohol swabs, and grimaces of pain every morning. Conversations of Kentucky and my uncertain future surfaced often. And that morning was no different.

"Thank you, Carolyn," I smiled, but focused on organizing that day's medication. "I so appreciate you and Ned, and everything you've done for me. I am still stunned by the whole thing. But it's time. I don't want to outwear my welcome."

"What will you do?" Carolyn asked.

"Oh, you never know," I said, trying to keep the conversation light so as to squelch my building fear and anxiety before it affected my sensitive nervous system. Then something came out of my mouth I didn't expect. "I just may be whisked off to Orcas Island and rent Pascal's cabin for the rest of the summer. It's available June 1st."

Did I just say that? Out loud? Why did I just say he had a cabin for rent—I don't know if his cabin is for rent! He hasn't even mentioned me coming to Orcas. Besides, why would I go there? Why on earth would I leave Carolyn's safe nest to live on some stranger's property?

"That could be nice for you," Carolyn replied, but although her tone felt supportive, it carried an undercurrent of sadness. She said again, "You know you can always stay here though."

I didn't respond, and her words seemed to dangle in the air along with my own words, which seemed to originate from a place other than my own brain. What I had just said felt like an outright lie.

Later that night, alone in the kitchen, my mind was still ruminating on what I'd told Carolyn. Instead of sitting in a chair to cook at the stove as I had done in Reno and at the Kula hermitage in Maui, I had found joy in making beautiful food again. I wasn't eating burnt pizza like I did on Christmas Eve; I could stand and make food with love, sing over my food, and even have the energy to do the dishes when I was done.

Singing to my food in gratitude, marveling at my journey that led me to that kitchen, and thinking about the intuitive words that spewed from my mouth a few hours prior, I dumped fresh green beans from Carolyn's garden into a hot cast iron skillet. The sear of the beans as it hit the hot oil merged with the chiming sound of my cell phone. I grabbed the phone to look as I stirred the beans. *I was multitasking better too*, I thought.

The text message was from Pascal: "Hey, looks like I got that sailing gig. You want to come care take my property for the month of June?"

Immediately, I felt a bolt of hot lightning course through me—from my crown chakra down through my toes, beyond the kitchen floor and straight into the core of the earth. At the same time, I heard a booming 'YES' resound throughout my cells. This time, instead of my soul falling on its knees, all of me fell to the kitchen floor, laughing hysterically. I laughed and laughed, rolling around with my puppies who joined in my gleeful celebration.

What could this be except another miracle from the Universe in the form of an invitation from another complete stranger to come live at his sanctuary? The sensation was still tingling throughout my body once I regained composure and finished cooking my dinner.

But as I began to seriously consider Pascal's offer, I felt the backwaters of fear and doubt riding along with the divine energy inside me. *Am I really going to do this? What if I'm wrong in trusting this decision? I'd be returning back to the Pacific Northwest. Now I'm not so sure about this.*

Before the text I was singing to my food, present with the life that was before me. Now, I was lost in the thoughts of my mind as I inhaled my food. I was no longer present, but rather, I was tripping through my future as I tried to envision it.

I knew I needed to sleep on it. *When I wake, I'll have my decision*, I intended. I wouldn't reply to Pascal until then.

The next morning I replied to Pascal as planned.

"This sounds amazing. It is highly possible, we should discuss this further." The proverbial 'Yes' was front and center in my heart and my mind upon waking, yet, fear quickly seeped in.

Suddenly I worried about his expectations if I agreed to his offer. *What if he has a huge physical project for me to tend to? What if he expects me to clean up his yard?* I knew I needed to be clear in communicating the state of my health. I may have been able to cook dinner and do some laundry, but I completed those tasks at my own pace, in my own time. I still rested when I needed to rest; I still had good days and bad days. But he responded to my apprehension with words of encouragement.

"I have a hot tub and wood burning sauna that can help you heal. There's nothing you have to do here except take care of yourself."

Later that day when we talked over the phone, he explained that all he needed me to care for was his cat and to make sure the technology of his off-grid home remained intact. But still I hesitated. After all, this was an invitation from a man I still hadn't met.

Any girl with a head on her shoulders would be weighing this decision heavily. My head wasn't quite all the way on my shoulders, my brain was still in repair, and I didn't fully trust myself yet. I may have trusted Spirit, but I needed to get past my own self-doubt.

But once again, Pascal intuited my hesitation.

"You should ask me the questions your father would ask me. That would be the smart thing to do." With total confidence he continued, "Trust me, I will pass the test." And although I did believe him, I knew myself enough to know that I preferred to ruminate on important decisions before committing to them. Even to that cautious response, Pascal revealed one of his own intuitive feelings.

"Look, I trust my gut, it doesn't lie. But I know you're coming home, I can feel it. You are totally going to do this."

Did he really say that word? Coming 'home'? There was no way he understood the significance of this word to me.

After we hung up with plans to reconvene in the morning, I stepped into the sanctuary of Carolyn's garden and caught sight of hummingbirds flitting about, drinking the nectar of the mauve flowers, and happily going about their business. My heart filled with their own joy and it reminded me that I could be in joy too and still make these decisions. My contemplation didn't need to be so dire and serious. My heart felt the resounding 'yes' of the Universe. I breathed a deep sigh; I was going to say yes to this crazy idea, I knew it already.

Orca Medicine

Orca whales are here to teach us how to understand the nature of our souls. They are creatures that embody the energies of both dolphins and whales with their playful spirit and how they move through the water with purpose. Just like their black and white markings, their presence reminds us that there is light and dark within each of us. Traversing this light and dark within our souls with playfulness and purpose is what Orca Medicine is here to teach us. Orca Medicine guides us to dive into the depths of who we are and allow the wisdom in our souls to surface into the light of our lives. *Are you able to apply the wisdom that is found in the depths of who you are to overcome the challenges and life tests you face now? Do you need time to submerge yourself in your thoughts in order to understand the behavior that has prevented you from reaching your destiny?* They migrate together over great distances and have done so for thousands of years. Orca Medicine summons the internal compass that is found in the heart and it is with a playful spirit that the compass will show the way. *Do you have a clear direction in life? Are you confused about which way to go?* Orca whales reveal the depth of our self-understanding, the lessons we've learned thus far, and they show us how to navigate through our present life with a playful curiosity instead of a rigid agenda. Embracing the black and white of our life allows joy to follow because it is in this embrace that self-love rises to the surface to lead the way. We must know the darkness so we can appreciate the light.

CHAPTER 28

Planes, Trains, and Orcas

ALONG WITH THE CABIN RENTAL that blurted out of my mouth to Carolyn, I also envisioned Pascal coming to Paradise to get me. I saw him driving my car. *Why? Why did I see these things that seemed so farfetched? Why on earth would someone who hasn't even met me do this, without expectation of something in return? What would compel him to do such a thing?* I kept pushing this image out of mind concluding this was ludicrous.

Still, after Daniele agreed to change course to help me get to Orcas Island instead of Kentucky, something didn't feel right. The accustomed light and energy I felt and saw around situations when they were about to happen, wasn't there. I did not see this familiar light when I tried to envision Daniele coming to get me. Instead, I saw a blackened reddish grey. Our agreed plans were not lining up with the powerful lightning bolt I felt only the day before, and I was perplexed as to why. *If Daniele's assistance wasn't happening, then what was going to happen*, I thought.

"I don't know why, but I don't feel Daniele coming to help me." I shared with Pascal as we talked more about this new, suddenly shared path of ours.

"Well, I have another proposal for you." With that statement, I felt the Universe stepping in once again to change the trajectory of my life.

"I know what you are going to say." I divulged, feeling the suppressed vision of Pascal driving my car surge up like a water-spout in the ocean.

"You do? If you know what I'm going to say, then say it." His very matter of fact tone indicated to me that I should not only trust, but *own* my prediction.

"You want me to say it?" *Oh, god, what if I'm wrong? I'll be mortified.*

"If you know what I'm going to say." He said again, firm, "Then you should just say it." He was making me accountable for my intuition.

"I think you're going to offer to fly down here to help me get up there," I said, straight as an arrow.

"No, that isn't what I was going to say," but it was as if I could see that sheepish grin of his showing itself through the phone. "I was going to take the train."

It wasn't a plane, but so what? My intuition had been right!

After Daniele's car broke down and my Plan B for getting to Orcas Island fell through, Pascal and I began to make official plans. As he suggested the proposal to meet in Eugene, Oregon where I would pick him up from the train station, I realized he had already thought all of this through. *Was this a romantic gesture?* I was so pensive about the decision, it hadn't occurred to me that he may be doing this because he genuinely liked me. Something was compelling him and I am not even sure he understood the reasons he was willing to travel land and sea to get to me.

The next day, with the car fully loaded, I walked into Carolyn's garden one last time to sit with all the beings that thrived in her sanctuary. I sat in the center of the garden on the mulched pathway, right in front of the Oregano flowers that first greeted me three weeks ago when I arrived. They were now brimming with full blossoms. *I wonder how much I have blossomed.*

I said hello to the honey bees dancing around the flowers, gathering their pollen. I had been meditating with them daily since my arrival in Paradise. I realized their steady murmurs were a hidden link to the spirit world, just like the buzzing of the refrigerator that night with the Star Beings.

Although I tried to settle into the calm of my meditation that morning before I departed, it seemed my body buzzed with anxiety. Merely observing and embracing what the buzzing contained: my fears, worries, doubts, courage, excitement, and the unknown of this decision to meet Pascal. They had taught me to keep listening to my own internal guidance system. And my internal guidance system kept thinking about the name, Orcas Island.

The waters that surrounded that island held the energy of the orca whale. The brethren to the humpback whales in Hawaii. *Could this be a coincidence?* I wondered. *Is there some connection to Hawaii? Why was I being guided to another island?*

The questions swirled around with the buzzing bees busy at work in what seemed to be playful purpose. I breathed in the aromatic scents of the flowers warming in the sun. The bees showed me images of the orcas swimming in the sea, talking to their humpback friends with some kind of intuitive sonar. Images of the whales conspiring to get me to Orcas Island flitted around my mind like the bees mingled in the flowers.

The possibility of the divine at work for my greatest and highest good mustered a confidence in me to take this next leap of faith. My fears and worries wanted to label my thoughts as ludicrous, but the compass of my heart felt like a sonar guiding me to these majestic creatures of the water. I couldn't help but to feel the light of my new life beginning to dawn with curiosity and potential. I was being led to a purposeful place on my soul's journey.

In my last moments in the garden, I received a sendoff and blessing from the plants and animals that had also become my friends during my time in Paradise. The bees' message on that day: I needed to keep my eyes and ears and heart opened to the journey and make sure I stopped to smell the roses and savor the honey of my life. Those whales were luring me north, back to an energy with which I resonated. Upon this realization I believed it to be true.

I settled into a strength and confidence that this was the right path and that I was capable of making the drive to Eugene, Oregon on my own. I was leaving on a new journey where I needed to rely on the Universe more than ever to navigate my course into the unknown.

Deer Medicine

Deer are gentle creatures that traverse the world with ease, grace, and peaceful foraging. The site of a deer causes one to pause, if only for a single moment, breathing with the wide eyes of a doe. Deer Medicine is here to teach us compassion, not just with others, but with ourselves. Their energy embodies a sense of tenderness in the way we could walk in the world. *Are you being too hard on yourself or on others? Are you frustrated about an area of your life? Could you love yourself a little bit more? Could you show more compassion for where you are right now on your journey?* Deer Medicine holds the wisdom that we are children of God, and reminds us that the love we feel from this higher power is the same love we must honor within ourselves. Deer remind us to find compassion and gentleness for the situation at hand, and to walk through life with kindness and sweet simplicity. Bucks also offer the medicine of strength in our purpose. The antlers are likened to a psychic antennae that connects us to our higher power, deeper wisdom, and a core strength that is capable of coursing through you once it is summoned. *Are you still listening with a tender heart to the strength that resounds in your soul?* Deer Medicine offers the balance of compassion, gentleness with strength and fortitude while we learn to understand our higher self. *Can you stand strong and be gentle at the same time?*

CHAPTER 29

The Driver's Seat

WITH PARADISE IN THE REARVIEW MIRROR, I set sail. Swallowing my fear and summoning my courage, I set sail north, to Eugene, Oregon to meet Pascal, the man who would then whisk me away to an island called Orcas. The drive along the I-5 corridor through Mount Shasta and into Oregon was the first major road trip I took on my own in over a year. As the asphalt unfurled before me, I felt the unknown paving the way into my new life. And this time I was in the driver's seat! Instead of fear coursing through me, I was in deep awe of the budding strength welling inside.

The powerful presence of Mount Shasta when she came into view took my breath away. Seeing her in her snow peaked glory, memories of my time on Haleakalā surfaced in my mind. Mana welled up inside me, and prayers to this Apu, Mount Shasta, passed my lips as I drove through the mountain pass. Reverence filled my heart in honor of the sage wisdom of all mountains that had taught me to find solidity deep inside my core.

Traversing the mountain passes and into the lush countryside of northern California and southern Oregon, a whole new world opened up before me; and with this new landscape was my newly transformed perspective from all that I had endured up to that moment.

Every cell of my being felt fresh with amazement. Jubilant tears fell from my cheeks over the magnificence that the beautiful Earth Mother,

Pachamama, created for her children to live upon. I could feel her love permeating the air from the countryside, and in the clouds, sun, and rain along that corridor.

I had experienced this same awakening once before, after being bedridden for two years from the same illness ten years prior. The same surrender that occurred on that drive also occurred then, along with the same feelings of love and beauty this surrender awakened in me. The success of taking a springtime walk after being bedridden for two years produced awe-inspiring tears to flow from the simple connection I felt when I saw a cherry blossom. The radiant, divine light pouring through those mauve petals overwhelmed my senses and connected me so deeply to my heart that I had no choice but to weep. Afterwards, I marveled at the honor it was to simply be alive.

But the sweet nectar of life I tasted through that cherry blossom slipped through my fingers when betrayals, heartache, illness, grief, and inner turmoil overtook the recesses in my heart. I had been on a quest to find and reclaim that sweet gratitude to be alive ever since.

Now, with the beauty of Mount Shasta in front of me and the presence of Earth Mother all around me, I found that divine love again. But it was more than a discovery; it was a deeply ingrained feeling. Every cell in my body could actually feel the love all around me! With that love, I felt free to BE, to FEEL the love everywhere and to GIVE my love in return. My body was a new vessel now, and deep inside was my soul, ready to realign with the energy of the earth. I was a part of her and she was a part of me; in all things, in all ways we were one. I had found my most authentic self. She was back!

My reconnection to the infinite love of the Universe kept me steady, in gratitude, and in love even though the long drive from Paradise to Eugene was beginning to take its toll on my recovering body. What was supposed to be a five-hour drive turned into ten hours, with delays from car wrecks, thunderstorms, and rush-hour traffic. My energy was spent, and I was relieved when I arrived at the retreat center where I had rented a two-bedroom yurt on the outskirts of Eugene. It was dusk, and two deer were eating grass just outside the entrance to the yurt. Seemingly unaltered by my presence as I pulled up, I sighed in relief and watched my gentle friends forage in the dimming light. It was a sweet place, full of wildflowers, wooded trails, and wildlife.

The sign at the yurt's entrance gave an auspicious greeting:

> If you walk in love, you walk with the angels.

Inside, another fortuitous picture greeted me with a radiant heart speaking of the lessons I had been asked to learned thus far:

> I have arrived. I am home.
> My destination is in each step.

Mana coursed through me as I read those signs, and I felt confirmed that I was on the right path. My journey was being wielded by the Divine; angels had brought me here. All was well at that moment, and no matter what happened with Pascal, what would transpire was already all right.

Outside the yurt, I watched more doe forage the lush, fresh grass as the sun set. They were everywhere, and their presence was a loving reminder to be gentle and kind to myself. I knew I'd pushed myself and my body to drive from Paradise to Eugene so I wouldn't disappoint Pascal, and I was all too aware that I had forgone some of the lessons I'd learned in order to do that. The tug-o-war of staying true to myself—my body *and* my heart—continued to play out inside of me while the deer offered the gentle reminder to have compassion for my body.

Later, as I tucked myself into bed that night, I made a strong intention for the following day:

You are going to love yourself fully, no matter what happens tomorrow. Listen to your body. You are beautiful on the inside and out. It doesn't mat-

ter what happens with this man. His offer to let me stay on his property is already a gift. Stay in your heart.

Sleep came easily to me after that, and I felt carried into the peaceful stillness of the woods.

The next day, I drove to the train station in downtown Eugene to await Pascal's arrival. Though a late spring thunderstorm had rumbled overhead the last two days, summer nipped at its heels. Lush and green, the landscape throughout the city filled my senses with every turn of my head. Buds swelled, ready to burst in gratitude for the rain. Flowers billowed from hanging baskets, trees were now in full foliage, birds sang their praises, and people hustled about.

The train station stood picturesque, seeming to be in its historical finest surrounded by older buildings. Perhaps the major hub of the city at one point, now it was part of a sprawling college town full of eateries, boutique shops, pubs, and university-style bungalow homes. As I approached the train station, movie scenes where people waited to be reunited with their loved ones on train platforms flooded my imagination, along with images of old time engines, steam spewing as they pulled into town. I could not help but be swept up in the romanticism of all those images in my mind. It was intoxicating, and yet, it left me pensive, nervous, excited, and at peace.

Waiting for Pascal's train to arrive, I sat on a bench to meditate, taking in the landscape and energy of my feelings over his impending arrival. With a long and slow exhale, I released all the nervous energy that had been building in me surrounding this date with destiny.

"I'm nervous," I texted Pascal.

He responded immediately.

"Don't be nervous. You are either about to make a really great friend or meet the love of your life." Though I was still filled with the feeling of butterflies flitting around my stomach, I smiled. He was on his way!

Forgetting the lessons learned thus far, my smile was trumping any signs that my symptoms were flaring though. I had made the drive to Eugene, but that morning at the yurt, my aching, fatigued body told me I expended far more energy than I intended. Teetering on the edge of exhaustion and a potential setback in my healing journey, I muffled the cries coming from my body, hoping to get through the next few hours of meeting Pascal. I tried to remain calm, knowing how important it was to keep my fragile nervous system on the right track. I knew that one emotional upset or unexpected physical demand could derail me.

Pascal's train was due any minute, the announcement had already come over the loud speaker guiding the departing passengers to the platform. People were hustling about, finishing their last cigarette, preparing their kids for the train, or waiting nervously for their loved one's arrival. But I tried to remain calm, sitting in deep presence on the bench, and continued to watch the bustling energy of the train station.

Finally the train made its grand arrival, seeming to go much farther past the point where I thought it would stop. It was a silver monstrosity of a machine: two stories high with tinted windows that I couldn't see into, and train conductors standing at every doorway. I had never seen such a train in my life! I had only ridden trains in South America, all of which were wooden, rickety, crowded and stinky. Once, in my youth, I rode on top of a train as it pushed through the Andes Mountains, and succumbed to vertigo when I looked over the edge. *That would never be allowed in the United States,* I thought. This train was a stark contrast to those trains I had ridden. It was big and tough and steel; definitely American made!

I should have come up with a backup outfit with Carolyn, I thought as I adjusted my blue, flowing prairie skirt. I didn't want Pascal to see my legs just yet, not as they were then—atrophied from months of neglect and swollen with lymphatic fluid.

In that moment, I was so very aware that I was being tested once again by the Universe to love me as I was, to accept myself where I was right there and then. But when the train arrived, all I thought was that I wanted to impress Pascal, and all my insecurities came flooding to the surface.

As I tried to look poised, confident, friendly, and calm, I was nervous he wouldn't like me. I wasn't sure how I was going to feel seeing Pascal either, but I was resolved to accept him no matter what. As determined as I was to love and accept all of my own imperfections, I was just as determined to love his. This was all part of the same test: to accept and love all beings, for we were perfect just as we were intended to be made. My lungs filled with a nervous breath as the metal monstrosity carrying Pascal chugged to a halt.

Can he see me from the tinted windows? What if he already saw me?

As the arriving passengers hurried past me in a blur, I began walking slowly against their current. Men darted by, but none were Pascal. People from all walks of life passed me searching for their own loved ones. Suitcases, people shouting, the gigantic engines settling down, train conductors yelling. It all whirred past my sensitive nervous system.

Then I saw him.

He was exactly as I imagined he would be, a sweet combination of a teddy bear, a hobbit, and a lumberjack. His neatly trimmed beard surrounded a smile that was sincere, boyish, happy, easily given, and tired from such a long journey. All the aspects about Pascal that I would have criticized before were now endearing to me. My superficial, school-girl perceptions no longer fit the current stage of my mind and my life.

Oh, he's cute, I thought as our eyes found each other for the first time.

"Hi," I said, noticing the overly friendly tone in my voice masked my nervousness.

"Hi," he responded, looking down at the ground, seemingly very serious and tired.

We exchanged a fleeting, superficial hug that was not at all the long and warm kind I normally give. In our brief embrace, I felt his reservation. *That's* okay, I thought. *This is new to us both.* This first encounter didn't carry the romantic energy I'd seen acted out in *Casablanca*, but what did I expect, fireworks upon first sight? That kind of love was as rare as finding jewels at the bottom of the ocean.

After we untangled our arms, I noticed Pascal had blue eyes. I'd thought they were brown from his pictures and our brief video chat, but I was wrong. They were blue, and also kind and engaging. His sweatshirt smelled of a bachelor, rancid and of wood smoke. He carried a soft leather briefcase for his laptop computer and a skimpy backpack.

"If I had just traveled by train across several states, the backpack I'd be carrying would be bursting at the seams," I joked with him as we walked out to the parking lot. "My car, Rupee, is over this way. You'll get to meet my wiener dogs."

We made pleasant conversation about both of our trips to Eugene on the way to the car but Pascal seemed tired and still a little guarded. When we got to the car, both of the dogs stayed in the backseat, surveying this new stranger that had landed in their midst.

I actually would have been more comfortable if he drove, but stubborn pride kept me from asking such a request so soon. My body's 'check engine' light had come on hours ago and my energetic tank of gas was empty. I was running out of steam, but I didn't dare show him this side of me yet. So I drove, and Pascal navigated us through the streets of Eugene and on a trip down his memory lane when he'd lived in Eugene briefly during his early twenties. Pointing out his old hangouts, houses he used to live in, the city layout, he told me stories of the hard time he'd had here and stories of the kind people that took him in. He, too, had experienced starting his life fresh again.

Over dinner at a Thai restaurant, we sat face-to-face for the first time. How different this experience was from only several days earlier when I'd tried ordering Thai food in Paradise. After incorrectly dialing the phone number several times, I'd driven 30 minutes to the restaurant only to discover that I'd left my purse, my wallet, and my money at Carolyn's house. And now I was eating Thai food again, only a few days later—and this time, I was not alone.

"There," Pascal said after a long contemplative pause. "Now I've told you all my family secrets."

His past was filled with difficult times, but I was used to hearing stories like this. Having provided healing work for over a decade I'd heard many outlandish, outrageous, shocking, jaw dropping stories from my patients. Was he expecting me to recoil at his family history? A month ago his stories may have rattled me. But now I was stronger. *He'll have to do more than that to rattle me now.*

*I felt my heart buoy back to the surface
where it found its home within me once more.*

Test Medicine

The journey of the soul is unique to each individual. Any journey we choose to take, whether an inward journey to heal the soul or an outward journey to exploring life, a test will ultimately come our way. We may choose to look at these tests with anxiety, as obstacles that must be tackled; or we can embrace them as opportunities to evolve. The Universe tests us on our journeys to help us learn our strengths and weaknesses, and how to have faith in what we have become. Test medicine isn't about passing or failing, but rather, becoming aware of the lessons that life is offering. *Is there a challenge you are facing right now that you aren't acknowledging as a life test? Do you usually look at a hardship in your life as if you are the victim? How could the situation change if you considered it as a life test rather than a hardship?* Life tests usually trigger old wounds, such as our self-perceptions and where we are afraid to grow. You will learn far more about yourself, who you are, and where you can grow from this vantage point with Test Medicine. To continue on your journey, use the lessons you've learned thus far and apply it to the life test in front of you.

CHAPTER 30

The Final Exam

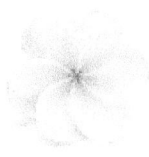"WOULD YOU LIKE ME TO DRIVE?" Pascal offered as we walked back to the car after dinner that first night. He might have arrived in Eugene tired, but even he could see my energy was like the waning moon descending at twilight. I graciously accepted his offer, as my body was already fighting off oncoming shakes from fatigue.

With him behind the wheel, we drove the meandering roads into the countryside where the two-bedroom yurt awaited us. We'd both agreed that we preferred this place, which was off-grid, in the woods, and without any pavement nearby, to a hotel by an expressway. This small agreement was just another check on the mental list I had started making of all the ways we were compatible.

Once inside, I set some mellow music to play in the background and then sat with Pascal on my bed, where we shared more stories of our travels, work, interests, family, and life. The two dogs lay in the space between us, already comfortable with Pascal. Our feet were gently touching one another's as we talked, and the gentle sensation of his foot to mine sent my body spinning with energy. Looking at the dogs, at Pascal, at the circular shape our bodies made together, I realized that it had been six months since a man had even touched my skin.

Though he was still little more than a stranger to me, I felt very comfortable being in a bedroom with Pascal; in fact, I felt more comfortable around him than I'd felt around a male in many years. I felt more comfortable with him than I'd felt even with Alex. It was all so soon!

Why do I feel so comfortable? Is it Pascal? Or is it the new me?

I felt stronger and more comfortable in my own skin now than before my treatment in Reno. I'd finally come to understand that I didn't need to impress someone with what I looked like, as long as I spoke the truth in my heart and honored my words. It was this sense of inner peace that made me comfortable, not just with Pascal, but with myself, I realized.

I also realized something else: *I like him.* It was a thought that surprised me, but it was true. *I actually like him.*

As we continued to talk, the early evening hours faded quickly. Soon the time was closing in on eleven o'clock, hours later than my bedtime over the past few months, and I was approaching my wall.

Well, I thought, *if something is going to happen between us, I better get this show on the road.* If a kiss was going to happen that night, the time to do it was now.

But before I could initiate a kiss, Pascal lifted a single finger and began to gently caress my arm. Thirsty for affection, my body responded like a withered plant finally given a drink. With that single touch I remembered my femininity and all the sexuality I still possessed. I needed to be kissed and soothed for a night, to be held the way I'd been craving for so long.

"You know," I said, "I haven't been touched like this in a very long time." My body's reaction to the caress of a single finger reminded me of how starved I'd been for any kind of touch, affection, and human connection. I savored his touch, and sunk into the sensations it produced throughout my body.

"I feel so connected to you," Pascal said. "This thing we have here is pretty unique. I feel like I can share anything with you."

His words came out in a quiver, which made my own intuitive antenna stand erect in forewarning. I felt a flood of nervous anxiety rush into the bedroom threatening to douse the sexual energy that had been building in me. Something was shifting in our little nest of intimacy, like a storm front closing in on a shore, and my sensitive body (made even more sensitive by Pascal's simple touch) felt it. A storm cloud was brewing within Pascal, and I knew from listening to his childhood stories, that this same stormy energy emerged from time to time throughout his life. It was a part of him, just as my intuition was a part of me.

Uh oh, I thought. I felt his darkened energy enshroud the room and I knew something was afoot before he even spoke.

"I feel like I need to tell you this," he said. "And I feel like I can tell you this because we can be so honest with each other." Pascal gently rubbed my arm as he spoke, and then began placing soft little kisses on my previously untouched flesh. It was a gesture of healing rather than of intimacy, as if he was already trying to soothe the hurt he was about to inflict on me. "But what I have to say may hurt you."

"Okay," I said, hesitantly, wondering what he could possibly say that could hurt me. He'd told me so much of his past already—his divorce, his family problems. What else did he have to tell me, and *why* did he have to say it now of all moments, right before our first kiss?

My anxiety was growing. I didn't even know this man other than a few of his stories. As a Scorpio, he was fully capable of carrying darkness inside of him as deep as the murky waters at the cold ocean floor. The mysterious energy swirled around me, and I felt like a ship at sea, shrouded in mist and fog, with no stars to navigate my way.

"Um," he stammered, "I think you're really beautiful." Then he paused, trying to find the words of his truth. "But I have never been with a woman your size before. You're bigger than anyone I've ever been with, and I am not sure I can do it."

The words flooded into my open heart and sunk me into the depths of his murky waters. The potential flame of sexual passion that had been smoldering inside of me was completely snuffed out now. Of all the buttons to push inside of me, this was the biggest button. This was the Big Red Button.

Oh my God! I cannot believe I am hearing this right now. I dropped my head into the pillow to hide from his words, but I could still hear his voice inflicting more verbal blows.

"I know you've been sick for a long time and you probably aren't in the best physical shape of your life, so maybe with a little exercise...."

His words floated through the murky energy around me, tossing me like a vessel thrown overboard in a storm. Warning bells shrieked in my head, and I was awash with an overwhelming siege of emotions. My fragile nervous system was being knocked around inside of me and there was nothing I could do to still it.

As quickly as I put my head in the pillow, my thoughts processed like a flash.

After all the torment I've been through, after all the hell, rebirthing, changing, clearing, and amalgamating I've done to love myself and accept my life and my body just as it is—now this man, this man who only a moment ago completed the circle with me and my dogs, this man has the audacity to insinuate I am not worthy of him! That I don't look good enough for him!

I could've easily countered Pascal's statement with an attack on his physical imperfections, but I'd already come to peace about that within myself. I didn't need to point out his imperfections because I knew he was perfect just as he was. It was a deep truth within me that could not be swayed, no matter what wounds he inflicted on me. I could've hurt him, but my words would not have been aligned with the Universe. They would not have been Pono. Still, waves of anger rose in me, and my heart sank in full despair.

Then, something inside me shifted, and somewhere in these choppy waters, I found my center again. I felt my open heart buoy back to the surface where it found its home within me once more. Two months ago, even one month ago, this surge of emotions and resurfacing of my heart could have taken hours, days, or even weeks. But in my newly awakened state of being, with my face still buried in the pillow, my heart found its home in a matter of seconds.

Carrying the realizations of the mountain strength within me, I lifted my head from the pillow and rose steady and strong. I could feel my inner strength, self-love and self-worth rise up through my heart and build in my throat to speak my truth. Words flowed through me without hesitation. I found my truth in a matter of moments, and I spoke it to him as such.

"You know," I said, "before Reno, I would have likely gone into the bathroom and cried after hearing that." And it was true. But I was stronger now; I was a survivor, not only of treatment, but of myself. I had survived my own inner storm, and I was strong enough to say so. "But after surviving treatment, I love myself enough and value myself enough to not need any validation of who I am and how I look based upon you or anyone else."

Even after I spoke, I continued feeling the anger ride the mountainous slopes within me. "I suspect your opinion is a projection of how you feel about yourself, and you are putting that onto me. And it is my guess," my voice was gathering power, "that with every relationship you've ever had, you've found one thing wrong in your partner and then knit picked it into the ground until it destroyed your relationship." The words flowed with such strength and clarity that I surprised myself. But I meant every word. They resounded like thunder in the clouds he'd brought into our retreated sanctuary.

I could tell he took in my words with care and thought, and I watched his emotions surface on his face until he was at the edge of tears.

"There might be some truth in what you say," he finally said.

Too bad. He blew it. It was a sad thought, but it was true.

My surging emotions drained every last drop of energy from my already ailing body. I no longer could keep up the façade that I wasn't totally exhausted. I was done. Fear was pouring into me, and I needed to sleep and ride out the storm on my own, without this man, who I could no longer trust.

"Pascal, look, it's been a long day for both of us. Tomorrow is another day. Let's go to sleep and see how things feel in the morning." I was trying to ease the tension that his words built, but the damage was already done. My nervous system was in a full Lyme flare and I didn't have the physical resources to go on.

"Are you still coming with me to Orcas?" he asked, which indicated to me that he also knew he blew it, and now he wasn't sure what to do next.

He hadn't wanted to hurt me, and he likely didn't expect the response I gave to him, but I could tell he meant what he said. His foot was already in his mouth, and no amount of back peddling could change what transpired. It was too late.

As Pascal left the room, I was grateful once again for that second bed in the yurt, I turned off the lights and I crawled under the covers with my dogs, who stayed on guard the entire night. Though Sampson usually slept under the covers where he burrowed down along my legs like most Dachshunds would do, this night he slept on top of the covers, on top of me, and kept his head in the guarded, alert position. Both he and Delilah knew they needed to guard me.

A few minutes after I'd turned the lights out, my heart jumped at the sound of footsteps approaching my bedroom.

Please go away, please go away. Leave me alone.

"Sahara?" Pascal's voice came as a whisper very close to my bed. I was terrified. I didn't know what this Scorpio was capable of doing, and the bits of Lyme bacteria still in my brain took me down dark alleys where horrible things happen. Sampson and Delilah could feel my fear, and they responded by sending low, guttural growls into the darkness. "Do you think we could cuddle for a little bit?"

"No," I coldly rejected him. "No, Pascal. Go to sleep."

"Are you sure? We could cuddle for just a minute."

He had no idea how badly my body was screaming for rest. My nervous system was completely shot, my whole body began shaking from head to toe, exhaustion clouded my mind, and I could no longer go on, not for one second more.

"Good night Pascal." I was firm in my words, and he dejectedly returned to his own bedroom for the remainder of the night.

I only needed to believe that good things were coming and the Universe would do the rest.

Grace Medicine

Whatever hardships that one must prevail over, grace offers us an opportunity to transcend into a place of the deepest surrender. Throughout the world Christian, Hindu, Buddhist, and Muslim faiths alike refer to their own state of grace as experiencing the transcendence of privation. It is in this surrender unto grace that leads us into the sanctity of Spirit, Allah, God, or Enlightenment. When the adversities on our life journey threaten to break down the illusionary boundaries we think keep us safe, it is time to allow Grace Medicine to step in and take over. Grace Medicine is a form of deep surrender, where our will, our way, our control, our transgressions are handed over to the Divine. It is in the act of handing over our last shred of dignity that the most miraculous love is capable of flowing through our hearts. *Are you feeling the pressure of your world changing around you but doing everything in your power to stop it? Do you feel you will fall apart if you let go of your control? What if something greater than what you can comprehend is waiting in the wings to carry you?* Grace Medicine is the Divine intervening when all avenues seem too difficult to travel alone. Through grace, our fears are relieved; through grace, we are led home. *Are you ready for the divine surrender found in Grace Medicine?*

CHAPTER 31

State of Grace

I AWOKE THE NEXT MORNING questioning everything. Though my body had ached for sleep last night, I barely slept at all. Instead, I lay there completely freaked out with what had just transpired: I'd left the safety of Carolyn and Ned's nest, driven ten hours to a foreign city to meet a man who I knew nothing about apparently. It seemed my heart had pounded all night long to the rhythm of my nervous system. At one point in the night, I imagined my body as a series of downed electrical wires unable to transmit signals over an expanse of rocky, shaking land. Every nerve seemed to be misfiring along the frayed wires that was my healing nervous system.

I had trusted Pascal completely to give me safe passage to his home in the woods on yet another island. Now regretting this decision, the light of romanticism was snuffed out into darkened fears where plausible tales of rape, murder, abuse and manipulation linger in the imagination.

On top of the exhaustion that weighed on my body when I tried to move the next morning, now I also had a severe case of doubt. I doubted my entire journey ahead; I even doubted whether I could listen to my guides in the coming days. I didn't want to go with Pascal to Orcas anymore. Trusting the 'yes' of the Universe seemed too great of a risk in my fragile state. Only one day after meeting Pascal, I had stepped into an emotional storm, and I had been whipped and tossed about. At first, the part of my mind that held my self-love and wisdom was victorious. My higher self recognized that love wasn't a package tied in a pretty bow, and it had spoken this truth out loud to Pascal. I was proud of myself for that, feeling like I had passed the final exam placed before me by the Universe.

But this morning, lying in bed, my higher self was nowhere to be found. Instead, the wounded little girl inside of me was front and center, and what she wanted was to crawl into a hole and die.

Although I felt I had passed the test the night before, the vulnerability that was inside couldn't shirk his words. I also interpreted his words as an indication that he didn't understand the physical toils I had been through.

Now, the familiar wall I had built around myself, to protect me from the hurt of being misunderstood because of this illness, had reinforced itself inside of me. I hadn't noticed the wall's presence until I woke up feeling exceptionally guarded. Like the Great Wall of China with a security breach, the wall stood impenetrable in me.

Physically, emotionally, mentally, I couldn't handle another blow or disappointment. I couldn't handle another person letting me down. Pascal was a good man. I knew this from the time we'd communicated through email until the day we met at the train station. I knew it by watching the way he carried himself, his simplicity, and his grounded nature. He spoke his truth the night before and I respected him for that. I still wanted to trust Pascal, who reasoned later that morning that I should still go to Orcas with him.

The person I didn't trust was me. I knew my track record; and now with the glaring mistake sleeping in the bedroom next to mine, I felt foolish for even agreeing to this insane idea of going anywhere with that man. I didn't trust my decisions anymore, not when my mind was still foggy from treatment and unable to make rational thoughts at times.

"Mikayla," I pleaded into the phone later that morning, "I need you to make this decision for me. My mind isn't working right and I don't trust myself to make this decision."

I needed counsel and Mikayla, already an angel on my journey, was the person I turned to. She'd stuck with me every step of the way, from the long phone conversations in Hawaii, to flying across the country to Seattle only to drive me to Reno for treatment. Then, while I was in treatment and she was back in Miami, she talked with me every single day on the phone. She understood the state of my ravaged mind, and I felt I needed her more than ever. Meanwhile, Pascal waited patiently outside the bedroom, so I had privacy to talk.

"Well," Mikayla said, "what do you feel?" Though I was trusting her to make this decision for me, I could tell she was trying to guide me to my own conclusion, not hers.

But I was desperate.

"YOU DON'T UNDERSTAND," I implored with every ounce of desperation I could muster in my voice. My pleas into the phone were like a gong sounding in her ear, I'm sure. "Seriously, I am not okay right now. My body is on the verge of collapse already. I'm too weak to decide this for myself. My brain isn't working right. I can't even see clearly right now. I'm not thinking straight and I know it. I need your help."

Even through the fog of my mind and my blurry vision, I could imagine Mikayla's stern look of concentration in my mind's eye. She was with me now, I felt it, and she understood the gravity of the situation. If I stayed in Eugene, I would be by myself in a city with absolutely no help. If I tried to get to Kentucky, I'd have to make the journey alone until someone could fly to the closest city on the path to join me. But who was there to help me that hadn't already helped? How could I have traveled any farther on my own in my condition?

Then there was Orcas. Going to Orcas was still an option.

"I don't know, Mikayla, I don't know what to do. I don't think I can handle another blow." My exasperated words only weighed the conversation more. I was already so very tired of my journey. *Where is my Shire?* I thought. *Please, God, help me find a safe place to land!*

Like usual, Mikayla listened so intently and so quietly that I had to check that she was still on the line. And like always, she still was. But the delay in her response, the silence—that moment when I thought there was no one listening on the other end—infuriated me even then. But as a Libra, I knew that Mikayla was someone who weighed things carefully. So, with no other choice, even though I felt the urgency as if I were in a sinking ship, even though I wanted to scream "mayday" to her over and over again, I waited in silence.

"Okay," she finally said. "Let me talk to him." So desperate for outside counsel, I was relieved that she was taking the reins. Someone besides me was going to size up this man now.

"Pascal?" I found him in the kitchen sitting quietly. Nothing on his face revealed what he was thinking. "Mikayla wants to talk to you." He cutely rolled his eyes, but then nodded his head and held out his hand for my cell phone.

They talked for some time, having a conversation that didn't seem meant for my ears. While they talked in the kitchen, I finished packing up my belongings, loading groceries into my car, and gathering dog toys with the little remaining energy I had left.

I was floating again like that same ghost who had returned from Hawaii to reclaim my dogs. Although floating with fatigue, packing had become a routine for the umpteenth time over the previous months, and still it took just as much of my energy. As I packed, my mind was spinning in its own orbit. I wasn't conscious of what I was packing, what Pascal and Mikayla were saying, or how I was even traversing through this world. I was out of my body floating in the ethers of the entire experience.

Finally, Pascal came into the bedroom and handed me the phone, before slipping quietly away so I could continue the conversation with my confidant.

"I think you need to go to Orcas." Mikayla said. "I think it's going to be okay for you there. It seems like the easiest path right now. No other path is going to be easy like this." She reminded me of Pascal's good qualities and the emotional support he'd given me while I was still in

California. She reminded me of the cabin that he offered to me.

Now it was my turn to fill the phone line with silence.

"Okay," I said finally. As soon as I spoke these words, I felt a settling inside of me that the decision had been made. I was too weak emotionally and physically to entertain the fear welling inside of me or to let it run me off my course. With the decision made, Mikayla and I said our goodbyes.

Then, I was back in the reality I had created for myself, in the middle of the woods with a man who blew it the night before. I picked up my suitcase to take it to the car. My gaze returned to the picture on the wall with words that I had embraced fully when I first arrived at the yurt: "With every step I am home."

Taking in the words for the second time, breathing peace and surrender into my body, I recalled the lessons of strength and courage that I'd learned to muster from the depths of my being thus far. Alone inside the yurt, holding the knob of the front door, I paused and whispered, *Please God, help me find the grace I need to take this next step. I can't do this without you.*

Bringing my awareness to my feet, I felt the earth under me and me on the earth as I walked out of the yurt for the last time. I felt the swirling energy of fear and uncertainty mix with my grounded stillness and recovering, frayed nervous system.

With a subtle nod, I signaled to Pascal that we were a go: I would go to Orcas with him, a man who found me unattractive. I was sad and dejected inside. The zest I felt only yesterday for the journey ahead had dulled, but the intentions I set about accepting the journey were still steering the course of my heart. I tried to reassure myself with reason: *If my prideful ego was in charge, I wouldn't be going with him.* Something else was wielding this entire experience, I knew it to be so, just like all the other steps along my journey. Likely unaware, what Pascal stirred in me was another wound that needed healing.

"Good," Pascal said, and with that one word, my decision was official. He nodded, gave me a thumbs-up and helped me load my suitcases into the car.

When he turned the ignition in my car, my music, all of which was spiritual on some level, began playing. "You know," he pondered as he turned off the stereo, "maybe I'm here to help you in the physical world and you're here to help me in the spiritual world."

Hearing this, I wondered if last night had impacted his soul as much as it did mine. Maybe I was here to teach him something too. Forces beyond our comprehension were wielding something, and I suddenly felt that he, too, felt our encounter was fated. I was intrigued by his comment, but too tired and guarded to properly engage with him at that point.

"Maybe," was all that I could muster in the moment.

So once again, I relinquished to being a passenger in my own car. Through the silence of our drive, with only the road noise to fill the void, I noticed that I felt at ease with Pascal. I felt a sense of peace and stability I hadn't known or felt in a previous partner, perhaps not ever. But he wasn't a potential partner; he made that clear on our first night together. Still, I felt an energy of attraction toward him, and I saw the same energy in his eyes whenever he looked at me. But, succumbing to my aching body, I put those thoughts on the back burner to contemplate later. My body was so very weak, I was walking such a fine line to collapse again that all I could do was allow this man to lead me to his home.

That night, Pascal and I stayed in Seattle after a long day's drive. My body didn't like being stuck in one position for so long in the car, not one bit. When we landed at Pascal's sister's condo, my legs were swollen and shaking with twitches. Still, I couldn't tell Pascal what was going on in my body. I rarely told anyone, much less a stranger. The only person who intimately witnessed the neurological ravage on my body was my ex-husband, John. And on that night, my own pride kept me from showing Pascal that I was still falling apart, at least for the moment.

Inside the condo, exasperated with fatigue and the effort to keep my pain hidden, I locked myself in the bathroom and let my sobs fall down my cheeks and into the shower drain. Later, when Pascal returned from a nearby store, he found me in the yoga pose I'd done a million times over the previous ten years: I was lying on a bed with my legs flat against the wall. Again and again I'd returned to this pose because it allowed the neurotoxins and lymphatic fluid to drain from my legs, and it always helped to recalibrate and settle the pain that often welled up in my legs. On really bad days, my leg muscles would twitch in what appeared to be a combination of Parkinson's disease and a seizure. And the pain, oh the pain. It was incomprehensible. At times, the simple touch of a blanket to my skin could send me reeling in agony. It was this kind of flare I was trying to avoid by settling with my legs against the wall.

Meanwhile, Pascal cooked dinner only a few feet away, not speaking, but seemingly content to be in silence with me. The solidity I'd felt in him from our first email encounter returned to me. Then, the rumblings in my body started again and I panicked.

"Oh shit!! Oh no!"

"What's going on?" Pascal hurried over to sit with me, but I didn't want him to see.

My pride sent me further into panic as he looked at my legs convulsing out of control. Having no other choice but to wait until they stopped, I watched helplessly and tried to hide my pain and embarrassment. But I was totally mortified. I'd been rejected by Alex, dejected by society for this misunderstood illness, neglected by so many friends and family, and now this. I was in an unfamiliar condo, with nowhere else to go. I couldn't run from the situation and now he was probably glad he wasn't attracted to me after seeing what a total mess I really was. It was all too much. I went reeling into emotional overload.

"This is too much," I finally said. "You didn't need to take this all on. This is way more than you bargained for. I shouldn't have traveled so soon. I'm still such a mess." By then, the convulsions in my legs began trembling through every cell in my body. I must have looked like I was getting punched in the gut. I felt like I was in many ways and the horrors of treatment in Reno flashed before me with my shaking body.

"What do you need? What do you need me to do right now?" Pascal was strong and confident as he helped me sit up. With that subtle movement, the room spun; I thought I was going to be sick. Whatever strength I had left in me released into his hands. Tears were threatening the dyke I had built around this illness, and I lacked the strength to keep it from overflowing. It was just another lesson from the Universe to show me how to surrender even deeper than I already had.

This has got to be the extra credit portion of the test.

Meanwhile, Pascal had enveloped me into his arms and held me there. As frightened as I was of him last night, I was equally as relieved by his embrace now. It was the first time I'd been held since Alex removed his huge arms from around me at the airport security checkpoint six months prior.

I had been hugged in friendship by many, in hellos and goodbyes, but not to be *held*. Someone was holding me. Really holding me, readying themselves for whatever pain that needed to be released from my soul. This was the first time someone let me fall apart in their arms since I stepped foot on that plane to warmer waters.

I sank into the reprieve of being held tight by Pascal's genuine embrace. His arms felt like a life preserver slid over me as I tossed around in the stormy sea of my journey. I wept uncontrollably in Pascal's arms, and all the while he held me patiently. The hurt I'd felt from his honest words the night before mingled in the tears of pain and embarrassment over my convulsions. I felt no resistance in those arms of his. He had taken me in, holding space for the emotions that flowed within my sobs.

"I'm so sorry Pascal," I wept desperately. "I'm not even used to people I know seeing this side of me. I don't know if I can do this with you. You don't want to deal with this..." But he responded immediately.

"Do you see me wavering at all?" He took my hands gently, and guided my face up to his so I could look him directly in the eyes. Two, clear blue seas shined back at me, and beckoned me to an inner calm. "I told you I would help you. I committed to doing this and I'm going to get you home. After seeing your physical state, I'm more certain now than ever."

I held on to this life preserver like it was the first mayday I'd sent that had been heard. "I can handle this. I'm here, I'm not going anywhere. You have to trust me. " Taking me into his arms again, he continued holding me.

I wept over everything that had occurred over the last six months. Up until that moment, I thought my ultimate surrender into grace was when I lay on that couch in Reno before heading to Paradise. But in Pascal's arms, between my heaving sobs, I felt the great wall in me begin to crumble.

This was an invitation from the Universe to embrace my vulnerability and let someone or some*thing* truly hold me. I sank into Pascal. I sank so deeply that the twenty-four year old dyke that I'd built around my disease broke. This wall of pride was the last barrier that stood between me and a replete, vulnerable surrender of accepting myself fully. The wall harbored the lingering wounds of abandonment, loneliness, and being misunderstood by a mystery illness. I surrendered again, and again, even deeper than I had before, into the hands of the Divine.

Pascal continued to hold me in silence, and as the longstanding and pent up emotions inside me gave way, I felt divine, compassionate, grace wash over me. With this grace, and the emotional liberation that came with it, I felt the final surge of neurological toxins flood out of me.

"You stopped shaking," Pascal whispered softly, and to my surprise, I realized it was true.

Belief Medicine

There is an elixir of mystery carried in the molecules of water throughout the world. No living creature on this earth can live or reproduce without water. Water is not only integral for our survival, but it also connects each being on the planet. It is in this aquatic substance that messages, intention, and miracles are carried around the globe. Water is the liquid web of life and it is in this substance that the power of belief courses through the seen and unseen forces that create this world. Belief Medicine holds the capacity to live with hope, possibility, and potential. Anything is possible if we believe. If a bird can fly, if the earth can heal, and if a broken bone can mend, then we must believe in the magic of the world. Having faith in your capacity to shine is the medicine that is being summoned when we believe. *Do you believe that you can change? Can you believe that miracles are everywhere? Do you believe that good things are coming? Or do you seek the half-empty glass instead of the full one?* Belief inspires our inner strength and courage, which allows us to transcend any obstacle we face. Belief Medicine is carried in the water which courses through every living thing and that in and of itself is a miracle to believe. *When was the last time you thought your life was a miracle? When was the last time you felt inspired?* Belief Medicine is here to impassion your heart, help you live your truth and help you trust that whatever you dare to dream might actually come true.

CHAPTER 32

A Worthy Vessel

THE NEXT DAY, OUR JOURNEY TRANSITIONED from land to sea on an hour-long ferry ride from Anacortes to Orcas Island. As the ferry chugged along, the chaotic energy of the mainland dissipated into the frigid waters of the Puget Sound. No more roadways, chain restaurants, the I-5 corridor, or the speed and pace of mainland America. The islands were ahead of me now. But instead of the palm trees and white beaches of the Hawaiian Islands, I was being carried to a magical rock whose habitat of towering cedars and rocky shorelines was already familiar to me.

I had been to Orcas Island a few years prior with Alex, so I knew when the ferry docked I would see open meadows and forested hiking trails, and feel the small island charm. Even though I had left Washington State behind me six months ago, abandoning the dreary cold in hopes to save my life, I savored the familiar sights and smells like a homecoming. I didn't want to be in the chaos of modern life anymore, and knot by knot, my body and my mind were comforted in seeing the ocean and familiar Pacific Northwest landscape once again.

From here on out, I wanted a clean connection to Pachamama's energy and to the rhythm of the tides, the moon, and the seasons. I knew from my time in Hawaii that I thrived best in a world based in nature, with fresh air and a slower pace. I needed this place to heal my nervous system and retrain my energy body to live differently, without Lyme disease and away from a fast-paced culture. Now, sitting quietly with Pascal on the ferry, I wondered if his comment the night before about his property being exactly what I needed was absolutely correct.

In Eugene, Pascal's comment about my weight had rattled me, but it hadn't changed the self-love and acceptance I'd found within myself after treatment. Nor did it change the reaction I felt when our eyes met. Seeming to oppose those words that had pushed my big red button, we still exchanged little glimmers of fondness for each other.

Content to be in each other's company, Pascal and I took in the sights through the ferry's windows in silence. Instead of the trepidation and fear that I felt when I first met this man, now I felt curious for the new adventure that awaited me. Anything seemed possible now that I was healing, and in those first few glimpses of island living, I felt the potential of all that I had ever asked for coming true.

My spirit had surrendered into God's grace the night before as my body sank into Pascal's arms. Every last brick of the wall I'd built around myself had been removed with my tears. I'd felt bare, open and ready to receive what the Universe offered me. And through all of my tears, Pascal offered me solace. Something forged between us in that moment—a gift I didn't know if I could ever repay. His chivalrous deeds had removed whatever doubts remained in me about this next step of my journey. What remained in me was a deep sense of calm.

I stepped out onto the bow of the ferry alone, and embraced the salty mist that settled on my skin. The wind blew my hair in chaotic whips, and I hugged myself to keep warm against the biting moisture in the air. But the Salish Sea was calm, it's still waters reflecting the light of the waxing moon; in return, I felt the same calmness reflected in me.

I had experienced the beauty of the human spirit through the kindness of strangers. The miracle of every synchronistic encounter, divine helper, and the strength to survive merged within me in that moment standing on the bow. Through all of my toils, I now felt a great life force coursing through me, my own Mana, connected to the Divine. I realized through this journey, it was one thing to conceptualize the vital power held within the soul, but it was another thing entirely to authentically emanate that loving power and soul strength that each one of us possesses. I knew that none of this would have happened had I shut down my broke-open heart.

My gaze lifted from the water upward, into those familiar lavender-grey heavens where the moon seemed to dangle with the stars. Like a graceful brushstroke, mist rolled through the trees on the distant islands and reflected the lavender-grey color onto the water below. Islands dotted the horizon near and far, and the oceanic energy encapsulated me in her presence.

Memories of where I had been only five weeks prior, in a hospital bed buried under blankets of sickness and despair in the dry desert, were quenched in the respite that I had made it back to the ocean once again. Only a few months ago I had floated in the ocean's warmer, South Pacific waters where the Mana of Hawaii coursed through me. It still coursed through me, and even as I stood on the bow of that ferry and looked out over the sea, I felt the Aloha spirit pulsating with my heartbeat.

The waters of the world, both before me and inside of me, were all connected. Contemplating how water molecules travel I knew the water now in the Salish Sea was once the humpback whales' playground in the warm Hawaiian sunshine at some point in time. Reflecting on this connection, I realized my journey was somehow coming full circle.

I was returning to the love of the ocean, the medicine of the whales, and island energy. Somewhere far below the ferry, orca whales were swimming deep within those cold waters. Those enchanted beings had lured me here, just as the humpback whales had lured me on the beach in Maui. I imagined them swimming along with the ferry, and I intuited their kindred connection with my journey to Orcas Island.

How did all of this happen? The realization of the divine guidance and grace that carried me throughout this journey left me awestruck. The complexity of the synchronistic connections and how God could wield such encounters was something I knew my human mind could never comprehend. If only I could stay in love with myself first and foremost, continue to see the love that emanated everywhere and in everything, I knew my life would be all right. I only needed to believe that good things were coming and the Universe would do the rest. I opened my arms wide, amazed at the miracle of this world before me. I was alive and healing, and that was enough.

My hands quickly gripped the bow's railing to steady my shaky legs as the boat continued its course to Orcas Island. The only sounds I heard were the persistent chugging of the ferry engine and the water breaking below. The sun was beginning to paint its colorful display against the clouds, blushing them in hues of magenta, yellow, and orange. And the magnificence of the air, sea, and sky set me ablaze with inspiration and love.

Then a voice came over the loudspeaker announcing our upcoming arrival to Orcas Island.

When the impressive silhouette of the island against the backdrop of the westward sun came into view, I couldn't help but to think of Maui. Both islands were shaped like horseshoes, and both had two adjacent eastward and westward mountains that ascended into the sky. Memories of Haleakalā, flying, the Star Beings, the whales, my Ohana family, and the healing that happened on Maui swirled around me in the whipping wind. The islands' similarities did not feel like a coincidence, but rather seemingly connected to the same magical energy that led me every step of this journey. I was given safe passage to another magical land, carried by a sailor out of my own storm.

As the ferry neared the rocky shore, I glimpsed the meandering roads that I would soon travel. With that glimpse, I understood the final lesson of this journey. Finally, this spirit of mine landed on the closest thing the Universe could find to the Shire—not Pascal's property on Orcas Island, but a little piece of paradise inside of me. It was in this paradise that I believed I was a worthy vessel, emptied now of the past and ready to be filled with a new life full of grace, love, and trust. My own worthy vessel had carried me home.

Acknowledgments

WITH MY DEEPEST AND MOST PROFOUND LOVE, I am so very grateful to share my arduous journey with you. The level of gratitude I have for those who have helped me on this journey is so immense I am fighting tears thinking about everyone. I had no idea I was writing a book when I wrote the first word of this story. Instead, I thought I was merely journaling my experiences as I have done throughout my life. Then one day while meditating, I realized that these writings were the beginnings of a book. I could not have written it without the divine connection and support I felt through all beings in all ways.

Each person I have included in this book has significantly impacted my life as I traversed from heartbreak and health issues and into divine connection. I could not have made this journey without each and every sympathetic touch, phone conversation, prayer, thought, energetic intention, and financial support. Any small and kind gesture was a miraculous gift to me and was paramount to my survival. If any intention of support, great or small, was given to me by you, I remember, I thank you and am so deeply grateful. I needed you at such a deep level to keep me alive. The people who helped me along the way are so many I don't dare list you individually. You know who you are. I survived this arduous journey because of you willing to ride out the storm with me. Thank you.

Thank you to all the healthcare professionals that held space for me during my time of illness. Thank you to Dr. Traci Taggart, my dear friend and colleague, who finally gave me the official diagnosis of Lyme disease. I would still be floundering with an unknown illness eating away my body if it wasn't for her. I also extend my deepest gratitude to Dr. Bruce Fong and Sierra Integrative Medicine in Reno, Nevada where I received medical treatment for the Lyme disease. Every single healthcare professional at the clinic deserves recognition for their dedication and hard work. It is, to this day, the single best decision I have made in my life.

To all the healing warriors out there with Lyme disease, thank you for your own courage to heal. You gave me the courage to put my story to paper. You are my inspiration! Those who are too sick to speak for themselves, I am honored to speak on your behalf here. Thank you and I love you.

Thank you to all the strangers that quickly became family to my wayward soul. They were all angels and I will never forget the deepest of kindness and support they offered to me during a most dire time in my life.

My parents deserve my deepest expression of love that I can give from my heart. I have been so blessed to have been raised by them. My father worked so hard his entire life to provide for his family. It was this fortitude and foresight that enabled me to seek medical treatment and recover. Thank you Mom and Dad, and my family. I love you. Thank you also to my spiritual family and the Ahunui tribe for your deep love, support, and embrace of me just as I am. Your love and the magic we share is sacred to me and I love you. Thank you for the gifts of being you and the lessons you taught me along the way.

I am grateful to my editor, Jill Twist, who helped me bring this story to life so that you could be an intimate part of this journey. She held my words in her heart with the deepest of intention to find the powerful messages that were between the lines. Thank you. I am equally grateful to my illustrator, Ardel Chisholm, who has not only been a steadfast friend, but an amazing artist who spins her wisdom, healing energy, and passion into her work. Thank you to my dogs, their undying devotion and love kept me alive. Thank you to Nahko Bear and Medicine for the People! I believed in the good things coming because of you. And to the one who broke open my heart, I am thankful because this book would not have been written if it wasn't for him.

The teachings of traditional Hawaiian words, ceremonies and spirituality have also deeply impacted my soul and shaped my life into something I could have never done on my own. I am not a scholar of Hawaiian traditions, nor do I claim to understand the breadth of its medicine and eternal lineage. I am humbly honored to be privy to some of the Hawaiian teachings. The Hawaiian traditions that I relay in this book are my own interpretations and understandings of this beautiful culture. I have done my best to speak with upmost respect, and hope that I have represented the Aloha traditions as authentically as possible. The magic of the Hawaiian Islands and its Aloha spirit have been integral in my healing, and it is a gift I simply want to pay forward. Thank you Maui, thank you for healing my heart and guiding me home.

And to all readers, thank you for being a witness to the baring of my soul. It is my love for you and desire to create a better world that I shared this with you. My only desire is that you find ways to open your own heart to share its amazing beauty with the world. And I trust that your own healing journey will lead you exactly where you need to be in order to heal. My own healing journey continues to this day. It is through this sharing of our hearts that healing will happen for all of humanity. Thank you, dear reader, for taking this journey with me. May you find your own beauty in these words to walk this earth in a sacred way.

Maholo Nui Loa. Aloha Nui Loa. A hui ho!

Sahara

Biography

SAHARA'S WRITING IS INSPIRED by the deep loving energy coursing through the natural world. Her work as an intuitive energy healer and 5 Element acupuncturist, along with her love of nature and understanding the energetic and soul connections of this earth and cosmos has shaped her writing and teaching. Sahara has also struggled with chronic Lyme disease her entire adult life serving as her greatest teacher. Her previous careers in medicinal plant research, teaching biology at the collegiate level, and her trainings in energy medicine, particularly Shamanic spiritual healing for over twenty years, has allowed her to create a system of healing that transcends the body and dives into healing the soul. It is the combination of this illness, her connection to the spirit world, and academic and medical training that has enabled the honing of her work to help others heal, including herself. She works with clients worldwide to transform their healing journey into living their most authentic, thriving life. She does this work in service for the betterment of the world. Since the publication of this book Sahara is still on her journey, letting Spirit lead, and continuing to heal her own body. One year after this story ends, her epic journey comes full circle to land on Maui with her two wiener dogs, where she continues to enjoy the island energy and Aloha spirit. She enjoys living sustainably, honoring the earth, loving many, and letting it all unfold one day at a time. For more information about Sahara Sun, her healing retreats, sessions, and additional publications please visit www.Sahara-Sun.com.

www.ingramcontent.com/pod-product-compliance
Lightning Source LLC
Chambersburg PA
CBHW080424230426
43662CB00015B/2208